El Béisbol

TRAVELS THROUGH
THE PAN-AMERICAN PASTIME

EL BÉISBOL

JOHN KRICH

THE ATLANTIC MONTHLY PRESS
NEW YORK

Published simultaneously in Canada
Printed in the United States of America
FIRST EDITION

Library of Congress Cataloging-in-Publication Data

Krich, John, 1951–
El béisbol : travels through the Pan-American pastime / John
Krich.—1st ed.
ISBN 0-87113-303-2
1. Baseball—America. 2. America—Description and travel—1981–
I. Title.
GV862.6.K75 1989   796.357'097—dc19   88-38032

The Atlantic Monthly Press
19 Union Square West
New York, NY 10003

Design by Laura Hough
FIRST PRINTING

FOR ALL THE DIVINE CRAZIES / PARA TODOS LOS
DIVINOS LOCOS

LINE-UP
ALINEACIÓN

Contents

Contents

ACKNOWLEDGMENTS

Baseball writers would not exist without baseball players. Fortunately, players are willing to concede the reverse to be true. There are no more helpful subjects than baseball people. And that is doubly true of those reared in the traditions of Latin America. At every point in my travels, I ruthlessly exploited their hospitality. In return, I offer added thanks to Luis Rodríguez Mayoral, Irene Lamsdorff, Nino Escalera, Pochi Castro, Ramón Genao, Vic Power, Rubén Gómez, Ramon Becerra Mijares, Winston Llenas, Tony Peña, César Gerónimo, Mario Guerrero, Joaquín Andújar, Tony Pérez, Carlos Cuadra; to the honorary Latins Jay and Ben Feldman, Soon Im, Howie Haak, Chuck Cary; to those *compañeros* who never made it into print, especially Rob Ruck, Paula Pettavino, Bernard Ohanian, Susan Meiselas, Ira Rothstein, Alison Ebata, Terry Clark, Julio Gonzales, Anthony Martínez, Chiori Santiago, Richard Grossinger, Steve Boros, Peggy Northrop, Rick Peterson, Soto Santos Sr., Emilio "Cuqui" Cordova, Bob Fontaine of the San Francisco Giants, and Jay Alves and Sandy Alderson of the Oakland A's. Finally, this book is offered as a tribute to Tim McGinnis, the editor, baseball nut, and friend whose irreverent spirit first encouraged this project. Without these coaches, I would never have made it around the bases of our American diamond.

PITCHER
LANZADOR
The American Diamond

"My favorite word in English is 'You never know.'"

—Joaquín Andújar

No one wants to take me to La Isabela. I've spent an entire morning trying to mount my own expedition to the first colonial settlement of the New World. You'd think this landing point where unoriginal Christopher Columbus laid out America's original European-style city limits is an ocean away, not forty miles as the parrot flies. Spoiled by easy pickings among the gringos, the cabbies outside the Playa Dorada Holiday Inn glare in disbelief, or quote astronomical fares to get out of brutalizing their shock absorbers on the Dominican Republic's notoriously untended back roads. Tour directors suggest snorkeling, golfing, or shopping for native jewelry. Every conceivable vacation activity has been quarantined within secure enclaves along the island's defenseless north shore, rechristened for package-deal conquistadores as the "Amber Coast." Why give up a day in the sun just to stare at a few mossy ruins? Don't I know there's not even a sewer line left to that Club Caribe founded on a "high season" January day like this one? *Nada.* Our self-proclaimed Admiral of the Ocean Seas never was much good on dry land. It was just like ol' Chris to decamp so far from a decent beach. He just wasn't a *playa* kind of guy.

Or maybe, like me, he was after something besides rays. I've come to discover why the place where America began is now known for a quintessentially American product: the baseball player. Before starting my research, I made the mistake of going to a Dominican consulate for some maps and brochures. "Ay no!" the receptionist told me. "You don't

3

have to worry about brochures. Our country safe for traveling. We don't have no brochures anymore." Yes, we have no brochures—only an occasional food riot. Also, "No problem." That's the motto printed on every T-shirt in Puerto Plata, only fifteen minutes from *gringolandia* but a century apart in attitudes and prices. "Money isn't everything," goes an old Dominican saying. "We'd rather be the head of a rat than the tail of a lion."

In ratty Puerto Rico, there's no problem a functioning economy wouldn't cure. No problem spotting the inactive cabbies milling about in the shadow of the pallid cathedral. No problem whatsoever settling on an eight dollar fare for a ride of four hours or more—if the route's passable. The only problem is waiting for my driver to return from his coffee. A negotiating team of cousins and car-washers keeps assuring me—as though the quality of a man's character is what keeps his engine running—that he's *"un hombre serio."* And one look at the man they call Samuel coming across the plaza tells me that his storm-tossed Chevy is going to make it, just like the *Santa María* made it. Responsibility is written in furrows across his nutmeg-colored brow. Best of all, he's wearing a facsimile hard black plastic California Angels batting helmet, complete with ear flap.

Could I have asked for a better Sancho Panza than this dour, moon-faced *taxista*? Or a more mythic means of conveyance than his '62 Caprice? The battered shell of this indefatigable bomber seems to have been remolded a dozen times and repainted, hubcaps and all, the sticky color of a lime lollipop. The upholstery I slide onto looks like it's been hit by a fragmentation bomb. The patch of windshield on the passenger side is not so much cracked as scarred. Stress lines fan out from a crescent-shaped hairline fracture, splitting the sunlight like a prism. A fuzzy stuffed tiger bobs on a string from the rear-view mirror. The cassette player in the dash works only when Samuel prods and jabs at a loose connection. Then I can just hear the tinkle of whipped-up merengue, such an urgent beat for so sleepy a country.

Though the air-conditioning in his cab must have given out around the time Mickey Mantle retired, Samuel looks perfectly comfortable in his molded cap. Mine is a fishnet weave that offers more cross-ventilation and bears the blue cursive insignia A.E. That's Azúcareros del Este, the Eastern Sugar Boys. Now there's a name for a franchise, a throwback to the utilitarian days of Brooklyn's Trolleydodgers and Boston's Beaneaters.

4

The American Diamond

In our complementary headgear, my cabbie and I are just two good ol'
boys rolling toward the next truckstop. Both of us display that peculiarly
American habit of taking our allegiances where we find them, though
the man at the wheel has to qualify as the true American. His ancestry
mixes Euro-, Indo-, and Afro-, and those ancestors got stranded here
much longer ago than mine. Yet my passport gives me claim to the full
hemispheric title, while Samuel's been cast as part of an obscure
subgroup, merely "Dominican." No wonder we're still groping toward
the sources of our shared identity, nearly five hundred years after
Columbus established the town where we're headed. Scanning the
horizon from under our visors, we're off to find where America got
found.

For all of eight dollars, this ride skirts the Pico Isabela de Torres,
leading up the Carretera Duarte through the Ingenio Amistad's fields
choked with the oversized, underpriced sugar cane that our bad boy
Chris first imported from the Canary Islands. Off the blacktop, we shoot
up and down undulating mounds dotted with long-necked royal palms—
just the sort of primeval scenery that inspired Columbus to jot in his
journal, "Española is a marvel, once seen, never to be forgotten . . .
fertile to a limitless degree . . . filled with trees of a thousand kinds and
tall, so that they seem to touch the sky. I am told that they never lose
their foliage, and this I can believe, for I saw them as green and lovely as
they are in Spain in May." In this discovery biz, what you don't know
can't hurt you. What sort of explorer am I, reeking of Royal Hawaiian
suntan oil, the taste of papaya enzyme and Kaopectate at the back of my
throat, Citicorp dollars in my kitbag! Would that I thought my God and
my breastplate were protection enough!

The word I use to satisfy this and every cabbie's curiosity about me is
periodista. I'm a journalist who works for no journal but sometimes keeps
one, a collector of the sort of facts that can't be confirmed by any sources
but my own heart, a historian who gathers footnotes on foot, does my
best research with the seat of my pants. No, don't call me "period
man"—though the shout of that single, unverified word is enough to get
me into the locker rooms of Latin America. I am not a fabricator of
conclusions, nor a specialist in knowing when to stop. Call me a
commatista, a hyphenista, a questionmarquero.

The farther we get from the highway, the softer and bumpier the gravel
becomes. But these roads hardly seem as bad as the lobby loungers

claimed. At the bottom of our first jungle hollow, a sparkling little creek crosses the one-laner. *"No problema,"* says Samuel, who fords it like he's on the Ventura Freeway. On the far side is the first of many settlements unmarked on any map but with a population density that attests to the length of human habitation here. The monotonous rows of one-room shacks, wooden or cinder block, are all freshly painted and lovingly surrounded by wild arrays of tropical flowers. Even the fenceposts around the traditional thatched *bohíos* are a Day-Glo pink. The golden tinsel of holiday decorations ripples in the heat miragelike.

I can only assume that we're nearing the ocean by the way the chalky pathways before us branch off crazily, a river of roads at its delta. With our low-rider suspension, it feels like a minefield. There's grass growing under our wheels. I sure wish Samuel's bomber was a Land Rover—but he knows better than I how to pretend that it is. Without apology or the slightest show of chagrin, my *taxista* follows one cow trail after another that turn out to be dead ends. On the way to the New World, Samuel has been blown off course. Like one of Cristóbal Colón's crew, he may have volunteered to come along because he couldn't imagine how far he'd have to go. It's been some years since my navigator was last required to come this way, and he's scratching his batting helmet.

The closer we get to the ocean, the more the landscape resembles a dry African savannah. Samuel's latest gamble comes to an abrupt end at a muddy watering hole where hunters might go to bag some wildebeest. It's hard to tell how deep this thick runoff might be. The bank is steep and a bluff on the other side looks more formidable. Where the roadbed used to lie, three naked youths are cavorting. Have we come so far to be turned back? An old woman shooing a herd of goats on the far shore beckons us with a languid wave. That's all the encouragement Samuel needs. My *taxista* still hasn't asked for an explanation of why I've got to get to this god-awful spot, but he sure isn't going to stop for one now. *"Paramos?* No! *Seguimos?* Sí!" The chorus repeats on his taped merengue. Do we stop? No! Shall we continue? Yes! The green Chevy turns amphibious and begins skidding its way across. Pebbles crunch beneath flaccid Goodyears, the water hits midwheel. Samuel gives me a *serio* nod, and smiles only when a pothole jogs his helmet's black brim down over his eyes.

The road follows a deeply carved creek bed that leads to the Atlantic. This *arroyo* dribbles into a pleasant cove where a small beach has formed around the outflow. A couple of sky-blue rowboats lie anchored, bobbing with the tide. The trail rises, curving parallel to the shore. We're cutting through a flat mesa guarded by two massive, palm-thatched *bohíos*, perhaps the manor house of the cattle ranch we've been crossing. From where we park to the shore, the bluff is covered with a lawn well-tended enough to be a patch of cemetery. Four or five bronze plaques, set into masonry work, add to the funereal air. Dotting this remote sculpture garden, these markers seem all the more inanimate against the fluid fields of ocean and cloud, as eerie as the megaliths of Easter Island.

Two flagpoles tower like galleon masts at the edge of the bluff, showing the pirate colors of Spain, the home banner of the Dominican. Like Cuba, like Puerto Rico, this flag of the sovereign republic waves red, white, and blue, our Stars 'n' Stripes scrambled. Surely, there must be more of an installation commemorating this opening of one-fourth of the earth to whatever havoc was to follow. At the least, an Iwo Jima bronze of the first trespass of the white boys. I'm outraged, rather than relieved, at the lack of a gift shop or Coke cooler. Out here, there are no racks of post cards, no embossed La Isabela mugs. "My Grandpa discovered America and all I got was this lousy T-shirt!"

Columbus himself was the first bumbling tourist, happier when he didn't know what he was seeing, content with cheap souvenirs. Gathering up the local wonders to show off back home, he loaded up for his return trip with useless plants like agave, false cinnamon and rhubarb, inedible nuts. He failed to notice coconuts, maize, cassava. Forget rubber or tobacco (though he took note of "some weeds which must be highly esteemed among the Indians"). He spent his wad of foreign currency on beads, the fifteenth-century equivalents of mugs and ashtrays. Beating against the tide for nearly as long as it had taken for him to come from Europe, he sought rumored inland gold fields. The spot Columbus chose for his resort was alongside a malaria-breeding swamp. All the guests came down with turista. If only he'd enlisted the native Taino Indians as waiters, bellhops, poolmen—brought them in to roast a pig on "Dominican" night instead of chopping off their hands when they didn't deliver a weekly quota of gold dust. No wonder it quickly became so difficult to get good help!

Whence, then, does the obligatory local guide emerge? From some lean-to? Or does this historian-for-hire sleep by the side of the road? These ubiquitous, self-appointed custodians of the world's tourist sites have more influence over our understanding of events than all the academics put together. It's their interpretations that become fixed along with our memories, their versions that we trot out to narrate our slides. At La Isabela, the saga of the first landfall in the New World has been left in the hands of a scrawny old man wearing an unraveling planter's hat, a dusty woven shirt, torn bell-bottoms, and Thom McAn tennis shoes without laces. His teeth are bad, his skin leathery, his nose bulbous, his eyes lit with a bumpkin's monomania.

I must be his first customer of the day, maybe the week. I've barely stepped out of the taxi when he scoots toward me, Groucho Marx–like, and begins jabbering. I hope Samuel will shoo the old man away, but my driver retreats to have a smoke in the shade of the field's single scrub oak. He isn't out here often enough to work in tandem with the fellow or get a commission. The guide doesn't bother to introduce himself, ask permission, or inquire about my Spanish. Fortunately, his dialect is nearly incomprehensible to me. Dropping his s's in typical Caribbean fashion, it sounds as if he's forgotten to put in his dentures. Speaking, like music-making, is accomplished with haste around here, a bluff of certitude that people expect to be called. I race off as soon as I've spotted the first outcroppings of an original settlement wall. But the old man follows, and waits patiently while I finish my tightrope walk along these mossy nubs.

I don't need his help to distinguish between the official headstones and the older rock beneath. In his mind, the former have clearly replaced the latter as the locality's raison d'être. I try to act attentive while the old man spews out word-for-word the dull proclamations inscribed on the plaques. The influential names at the bottom include a roll call of recent corrupt *presidentes*. You would think something might have been done about the roads for the sake of these visiting dignitaries. One plaque has been erected by a historical society known as Los Amantes de la Luz, the lovers of light. Sounds just mystic enough to cover for a death squad. But I don't ask for an explanation. I wouldn't understand, and anyhow he has none to offer. When I interrupt his oft-rehearsed recitation, the old man takes it once more from the top. He's memorized by rote and can't simply refer to the sentence where I point. It takes me several questions to realize that my guide does not know how to read the inscriptions he spends his life repeating. No wonder then that for him the road signs have become the monuments.

The American Diamond

I don't see any tablet erected by Rafael Leónidas Trujillo Molina, the former Dominican dictator who specialized in erections public and private. Here, as elsewhere, any trace of his thirty-year domination has vanished, the way a dream evaporates. With some prodding, the old man relents enough to utter Trujillo's name. I don't quite catch the gist of the guide's accusations, but the island's glorified straw boss had as little feeling for archeology as he did for the masses. In a country where peasants were required to post signs that read, "Trujillo brings the rain, Trujillo waters our crop," he could not be upstaged by some upstart named Columbus. Apparently, the generalissimo had some of the most precious relics bulldozed into the sea. But this custodian's condemnation is so automatic that I feel he probably has a more laudatory spiel still stored in the back of his mnemonic mind.

When his tour proceeds to a perfunctory stroll around the outlines of the first colonial buildings, the guide drones on about how the Spaniards made their building material. These blocks have stood the test of time because of the proper mixture of water, stone, and, apparently, flour. I hear the word *harina* so often that I'm beginning to think he's offering me a recipe for tortillas. Maybe the whole town was made from Bisquick. I wish that the guide had something to say about the Spaniards' need for such permanence. Did it have anything to do with the first word adopted from the indigenous Taino Indians, namely *hurricane*? Clearly, the Spaniards weren't settling for anything thatched. They weren't going native but they were here to stay. This was no tentative foothold they were building, no experimental space lab. The conquest's most amazing aspect was how bent the Spaniards seemed on making local conditions adapt to them. The idea was to stay Spanish and feudal at all costs, only richer. With the arrogance and the blindness of gods they went around renaming the void after themselves. The gall of calling it a new world! Like today's space explorers, the conquistadores carried their environment with them, traveled in their cocoon of prejudices. "In the Island of Hispaniola, to which the Spaniards first came," wrote the monk Bartolomé de las Casas in *The Tears of the Indians*, "these slaughters and ruins of mankind took their beginning."

Almost at the edge of the bluff, I stumble upon the foundations of the first church. It's an irregular rectangle with a curved nave at one end, big enough for a single altar and a congregation of fifty (not including newly converted concubines). No more than twenty feet inland did those brave

9

explorers venture before figuring they had better seek the aid of the One who got them into this. On a sunny Sunday like this one, in January of 1494, just before the worshippers began slaughtering the unconverted, the first Catholic mass on heathen soil was celebrated.

The inheritor of this history offers a tidy progression of edicts, works, noble motives. I hear about the first meeting of a civic council, 1494, but nothing about this town's other fabulous firsts—the first venereal epidemics, the first corruption scandals and ensuing mutinies, the first "What the hell are we doing here?" Columbus, for one, thought he'd landed in Japan, then referred to as Cipangu. When the Indian caciques told him about the inland valley of the Cibao, meaning "rocky place," the arrogant admiral assumed that they were mispronouncing the name of their own country. "We are good, we are good!" is how the Spaniards translated the greeting they got from the native Tainos. In fifty years, these helpful hosts would be wiped off the face of this ocean refuge they called Bohío—the mountainous eastern third, Haiti or "high ground," the fertile two thirds, Quisqueya meaning "mother of nations." Since then, it's been known variously as La Española, Hispaniola, San Domingo, Saint-Domingue, Santo Domingo, the D.R. Too many names for so small a place, too many conquerors.

Beside the church, there's a low hut of thatch over tree trunks. I assume this is some herdsmen's prime one-bedroom-with-view until the old man holds open a plastic flap that guards the entrance. Inside, unlabeled and unprotected, are the results of an archeological dig. The bones and artifacts of the first settlers lie here and there in scooped-out tureens of red earth. There are no identifying tags on these finds. My guide is careful to point out every rib and joint of what he claims is the full skeleton of a Spanish woman—though there were no females among La Isabela's civic founders. The next skull he shows me is identifiable as native by the compressed temples, a product of the bracelike headgear worn by Taino children. These remains seem so neglected and randomly arranged I suspect they've been dug up from some local graveyard. I half expect to see "Juan loves Lupe" carved into one of the pelvic bones.

La Isabela, the Dominican Republic, all Latin America makes us confront the possibility that America is a place where everything has gone wrong, was irretrievably off course from the very beginning. The promised land as the land of false promises. It's not rock mixed with flour that this fortress is built upon, but illusions—from the illusion of "the discovery" to the illusive quest for El Dorado to the self-deceptions that justified slavery to the current-day delusions of "the land of the free and the home of the Braves." If only we could peel back the strata of deceit, one fine tissue at a time, until we arrived back at this landfall.

Columbus was the first American not merely because he was striking out for "opportunity" but because he was the first hustler, the guy who could sell you a vacuum cleaner or a Veg-a-Matic, even talk a queen into making him Admiral of the Ocean Seas. He thought big and worried about the consequences later. Do now, pay later. As with most great men, all that endures—and, as La Isabela shows me, the only thing worth inspecting—is the obstinacy of his delusions. The man wasn't quite sure what he was after. He just knew it had to be something new and improved. What's an American anyhow if not someone with a chronic Columbus complex—a man who thinks there's something better around the next cape, canyon, or turnpike curve? An American is someone doomed to keep recapitulating this voyage of exploration. An American is someone who keeps talking about the future because he's drowning in the past, who keeps looking for the reason he's here because the reasons his ancestors came are no longer his own. An American is someone always lying in wait for the big idea, a chance to take his cuts in the ninth inning with the bases loaded.

Standing on the spot whence it all unfolded, I have a vision of myself on the bridge of the first ship. I'm Rodrigo de Triano, a rather dubious fellow rumored to be a Jew, who was the first to spot the outlines of land at Samaná Cay. Perhaps this adjutant couched his cry of discovery as a warning: "I see a city in Ohio named after thee, Admiral! I see parades every year on this date with politicians waving from convertibles, Chinese drill teams, drum majorettes, the descendants of slaves in fife-and-drum corps, beauty queens, disc jockeys, innoculation units, glockenspiels!" When Columbus committed the first injustice of the New World, awarding himself fifty gold *maravedis* because he claimed to have seen a "holy light" on the horizon the previous night, Triano must have protested with the first egalitarian cry, "Kill the ump!" The naked savages probably joined him in the first bleacher chant of "We wuz robbed!"

Could the conquistadores have guessed that a more recent conquest would make the national pastime of the United States a national obsession here? That a nonterritorial sport would put this singular bit of terra firma on early navigational charts back on the map? Thanks to baseball,

American history has come full circle—and what history! I wonder if that lookout had a vision of all that was to come: of baseball and burgers, corn for tortillas, cane for rum, potatoes for fries, hot Chevies and quickie franchises, juntas and multinationals, banana dictators and tobacco liberators, cowboys and gauchos and G.I. Joes, cocaine and Chiclets, the cramped hovels and the holy mysteries, the beat of *charanga* and Motown, Carmen Miranda and Marilyn Monroe, the miners of Peru and Harlan County, garage-door openers and death squads, the Pentagon and the Amazon and the Bay of Pigs, encounter groups and hot tubs and blue jeans and Irishmen making pizza and Greeks dishing out chop suey and every new arrival having to eat everything, want everything, get everything until they know everything except who they are.

To discover America, Columbus needed three stout ships and a good wind. I have a ballpark. For me, the first dazzling landfall of discovery can be sighted from the bridge of row seventeen, section twenty-two, upper deck grandstand unreserved. Terra firma is that patch of green growing outfield sweep, suggesting frontier spaces and vast possibilities. If there's a New World that strikes me as habitable then it must be this gentle terrain bounded by foul lines, the safe harbor of bases. I feel welcomed by a sport that exists within the promise of languid, carefree summers on a bountiful continent. I sniff my way along paths scented with sausage and peanuts (that American seed!). My native tribe spits tobacco (that American leaf!) and squints toward uncharted horizons. My native tongue is the sonorous cries of vendors, the disappointed moans among the bleacher bums, the wry tales of raconteurs who use this sport's built-in silences as their amplification, with an indigenous vocabulary of "Hey, batta, batta!" and "You're outta there, ya bum!"

Love America and hate baseball? Love baseball and hate America? Neither is possible, except in the abstract. What better expression is there of a continent restless for bigger and grander things than this diversion constructed of infinite options? What better comment on a nation that has never been forced to accept its own limits and does not know its true intentions than this pastime's open-endedness, ominous pauses, piling on of might-have-beens? Or the fact that, in the vast green space allotted, he-men must nonetheless skitter from base to base where they can cling to the safe haven of old opinions, old customs?

Where else but the stadium could a New York schoolboy go in the fifties to get hard information about our neighbors to the South? Latin America certainly wasn't part of my curriculum. The vision of history presented in school went east-west, not north-south. Aside from the Declaration of Independence and battles at Valley Forge and Antietam, it seemed that the only events worth recording had occurred somewhere between the Euphrates and the Thames. So I memorized all the kings of England, discovered that flush toilets were invented for Crete's palace of Knossos, but was never given a word to read about the technology of the Incas or the contorted genealogy of the emperors of Brazil. *Beowulf* and *Gilgamesh* constituted epic poetry—forget the ten thousand *versos libres* of José Martí! Simón Bolívar was the poor man's George Washington, though he fathered more countries for nobler aims. "In 1492, Columbus sailed the ocean blue," but after that was a gap of several hundred years or so before the Pilgrims completed the job. The fact that Spaniards laid claim to a territory three times our own in half the time was apparently not worth considering. The rape of Mayan maidens and Queen Anaconda was edited out in favor of sexless Betsy Ross. All we heard was that Ponce de León sought the fountain of youth. Oh, those whimsical, impractical Latins! I remember a review quiz on that meanie General Santa Anna. How dare he skin Davy Crockett's coonskin cap at the Alamo? But not a single study session, not a textbook paragraph on all the martyrs beloved by those to the south!

Baseball's Hall of Fame suffers from a similar myopia. The "foreign baseball" section holds exhibits about Korea and Italy and Japan. Is this all the result of a rather natural unwillingness to take a hard look at the people on the planet most like ourselves? Or to keep Uncle Sam from being shown with his hand in the cookie jar? Baseball, that open-ended game, came to popularity at the heights of American expansionism around the turn of the century. Unwittingly, this nonmilitaristic sport would be spread through intervention and occupation. My first inklings of our continental neighbors came from the glorified seasonal workers who traveled North following the summer game, the migrant *braceros* who helped pick crops in green outfields. Suddenly, I was having to make so many incongruous insertions in my lineup card: daring pinch hitters who bore unpronounceable names, game-day replacements who flashed bad teeth and couched their wry humor in funny accents, bubble-gum idols with pencil-thin mustaches who came in an array of skin colors that attested to a genetic melting pot far more efficient than the one my civics classes extolled. I got my best geography lesson from the birthplaces listed on the team rosters: "Matanzas, Cuba . . . Maracaibo, Ven." How could there be people so different they did not speak our language and so alike they played our game?

Not until I was nearly an adult did I fully realize there was a Palm Tree Circuit to go with our Grapefruit and Cactus leagues. Between big-league campaigns, the Latin players returned to their home countries' winter seasons, which had histories as lengthy and fabled as our own. These players had dual careers, swung their bats while astride several worlds! Many of the greatest North American stars, especially those of the Negro Leagues, performed regularly and with greater adulation in Latin America. In Cuba, they still talk about Gorgeous George Sisler; in Puerto Rico, the black star Willard Brown; in Nicaragua, of all people, Marvelous Marv Throneberry! And these leagues presented a style of play and rooting as bizarre and joyous as the culture that housed them. There were two kinds of baseball just as there were two Americas.

That's why I've set out to record the American game's second season. As I follow one winter's arc, I'm attempting to trace the parameters of Yankee influence. I'll go wherever I can still find a baseball diamond—that Yankee brand left in the flanks of various lands, that curious formation which is the most distinctive feature of the New World landscape. And like a diamond we might lay out in our backyard, aligning pillow cases or garbage lids as best we can, so the dimensions of our American diamond are expandable, portable, and stretch far past the foul lines of our borders. Rounding the bases of this metaphoric playing field, I'm on a journey to the end of baseball. And like any baserunner, I'm doing no more than trying to find my way home.

The custodian of La Isabela jolts me out of my meditation. He's gone across the road to fetch something and now staggers down the lawn toward the sea under the weight of a huge, dusty ledger. Who knows where he keeps the thing? Perhaps under some laying hens. This guest book has to be at least thirty years old. So is the pen he excavates from his bell-bottoms. Now he presents both to me, like a French maître d' proud of his menu, holding the book open to the first blank page. On the opposite leaf are addresses from Chile, I read Puerto Rico, Brazil. Suddenly, I realize just how many people have braved the roads to fill up this book. Who knows how many Americans have been disappointed in their search? But I'm not disappointed in the least. I want to flip through to see if the autographs led straight back to de Triano, to Diego Columbus and Nicolás de Oviedo, to the monk Las Casas who first exposed the extermination of the Indians and first proposed that sturdier Africans take their place in the fields, to that first uprooted slave, the first buccaneer, the first marine, the first ballplayer, and especially the first coach, manager, peanut vendor, the first *caudillo*, the first CIA bureau chief. We're all temporary visitors in America, and we must all sign in. But the guide keeps a hard grip on the corners of his book, keeping me from skimming through the back pages. It's hot and he's laboring under *el guest list grande*.

I sign, then tip him with the first denomination of bill out of my wallet. The old man looks more stunned than grateful. He calls me "Caballero," a title that once connoted noble stature, now bought with meager gratuities. I nod toward Samuel, who's removed his batting helmet at last and waits in his precious patch of shade. His long, brown face bespeaks bemusement and bored millenia of hanging out. His glance seeks confirmation that I've gotten what I came for. Now it's time to roll, time to head off down the trail and sling our feet up on the dash and scrunch our caps low down over perplexed brows. Samuel and I are both Americans in this way, too. Any excuse is good enough to hit the road, no questions asked. *No problema.*

FIRST BASE
PRIMERA BASE
Mexico

"He who shuns the 'bad taste' of things will fall on his face in the snow."

—Pablo Neruda

THE OTHER SIDE
OF THE TORTILLA

Every journey requires its unique phrasebook: a pocket-sized lexicon, a desperately thumbed dictionary of everyday interchange, trusty life raft of the communicable, one reference work to swipe off the shelves and lug in the streets. Give us this fifty-dollar-a-day our glossary of terms—complete with common forms of greeting and swindle, a phonetic guide to retail and wholesale distress. "At the hotel, at the store, at the hospital . . ." The key to pronunciation is the key to survival. Better not stumble over improper nouns, lose our way, or forget the first-person. This trip's no exception, though the language to master is but an Iberian twist on the most hallowed American vernacular.

Our quickie Berlitz course begins with what's most readily graspable, which is the ball, still five-and-a-quarter ounces and nine-and-a-quarter inches around. Please say *bola* or, more formally, *pelota*. This makes those who fling and pursue said object *peloteros* or sometimes *béisboleros*. They do their work in studded shoes the stuttering natives call "es-pikes." Does this lyrical Latinate vocabulary change the rules of the game or just our perception? The point, whether or not you trill your *r*'s, is still to scramble around those *senderos* until you score some *carreras*. Just ask the winning *equipo*. Avoid the *blanqueo*, that's shutout, and the *poncho*, that's strikeout. When in doubt, try to *caminar* your way on, so you can become a *robador de bases*. Or lay down a *toque* (just a touch), which stands for tag as well as bunt. If the call is *malo*, scream your favorite international epithet toward the *árbitro*.

19

Mata the ump! Take me out to the *diamante!* For manager, *manajer*—gosh, this is easy. But remember a *coche* doesn't smear signals across his jersey, a *coche* is a bus! And this sport's *camarero* isn't a waiter, but the second baseman. At third, there's an *antesalista*, and the catcher, passive squatter, is, of course, the *receptor.* Score a hit by saying *dobley, tripley,* that's not so tough. Neither is *terreno de foul* for foul territory, *jonron* for the trip that takes every hero right back home. And isn't the activity of outfielders more pastoral when the patch of green they tend is a *jardín?* The Hispanic urge toward embellishment takes over when a spitter becomes *una bola de ensalivada,* the dugout *madriguera,* a wild pitch is so much wilder as a *lanzamiento descontrolado.*

Playful play-by-play men trade old slang for new. Stengelese turns Spanglish. In Cuba, it's "four fish in the pan" instead of "bases loaded." *Bésela!* means, roughly, "Kiss that baby goodbye!" A one-two-three-inning goes by at *el paso de conga,* the pace of the conga drums. But *pasó la noche la pelota* means a pitch so fast it passed through the night. Throughout the hegemony of baseball, the sports pages are a snap, and the homesick fan's secret joy. To look for a nation's working allegiance, look at the ways they play. You'll find the box scores don't look any different in the *International Herald-Tribune* than in the official organ of the Sandinista Front for National Liberation. Headlines are easily decipherable when they tell you who's been voted *más valioso* or which team managed to *vanqueo* which in the *Serie del Mundo.* It's simple enough to check the standings for the summer progress of los Esquivadores (Dodgers), Serafinos (Angels), Medias Rojas (Red Sox), Azulejos (Blue Jays), Llaneros (Rangers), or the local frontrunners among winter's cast of Southern Alligators (Caimanes del Sur), Crabbers (Cangrejeros), and Creoles (Criollos). Merely adjust all accounts for hyperbole. In realms where style counts over results, each routine task executed with flair is *tremendo,* every bloop hit's *magnífico* or a cause for *ovaciones,* a good catch is a mortal jab at the *toro,* and anyone who distinguishes his *patria* in the stadiums to the North becomes an instant *inmortal.* Gringo or spic, have no fear that you can't speak the language—not where tourist and native care just as passionately about the final score. Only South of the Border, they spell it *el béisbol.*

Spit out your tobaccy and repeat after me: *Qué es el béisbol?* Kay ess el bayze-ball? *El béisbol* is the national pastime of nations we hardly recognize. *El béisbol* is a subcontinent straining to make the majors. *El*

The Other Side of the Tortilla

béisbol is a geography primer, a peek into our neighbors' house. *El béisbol* is arguably the most benign gift the one America has presented the other. *El béisbol* is the other side of the tortilla.

And that other side is only as far away as the checkerboard of parking lots and tattoo parlors and office towers burnished by downtown San Diego's cold sun. The moment Kim and I board the Tijuana Trolley, a two-car rail shuttle far more streamlined than the name suggests, we're on a track that leads straight to Machu Picchu. The platform signs announcing these last Californian stops should carry warnings: last sprinklers and burglar alarms for eight thousand miles, last Slurpees, last stable currency. Suddenly, the public-service announcements seem irrelevant, the straps and hand-rails and wheelchair access seating inadequate. The aisles are crammed with plastic sacks and canned goods and food smells, women overladen with babies and chatter, raucous laughter, and occasionally, a devastating silence. On this evening commute, most of the passengers look like they've already been to the end of the line. And we're still five miles from *la frontera*.

"Is it Messico yet?" my companion whispers. By chance, I'm crossing over with someone whose English is as shaky as her standing with the Immigration and Naturalization Service. Kim is a Korean artist in the States on a work-study visa who lives in my building. I surmised she was from Korea by the name on our joint mailbox, where we'd met while retrieving our meagre correspondence from a neighbor's slag of Hallmark cards. I could tell Kim was an artist because she wears her jumpsuits sewn from surplus parachutes, plastic jelly sandals, and a black cape that shrouds her like some haute couture monk—also by the etching press she moved into our basement. And she seemed to be the only person in sight who cared less about Christmas than I do. On an impulse, I invited her along.

"Tee-wanney? They have pyramids there?" She doesn't have the slightest idea that she's entering the world capital of pandering, miracle cures, and cheap pharmaceuticals.

"No pyramids. Tacos. And beggars. And baseball."

"My brother, he play in Little League!" Of course, there's baseball in Korea! "Mess-ico, land of primary colors! Diego Rivera . . ."

And also the Liga Mexicana del Pacífico, the nearest winter ball. By December, a Stateside *béisbolista* is either in deep hibernation or despair. The previous season's averages and percentages have been duly recom-

21

bined in every trigonometric permutation. Each fan's private highlight reel of team bobbles and comebacks and oddities, seconds gleaned from listless, sun-drenched hours in bleacher or box seat, has been replayed ad infinitum. A desperate few may have begun sowing the ground for next year, scratching out projected lineups and starting rotations, a private solstice ritual meant to tend the seeds of the coming spring. Now trade rumors move like slugs. The owners' winter meetings are already over by the time winter actually arrives, leaving in their wake a smattering of transactions to keep the so-called hot-stove league from going tepid. We've finished tracing how the movement of our favorite constellations may alter our cosmos, measured in millimeters rather than light years the delicate shifts of balance in the National League East. At this time of year, no news of the home team is good news.

Never mind two shopping days until Christmas. Four months until opening day! For more seasons than I care to count, I've charted my own wins and losses through the ups and down of the Oakland A's, those swingin' A's! We were both transplants to this black sheep city by the Bay. My first opener was the year of their first championship, the month McGovern and Humphrey were pitted against each other in the primaries while Nixon strode confidently toward "four more years" and the North Vietnamese had staged yet another of their surprisingly powerful offensives. The Vietcong, like the A's, were vastly underrated by the Eastern press. In those days, it was still possible to think that politics could find application anywhere. That first spring, I made a banner. I was used to painting slogans on old sheets. Like so many proclamations in the wind, this one was forthright enough that I was embarrassed to unfurl it. But I did, with a little help from my friends. In the bleachers, I held aloft, "VIDA SÍ, CHARLIE NO!" With apologies to the Cubans. Since then, I've moved from the bleachers to the press box. Baseball sure cranks around, don't it? A sport whose start-up is powered by celestial gears. Kiss my A's! This game is the game of renewal.

Right when we've begun to doubt that we'll fight our way through sniffles and snowdrifts to another opening day, vacation promos remind us that it's perpetually warm in some other parts of the planet. Like its devotees, baseball refuses to take a holiday—offering an escape from Ole Miss cheerleaders and Yuletide travesties. One can wake almost anywhere in Disneylandia and catch a game at the first Latin diamond that evening. According to the mimeographed sheet I've been sent, the Tijuana

The Other Side of the Tortilla

Potros—that's Ponies—and the Yaquis—not Yankees—of Ciudad Obregón are playing the next-to-last game of their season. That's why a T.J. Christmas, sacrilegious to some, sounds to me like a shortcut to redemption.

"Bye-bye America!" Kim calls, waving one floppy wing-flap of her black winter wrap.

The trolley's last stop nestles under the big gray armpit of the last wide freeway curve on the way to the drive-through customs station. But the asphalt arm's gone, amputated. No attempt has been made to blunt this stump of America. Too many lanes go nowhere, sit on too many stanchions, making this look like some over-inflated rubber highway. On the other side, the lane markers don't glisten, and there just aren't enough cars. The frontage roads are lined with shanties and *yonkerías*—the closest transliteration of junkshop. Just in case anyone has a case of cholesterol panic, there's a McDonald's a dozen steps or so from the border crossing. It's only a few steps more to ground chili and lime on everything. A stroll through one linoleum corridor and at the end, chaos. No amount of posted officialese can smooth the abruptness of this most-traversed demarcation between First and Third Worlds, soften the sharp distinction between two ways of being on the planet. Maybe the world's think tanks ought to be located here—where we confront the "other" and make sure its papers are in order.

But I've come for a ballgame! Our *taxista* balks at first, explaining that the stadium is located far beyond the Tijuana city limits. He follows the main highway out of town past fitful attempts at suburbs, stopping three times to get directions from roadside gypsies huddled by garbage can bonfires in the dusk. At last, he finds the correct way up the hump of a canyon wall. The road turns to dirt as soon as the civilized world can't see. A tract subdivision claims one side of the dark chasm. The staggered boxes climb one front door at the level of the next one's roof. One good rain could wash away their bare front yards. Momentarily, the taxi spins its wheels in a mudhole. Looking toward the top of the crest, I spy a familiarly circular form hovering ominously. Though it's taken a half hour to get here, a coil of concrete is nuzzled below a craggy ridge that must be back in California. The first ballpark in Latin America sits less than a Dave Kingman poke from the U.S. This could be where illegals gather to make their midnight dash. Unfortunately, the stadium, light towers and all, squats in the dark. The bulldozed shelf of dirt lots is

23

empty. My league schedule has obviously been revised. Already Latin America conspires to spoil my best-laid plans.

"Mañana," the driver announces, my first of many mañanas. My sidekick doesn't care if the game's on or off. This is her first archeological site and Kim insists on taking a turn around the turnstiles, the ticket booths, the smooth, graded slopes of grandstand. "Pyramids!" she cries out, as though I've led her to Chichén Itzá.

The driver drops us along the Avenida de la Revolución. "Which revolution?" Kim wants to know. With Woolworth's and Denny's and two-storied stucco lawyers' offices, this could be broad, well-lit Main Street in any California valley town. Only a few basement-level strip-joints, with suggestive names like El Unicorno, remain from the heyday of Tijuana's sex industry. In this area, too, Mexico can't compete with the productivity across the border. Our peep show houses, take-home porn videos, and phone fantasy party lines deliver the explicit with greater efficiency. Kim and I stumble past ghostly warehouses of blankets and pottery, a glut of liquor stores offering deals on mezcal, *farmacias* well-stocked in medicines which the FDA hasn't yet approved. These have become more typically Mexican sights than the street photographers who wait patiently to snap Mom and Pop in sombreros.

"Is Mess-ico only Polaroid?"

Mexico is probably the most mysterious of our Latin neighbors because it's so shrouded in false images. We know this place least because we think we know it best. Tijuana, for instance, has for some time been the fastest growing city in North America. A local economy revved up with oil revenues and the pocket change of immigrants gathered at the edge of el Norte has turned Sin City into a boom town. It sprawls down a narrow valley in huge boulevards that replicate the American West's grimy fast-food, oil-and-lube strips—except that here the rotating neon needs translation. Tijuana is also visited by more Americans than any other destination outside the States. More than London, Jamaica, Tokyo. T.J. provides more U.S. passport holders with their image of foreignness, one day-trip at a time. And what is that image? If first impressions are to be trusted, and most Americans go no further, then Latin America must be the realm created to straighten whatever we've made crooked. The disordered, hilly grid of downtown is crammed with auto body shops, cut-rate dentists, and plastic surgeons. "Give us your dented, your misshapen masses!" says the Mexican Lady Liberty.

The Other Side of the Tortilla

We wind up in Tijuana Tillie's, one of those posh, stage-set versions of a *bandidos'* watering hole. At one end of the broad-beamed dining room, mariachis blare; on the other, a six-foot projection TV screen shows rock videos. Neither noisy side manages total victory. The few college kids engaged in their time-honored semester-break rituals couldn't care about atmosphere. One frosh after another leans back in his seat and opens his gullet while an obliging waiter pours the José Cuervo down. I hope these are the fraternity's all-star guzzlers. Their brothers count off booze consumed in seconds, not ounces. "Ten-elephant, twenty-elephant, thirty-elephant. . . ."

Once we've polished off *chimichangas* in puff pastry cups shaped like coffee filters, my escort asks, "Can you show artist true Mess-ico?" I drag Kim toward the Zona Norte's unpaved mire of flophouses and cantinas. Here, the sidestreets are thick with vendors shucking *mariscos*, shoeshine boys selling a tenth of a tenth of a prayer at the *lotería*, hoboes sprawled where they can find solid pavement. Well-placed puddles cushion the fall of *borrachos* bounced out flapping red saloon doors. The poverty here is so Hollywood perfect that I feel like complimenting the wardrobe and makeup departments. The Mexicans know better than anyone how to infuse dramatic charge into personal defeat. Nowhere do people fall so low or wallow so magnificently. Their mean guys look the meanest, nasty the nastiest, heartbroken the brokenest.

Kim coaxes me into one tavern that promises to offer a tableau of "The Lower Depths." The action inside turns out be as innocent as a junior high prom. A balcony encircles the oval-shaped dancing pit, like an indoor track above a YMCA gym. Up top, an all-brass orchestra in secondhand military regalia pumps out the outlandishly blaring, pathos-filled oompah-pahs of its Germanic-based Norteño ballads. The throb in the horns is all Mexican, but the beat's a reminder that this territory was once claimed by the Austro-Hungarian Empire. Below, a number of cowpokes are doing the fox-trot. In formal, mournful coats, buttoned down to their knees, these men look like nineteenth-century hands just off a long cattle drive. They wear Stetson hats with various tassels attached. A tassel earned for each season on the range, I like to imagine, each duel with a *mal hombre*. As they do their best two-step sashay, the men barely smile, make no attempt at hanky-panky with for-hire escorts who barely reach up to their waists. The roly-poly, peso-a-dance squaws wrap their dark manes in buns; the lanky men sport bushy handlebars that seem to have collected the dust of the trail. The fleeting connection between these gents and ladies is effected with scrupulous dignity.

"Seen enough?"

"Artist must see world."

So we cross the alley and head for a classier joint with mock Arabesque facade, poke our heads through padded doors that were the height of forties elegance. "A Thousand and One Nights" is apparently under new management. Leatherette booths, the loud, lucky red of a Confucian temple, are claimed entirely by Chinese men. Three male generations of the growing Chinese clan in Tijuana, from graybeards to bespectacled young clerks, sit absolutely silent amidst the lurid decor, nursing drinks they don't seem to want to touch, waiting for a pageant of harem girls that's long been cancelled. It's as if they've come here to rehearse being Latin but their hearts just aren't in it. I doubt any of them will work his way up to hooting, "Ay, *caramba!*" Perhaps they're consoled by the sight of one another's discomfort. Hesitating at the door, I soon realize that I've made their evening by importing Kim. The men can't help turning their heads in unison. They must not have seen an unclaimed, unfamiliar Asian female in decades. "Very bad!" Kim whispers. "We go now!"

We check into the Hotel Caesar, where the salad of the same name was invented. Today, the place doesn't even have a restaurant, let alone room service. Do we ask for singles or a double? Is this terminology from baseball, too? I discover that a Korean lady's idea of what to do in a fleabag hotel with a strange older man is pluck the first hints of gray out of his head, one strand at a time. I'm unhappy only because she finds so many. Mexican late-night TV shows José Feliciano doing "Jingle Bells," ads for canned lard. No carolers, no make-believe families sipping mulled cider, no pine needles on the carpet! This Christmas in Tijuana may be the best Christmas I've ever had.

THE DAY
OF THE FANATICS

Kim was right. By day, the Tijuana
stadium is a Mayan ziggurat placating the gods of the barren West. There
is something pre-Columbian about the whole affair. The oval grandstand
slopes upward in steep slabs, perfect for sacrificing virgins, or sending
packs of kids sliding down on the seats of their size two Wranglers. The
base is striped with tan, orange, and purple. Either the park is supposed
to look like a big tequila sunrise or those are the hometown Ponies' high
desert colors.

A banner strung over the ticket booth rechristens Christmas "El Día
de Los Fanáticos," the Day of the Fanatics. It sounds like some rediscov-
ered García Márquez epic. After the foretold hot dog, a hundred years of
indigestion! Once the announcements begin, I realize that my translation
is, like most things literal, wholly misleading. "El Día de Los Fanáticos"
is the Hispanic transcription of "Fan Appreciation Day." The Tijuana
franchise, like its counterparts across the border, will be rewarding its
loyal patrons with giveaways between every inning—a merchandising
trick to attract spectators for a final game unlikely to have a bearing on
the standings. I don't see anybody among this subdued crowd of five
thousand checking frantically for a winning number on his ticket stub.
Those who've chosen to be here on their holy day are fanatics in the
original sense of the word, connoting attachment to the sacred. From
the Latin *fanum*, meaning temple.

"Every day's a good day for a ballgame" is the gospel according to

27

Ernie Banks. So why not this Navidad morn that breaks chilly and serene, with visibility all the way to the land of opportunity? Pope John XXIII was only plagiarizing a Chicago dugout cry when he declared, "Every day's a good day to be born and a good day to die." My religion begins and ends with Mister Cub's single commandment, "Let's play two!" A doubleheader is on tap for this final day of the Mexican season.

"Please explain!" is Kim's battle cry.

The rules of the game are difficult enough, but how do I tell her about the quiet joy I feel claiming our place in the sun? That first glimpse of smooth maternal infield curves, the comfortingly symmetric alignment of bases, always feels like the first and the ten-millionth time. This vision of green patch captured for my private use summons up the memories, dreary and magnificent, a remembrance of games past all the way back to the first time I stumbled down an Ebbets Field aisle holding my father's hand and couldn't believe I'd been let in on something so arcane yet intimately within my grasp.

Every ballpark is a nation unto itself: each with its own diverse citizenry, its unique customs of feeding, its distinct tenor of absorption and purpose, its disputed borders and one-of-a-kind vistas, its downtown box seats and remote bleacher cantons. The particular pitch and twitter of "hey-batta-batta" are no less clues to the native species than a forest glen's murmurings. What a wise sport in which the venues not only influence outcomes but our experience! They become a part of what we come to gape at, rate, and rank. Think of the subway cars chugging back and forth behind the Yankee Stadium bleachers; the redbrick confines of Wrigley, somber as a Chicago slaughterhouse; the Cecil B. DeMille palms that fan Dodger Stadium, with its seats powder-blue as a leisure suit. Think of the churchyards or shopping malls adjoining the sandlots where you played Little League or Sunday morning softball. Like its crystalline counterpart, the baseball diamond changes with its surroundings. No two jewels alike, that's the game's unspoken guarantee.

Here, the grass is well-tended and particularly verdant against the mesa-brown backdrop. Wide-bodied lady vendors in flowery aprons prowl the red seats bearing trays full of *tortas* stuffed with pork *carnitas*, the Mexican equivalent of corned beef and onion roll, enchiladas that are mostly onion and cilantro, pig's knuckles in gelatin, and a half-hardened creation in plastic containers that I take to be a fruit drink. The stands are dotted with more Padre caps than Los Potros headgear. I keep forgetting that San Diego is just over the next hill. The Ponies also offer their version of the San Diego Chicken. This mascot neighs from under an equine head, looking more like Bottom in a college production of *A Midsummer Night's Dream.* In addition, a local quick-change artist entertained the crowds from foul territory, first in drag as Cleopatra with her asp, next as Michael Jackson moonwalking, then satirizing the patrician image of former Mexican President López Portillo, a modern emperor with no clothes but Roman toga and laurel wreath.

Mexican baseball, like the Mexican economy, is just a half-step ahead of the creditors. The precipitous decline of the peso against the dollar has virtually destroyed the league's ability to attract decent U.S. talent. Complicating matters further, Mexico is the only Latin country with two professional seasons. The Pacific League operates in the winter, representing the main towns along the Northern coast. The more popular and established league plays all summer, running its games concurrently, defiantly, with the majors up North. Out of stubbornness, pride, or custom, Mexican baseball owners rarely allow the U.S. major leagues to supersede their contractual rights. So Mexican players can only sign with big league organizations once they've paid some owner for their liberty. The gringos have to pay what amounts to a finder's fee, and often it is a steep one. This is the only Latin ballplaying realm that's not free territory for scouts. The condition of its winter leagues perfectly exemplifies the country's relationship to the United States. Mexico refuses to admit that it's a colony, though the nation might be better off to quit standing on ceremony.

For every Aurelio ("Señor Smoke") López, there are dozens of outstanding players—including one slugger known as the "Babe Ruth of Mexico"—who've been forced to spend their careers on bus rides between Hermosillo and Mazatlán. Those few who get to play in the States are therefore all the more celebrated. The Mexicans' current duo of burly lefthanders, Fernando Valenzuela and Teddy Higuera (whose middle name is also Valenzuela), upstage the Mexican president whenever they appear in motorcades. Certainly, these pitchers' economic houses seem to be in better order. As Babe Ruth once said when asked why he was being paid more than President Hoover, "I had a better year."

Valenzuela has even been made into a comic strip character called El Toro. One of his cartoon followers declares that this folk hero is *"más popular que la leche adulterada y que los kilos de 950 gramos."* Both

29

leading Mexican stars are "more common than diluted milk or kilos of only 950 grams" because they emerged from peasant families living in back reaches of the Sonoran desert. Raised in a house without electricity or running water, Valenzuela is the youngest of twelve brothers; all played on a team representing their *pueblito* of Etchouaquila. Fernando the Bull has taken on godlike stature not only because of his eyes-to-the-heavens delivery and six varieties of screwball but because he plays in Los Angeles, a half-Mexican town where the Dodgers have been adopted as the unofficial national Mexican team. Los Esquivadores, as they're translated, were the first U.S. team to offer Spanish-language broadcasts and have always made more of a conscious effort than other franchises to attract the Latin fans. Valenzuela, the pitching embodiment of the Mexican exodus, gives them a perfect box-office draw. With his pug nose, puffy baby face, and beer belly, he even looks like an *indio* Babe Ruth. Like Ruth, Fernando stands as living proof that almost anyone can master this sport. Flesh and sinew can go to seed, because the trick is all in the hand, in the eye, and most especially, in the nerves. Baseball is all psyche and Latins especially admire those like Valenzuela, who can quietly, charmingly, pull off the ultimate bluff.

El béisbol, after all, is about beating the Yankees at their own game. And Latin players seem to do this with a flair and zest that's a throwback to the sport's early, freewheeling days. The sport seems to have been invented for Latin America and its play-ball climate, its emphasis on individual bravado. Latin players who are regularly branded "hot dogs," or show-offs, are merely relishing the game the way scrappers like Wee Willie Keeler or Three Finger Brown did at the turn of the century. Baseball is a game that encourages eccentricity: Jesus Alou's preswing neck-twisting, Roberto Clemente's three-hundred-sixty-degree *torero* spins, Vic Davalillo's leg-lift, Juan Marichal's patented high kick, Luis Tiant's gravity-defying gyrations and victory cigar smoked in the whirl-pool. Baseball lore offers numerous tales of Latin pride runneth over—like Rusty Torres's dugout brandishing of a revolver—as well as Latin values asserted. When, after a frustrating loss, Giants Manager Alvin Dark tossed a post-game supper of cold cuts onto the locker room tile, a defiant Felipe Alou began eating off the floor—as though to say, in the words of his Dominican pal Juan Marichal, "Win or lose, you do not throw away food."

Tijuana's Potros have to win this contest to secure the final berth in the upcoming playoffs, but that's hardly something I can get whipped up over. When Flaco Jiménez takes too wide a turn and gets picked off third, I have no way of knowing if that's one of Flaco's tendencies. A weakness is only interesting if it's predictable. I am thrown back to studying my siblings in the family of fan. A ticket to the bleachers offers total transcendence of the self at almost no risk. Can more be said of any of the major religions? The occasions that make us rise out of our seats and wave our banners—they're what count. The rest of our lives is the game. By refusing, for even one moment, to forget about it, I keep baseball in very high company. The opiates that ensnare us—those are what define us more surely than any claims we might make for ourselves. The Day of the Fanatics makes me think of Hemingway's questions: "Why should the people be operated on without an anesthetic? Why are not all opiums of the people good? What do you want to do with the people?"

For now, I want to join them in their yays and boos. I want to loll where small-time, scratching-it-out America eases back for a rest. Where America clears its throat and bellows. Where all America is on familiar ground and everyone is an expert, everyone an American—even Kim! The story goes that after being taken to his first baseball game, psychologist Carl Jung made the pronouncement that Americans are people with the minds of Europeans, the souls of Indians, and the public behavior of Africans. Sounds good, except that Europeans act rowdier at their soccer matches than do the mellow black old-timers nursing hip flasks who populate baseball bleachers. Leaning back, unloosening the starched business shirts they wear beneath their Levi jackets, the Tijuana fans fill the air with sighs instead of hollers. I can't tell if these groups of buddies escaping their families are holiday respectful, or just holiday weary. These Mexicans display the Indian stoicism, an accusatory quiet. Given a style of play that stresses speed and defense, the grandstanders find their excitement not so much in brute force as in proper execution. They wait for a steal of home plate, even a meager single, the way their ancestors must have waited for the rain during a drought. They give thanks in the same time-honored way, not with howls or even chanting, but with knowing nods, nearly imperceptible twitches.

"Baseball good for looking," says Kim. "But nothing happen!" The usual plaint of the baseball virgin. And it's true—nothing happens, until things happen so fast that you can barely keep up. I can only tell her,

"Baseball is a waiting game." It begins with the catcher, mum as a movie Indian, settling on haunches and adjusting his ceremonial padding, beckoning in sign language toward the next sentry. A sturdy ump shares the vigil, stooping to see as the mitt sees, guarding his zone of air yet eager for its violation, trained to serve as judge in this trial of patience yet unable to speed his verdict. The hitter needs time each time to rediscover what dirt feels like in his palms, what wood feels like in his grip. He must align elbows and tendons with his telescopic sight, adjust testicles and superstitions, bounce on heels to keep his span in the box from becoming a sentence in a cage. Nobody's in any rush to begin what must end too quickly.

The pitcher remains king of the hill, invulnerable on his sandbox mound, clutching the power to relieve all his adjutants of their poised attendance until the ball's released. It's not easy to heave away superiority, and before he does he will squint in search of the catcher's coded command, fidget with his cap's bill just to share the fun, toy with resin bag and suspense, hope for an encouraging configuration of shadow and windblown hot dog wrappers, seek the extra heft of an inner gust. Behind him, the infielders gauge barometric clouds, shift gloves, sweep semicircles in the dust. Between expectant crouches, these human springs resting on tolerant knees will try anything to uncoil. Banished to the farthest reaches of vigilhood, isolated as frontier sheriffs by the distance they patrol, the outfielders are pitifully alone on their watch. They do not catch the ball as much as the ball catches them. The traveling orb's a spotlight that shines only fleetingly on these vaudevillians in cut-off trousers. An arc of horsehide in their direction is the cue for soft-shoe routines meant to contain the moving prop sent their way.

In the wings waits a chorus line of leathery *poupées mécaniques*, set to pop into action as the lineup turns. With bubble-blowing dalliance, they stroll from dugout to bat rack to on-deck prayer circle. One by one, each steps forward gallantly, foolishly, so relieved to be done with his anticipation that he's willing to step through a hoop of fastballing fire. Bench to batting box, they dance a severe minuet, a grim promenade which ends with most of the club-bearers returning to their seats, like wallflowers at a teen dance damning the whole awkward ritual while itching to get asked to rise from the bench once again. But more often than not, nothing happens except an almost indiscernible discernment, the refusal to act just quite yet, a flinch or a turning aside pitch after pitch. And the waiting continues.

In what other sport does warming up entail slowing down? Before each contest, teams must relearn how to move to the gentle and archaic meter dictated by the game's measured tasks. The players honor an unwritten code no less strict or convoluted than the official rulebook: when to catch and when to soak mitts in cow's milk, where to scuff shoes in the clay and where to test the traction of the Bermuda grass, when to spit tobacco juice, when to put dirt in their back pockets, when to sit cross-legged, turn their caps backwards and meditate upon all this foolishness, when to strut in the sunlight. None of these mercenaries ever looks too studious, too overwrought.

Baseball's delight is in the unrealized, in the infinite rotating of situations rather than its limited results. In this sport, as in life, the ratio of event to expectation is impossibly large. The wait is often better than what we're waiting for. Baseball teaches its devotees to refrain from heaping too many expectations on one play or one game or one lifetime. Resigned to the mundane, yet always on the lookout for the inevitable mysteries to come, the fans wait, as the catcher waits, ump waits, batter and pitcher wait, fielders and batboys and benchwarmers wait. Because the distinctions that ultimately get made—the hesitant embarrassed undemocratic culling of champ from chump, Hall of Famer from Alibi Ike—are minute and highly cumulative, judgments that only all the waiting, all that time can provide. Baseball—the creation of a young nation with time on its hands—defeats empty time, perfects the waiting until it no longer feels like waiting at all.

There's a saying that hours spent at the ballpark are never subtracted from one's lifespan. Baseball, the sport with no clock, is exempt from time's merciless progression. Dream time. And, if that's so, then watching baseball in Latin America is doubly dreamy. Never mind if I pass on the pig's knuckles. Or if I've got to protect Kim from the attentions of benchwarmers and bat boys who've noticed this exotic good-luck charm in the stands and want to pose for pictures with her at game's end. Lounging in the December balm, I can't squelch a grin. This is cheating. It feels like I've laid down a bunt on the universe.

Back in town, we follow the celebrants toward a *feria* around the cathedral. Everyone crisscrosses the plaza hurrying to be with family. Pig-tailed girls carry sparklers, trinkets, plastic sacks of spongy cake from the *panaderías*. Blocks around are clogged with toy vendors, carnival games, and stands frying up deep bucketsful of the horsetailed doughnuts called *churros*. Husbands and wives behave stiffly, awkwardly, unused to letting go their separate burdens of subsistence. The children, many children to each pair, point without much hope toward bins of toy dump trucks and rubber U.S. infantrymen. They may have to wait until Epiphany, the big day for gift-giving in Latin America. Wafting over the cries of the vendors, the controlled clamoring of the children, the hubbub of bartering, is the Gabriel call of the mariachis. This holy night is hardly a silent night. Here, there's no false separation between the sacred and the mundane. The church bells drown out the honky-tonk. A magnificent sunset radiates from the hills, like the last wail of a cowboy ballad. The chill of semiwinter descends. Somehow, the world seems in its place. It's for these people that carolers and pontificators everywhere intone "Peace on Earth." Maybe this isn't *Miracle on Thirty-Fourth Street*—but it's close enough.

And this is most definitely *el mundo Latino*, though I can't tell exactly what makes me know I've wandered into the jaws of a cultural monster that won't let go from here to Tierra del Fuego. Could it be *la raza's* arresting faces, well worth a second and third stare, faces that show more than a hint of red clay and raw suffering, faces where that suffering emerges as faint illumination in the eyes, wistfulness in the smile, creases that form a road map to inarticulate wisdoms? Or could it be the planters filled with cacti that frame lurid portraits of the Virgin Mary tacked to the windows above? An emerald-colored shed that proclaims itself the Garage Los Tigres? The elegant sidewalk stacks of cowboy hats and silver belt buckles? The dusty and nearly unstocked hardware stores, the *torta* shops exuding smells of rancid pork fat and cumin? Is it the daubs of color applied wherever there's room, as though to cover some inherent blemish? Is it the fraying around the edges, the ribs showing on the dogs? Is it the comforting transparency of all pretensions, the sense that culture here is but a string of colored bulbs draped on a tar-paper shack?

"Is like a painting to walk through," says Kim. "Is Paul Klee, is Kandinsky."

Certain places stay with you forever, even if you only pass by them for an instant. It's almost as though some destinations have been waiting all along to be found, like unglimpsed potentialities within ourselves. This is when we know why we travel. These are the moments that remind us nothing is ever so familiar as the strange. For me, each turn around the plaza tells me I can't properly define myself anywhere else.

Then why am I so concerned about getting back across the border? The excuse is that we've got a flight to catch and Kim must return to her classes. The dozen or so lanes of traffic are backed up like rush hour on the Triboro Bridge, but pedestrians form an "express" line at the supermarket of dreams. The secret, when it comes to bureaucrats, is not to provide them with anything to check. But Kim's work-study visa and Korean passport are unlike anything the Tijuana rubber-stampers have seen. "Don't worry," I tell her. "Nobody ever got barred for the crime of going to watch a baseball game." She's reassured further by the treatment of the two scraggly *chicos* filing up to the single counter ahead of us. Without luggage or passports, they strike me as prime suspects for *la migración*. At the formica portals, I hear one claim he's a senior at Escondido High on a day-trip, though his school ID is *escondido* somewhere. The second says he's running an errand for a sick aunt. Both are waved through with me. The harried clerks won't let me stay by Kim's side and argue her case. Powerless, I have to wait on the American side of the revolving door. While minutes go by, an unbreachable torrent of Mexicans washes past.

I comfort myself by pondering baseball's remarkably proportioned architecture, with its ability to make apparent the minute amount of leeway within which all human activity takes place. If the strike zone were a millimeter wider or the bats six inches longer or the mound a foot shorter or the bases a foot farther apart, then the advantage would swing to either offense or defense. How could this precarious balance of forces and dimensions have been devised without computer imaging or, at the very least, a crew of statistical engineers? Yet the first foul lines were crooked, the field paced out, the floppy bases flung here and there. So it is with the balance of payments, the adjustment of currencies and wages against the dollar. Were the peso worth even a smaller portion of a penny than it is there would be rioting and social upheaval; worth a few more and the flow at the great border station might turn the other way. The web that holds rich and poor in place is no less fragile than the design that keeps a hitter from beating out a ground ball by less than a single step. The real games of inches are politics and diplomacy and economics—but also friendship, courtship, and reproduction, a game of uterine inches. Every game, in a sense, is a tacit acknowledgment of the fact that nothing would be possible if we did not wake up each morning to the same general set of ground rules. That's what keeps us abiding by even the most oppressive of rulebooks, and makes us shudder to think of what might be let loose should our common field of play be redrawn.

"Kim can be crossing! America says okay!"

But exact fare is required for the automatic trolley, and all we have are centavos. While Kim waits, shivering at the turnaround, I try McDonald's, Wendy's, Sambo's. The cardboard signs scotch-taped to the cash registers say "No change." And they mean it.

RIGHT FIELD
JARDÍN DERECHO
Puerto Rico

"For me, I am the best."

—Roberto Clemente

BOSS, ME NO FEEL LIKE HOME RUN

Every time I get on an airplane, I think of Roberto Clemente. At takeoff, feminists may seek the vanished spirit of Amelia Earhart, soul singers may reach for the final crescendo of the Big Bopper. For a ball fan, the great Pittsburgh Pirate right fielder serves as the friendly skies' emblematic fatality. On New Year's Eve in 1972, Clemente and a cargo of humanitarian relief for Nicaraguan earthquake victims dropped into the ocean just offshore from his beloved Puerto Rico. Though I've purposely timed my flight around the disaster's anniversary, I cross my fingers until we've reached cruising altitude. Never mind that Clemente was traveling in a prop charter of dubious registry while I'm on the midnight run of a commercial jet shuttle, that his hold was overloaded with baby formula while mine is crammed with bulging cartons of holiday loot from relatives in Nueva York, or that he was on a mission of mercy while I'm after the intangible rewards of idolatry.

Were it not for Roberto Clemente, I might never have been compelled to patrol this part of the world's turf. At what age did I first anoint him as my hero *número uno*? Clearly, I'd already formed enough of a world view that I sought to identify with angry underdogs—the further under, the better—and in Clemente I discovered a player who was as adept at brooding as batting. Yet I must have been old enough to have developed some aesthetic sense, an appreciation of just how balletic baseball could be when performed by a master. Closing my eyes while my Walkman pounds out a Rubén Blades tune, I can still summon up images of the fluid one-handed running catches followed by three-hundred-sixty degree pivots and the spinning fandango heaves that punctuated Clemente's dance to a different drummer. His eighteen-year career was encapsulated in the very first assessment of Al Campanis, the Dodger scout who signed him: "Hell, you can't gild a lily!"

For Clemente, baseball was nationalism with ground rules. Starting out in the fifties, when play-by-play announcers were still trying to rename him "Bob," Clemente showed as little fear of opposing pitchers as he did of speaking out every time he felt Latin players were underpaid, ignored in All-Star selections, stereotyped as hotheads, or belittled for their broken English. "Some people act as though they think I lived in a jungle," he'd remark, challenging reporters who misquoted him to try their hand at Spanish. After he turned the 1971 World Series into an extended showcase of his skills, Clemente became the first Latin player to dare break into his native tongue during the nationally televised locker room celebrations—so he could ask his parents' blessing and dedicate his victory to Puerto Rico. Only Clemente could have interrupted yet another drearily predictable jock interview to declare, "I love the poor people, the workers, the minority people, the ones who suffer. They have a different outlook on life."

Fourteen years after Clemente's martyrdom, I've come to see how his favorite people have been getting along without him. What has Puerto Rico's "economic miracle" done for "the ones who suffer"? What "different outlook" survives when over half the population has been impelled to look North for their American dream? Heading down for our landing, I'm listening to "Todos Vuelven," or "Everyone Returns." The song is a kind of unofficial anthem of the Puerto Rican diaspora: "Everyone returns to the land where they were born, to the incomparable bewitching attraction of its sun. Everyone returns through the route of remembering, but the time of love returns no more. Everyone returns . . . to the perfume of a woman. Everyone returns . . . because memory lives free." If Roberto Clemente remains el Inolvidable—the Unforgettable One—to what use is his memory put?

The lights of San Juan's beachfront towers snake through the night like a conga line. My plane resists a midnight plunge into the black breakers. After an hour scanning the Christmas goodies, the VCRs and toaster ovens spinning around the baggage carousel, I realize that the only accident to befall me is the loss of my luggage. My supreme sacrifice will be two days without organic tanning lotion or designer khakis. At least I've got a reservation at some bargain hostel. My taxi driver has trouble finding the right driveway down a sidestreet in the shadow of the mosque-white skyscrapers of the Condado. Nobody answers the night bell. Just when I'm about to make for a Best Western, the proprietor rises from his slumber, unlocking the iron gate in his boxer shorts and a *guayabera*. He acts annoyed that I didn't wait outside until morning.

I wake to the jackdaw cry of pneumatic hammers, not the rustle of palms. My continental breakfast consists of instant Sanka and stale raisin bread. My "beach access" is through a row of construction sites for twenty-story stacks of fly-paper condos. Somehow, I don't feel like a swim, and, thanks to the airlines, I have no suit. I walk six blocks to find a booth where I can place calls to my few precious baseball "contacts." In the next few days, I'll get to know every available pay phone within a twenty-block radius. These seem to be the only North American amenities in short supply. On all sides, there's a cavalcade of fast-food parlors, the best of *gringolandia*. These are patronized by local teenagers, not homesick travelers. After all, what's there to get homesick about? Here and there, I find pockets of tinder-box stationers and grimy *farmacias*, open-air lunch counters featuring tropical fruit drinks and flies. But I have to do more than sip blended papaya to convince myself this isn't 1954 and I'm not reliving an annual Christmas visit to my grandmother's boarding house in Miami Beach. This is Miami without Mr. Clean, without miniature golf, without the chocolate waffles I dreamed about every year, without the pumpernickel rolls in the Jewish delis, without Jews.

The only way to end my disorientation is to find some speck of foreignness that might justify it. I'm not usually one to make straight for the cannons or stockade recreations—but I need the feel of old San Juan's cobblestones underfoot to convince myself I've arrived somewhere. Except for the fluted guard turrets erected by Ponce de León to survey his "rich port," the place provides little clue of colonial days. A few white linen restaurants remain as evidence of nineteenth-century sugar barons' privilege. Luncheonettes with becapped countermen and fountain syrups attest to a gentility more recently extinct. The lanes are crammed with gift shops and hole-in-the-wall bars where a clientele that's dropped in from Maui guzzles trendy imbibements like "Sex on the Beach." I'd prefer to wander the *barrio* of ferocious lovers and indestructible whores captured in Oscar Lewis's *La Vida*. It's probably been bulldozed to make way for a mall. Besides, my guidebook does not map out a walking tour of such places. What's needed for the sort of tourism I practice, call it antitourism, is a Baedeker to the slums, rated with one to four forks for their show of humanity amidst squalor. Where's the *Guide Michelin* for travelers who find no sight as dazzling as the genuinely dismal, no destination more exotic than the realm of emergency?

The radio in the cab back to my hotel is tuned to a call-in show that's immediately recognizable as the local variant of North American "sports talk." The tip-off isn't just the words *pitchey* and *e-short e-stop*, but the obsessive urgency, the earnestness, at once touching and ludicrous, with which the host and his phone pals debate the match-up of starting pitchers for tonight's contests in the six-team winter league. As though our planetary fate hinged on the outcome of Ponce Leónes versus the Arecibo Lobos! Or the Caguas Criollos versus the Santurce Cangrejeros (who can hardly inspire cheers of "Go, Crabbers, Go!"). I've read reports of a recent, precipitous decline in support for the league, but discounted these as exaggerations. I take this on-air jock session as a first indication that there are still some fans out there. It does seem odd that the discussion isn't focused on a manager's strategy but on the recent death of a Ponce player in a car crash. Caller and announcer agree that team management was to blame for excusing him from traveling on the team bus. I'm just getting excited about catching tonight's game between San Juan and Mayagüez when the driver flips the dial. Like *taxistas* everywhere, this one will prove to be a fair representative of all the rest. In San Juan, they prefer Frank Sinatra while driving. Even the cabbies have turned away from the game.

The professional teams have fared poorly in the years since Clemente, and I'm beginning to see how poorly. Is it possible that the very existence of the sport is threatened in a place that's been a baseball hotbed since before the Spanish-American War? For decades, Puerto Rico was a prime stop on the Caribbean circuit. In its heyday, Puerto Rico produced a host of stars besides Clemente, including Orlando ("Baby Bull") Cepeda—called Peruchín here because his father Perucho was also a great player. Once upon a time, small ballparks graced downtown neighborhoods. As up North, they've been gradually replaced by "improved" facilities which are grand, impersonal, suburban. Back in my room, I plot out the bus routes that can take me to Hiram Bluthorn Stadium. The home of the Metros, named after the first Puerto Rican to sneak through the big leagues' color barrier, is located near a freeway exit on the southern edge of San Juan's sprawl.

Fortunately, one of the messages I've left yields a last-minute offer of a ride from the Giants' chief scout for Latin America, Nino Escalera. "Always at the service of San Francisco sportswriters," he tells me on the phone. "*Chronicle* man, *Examiner* man, Nino knows them all!" I'm a bit chagrined when he rolls up to my cruddy guest house in a brand-new white Buick Electra. If I'm not the expense-account journalist he expects, he's not quite as he appears either. It's hard to guess the age of this lanky old-timer shrinking away inside a finely tailored linen jacket. He sure drives older than he looks, tooling down the six-lane highway as if we're out for a Sunday jaunt. Escalera's bushy white mustache completes a pitcher's face: wily and foxlike, with a self-preoccupation only occasionally disturbed by a gap-toothed grin of self-satisfaction. I've barely settled into the air conditioning when the scout works our conversation around to remind me that he was one of Puerto Rico's all-time great *zurditos*, that's lefthanders. I'm afraid to admit that I've never heard of him. And when I get home, I can't find any "Escalera, Saturnino" listed in my encyclopedia of major league records. Eventually, I'll be able to assemble an all-star team from the Latin legends who take it upon themselves to be my chauffeurs! But Nino must have done all his pitching down here, or in the minors. He relishes my visit as an opportunity to show off whatever status he can throw around. He demonstrates his power windows and car stereo, and, within minutes, manages to flash the World Series ring—a diamond for every base, or are they cubic zirconium?—which he earned in a previous tour of scouting for the Mets. "Now the Giants," he plugs shamelessly, "they treat me first-class all the way." Yet Nino's cruising on empty. He passes several brand-name gas stations before waiting in line for fifteen minutes to save a few pennies at the discount pumps of some company with a name like Pedro's Petrol. Still, he won't let me pay for a drop. And when I wonder if we'll get to the park too late for good seats, he winks and says, "You leave that to Nino."

From the raised freeway, I finally spot the stadium lights. The circles of blacktop surrounding the park are shockingly unclaimed. There are far more cars across the boulevard at Plaza Las Américas, billed as the largest shopping mall south of Florida. Maybe the fans of yore are in

Florida, too—or freezing in the South Bronx. Evidently, J.C. Penney is outdrawing José "Cheo" Cruz, the underrated outfielder who's the best of the post-Clemente crop. Nino beams proudly when we're waved through by the teenage girl who guards the empty lot. He insists on searching for the VIP parking section though there isn't any point. Now I see why Nino didn't need to hurry. With him, though, I don't need a ticket. I try to look properly impressed when the head usher lets us through the turnstiles with a resigned shrug.

Maybe the game is delayed Latin American–style, scheduled on mañana time. There are no lines at the stands for pizza or *empanadillas*—small meat pies served by ladies in hygienic paper hats—or "Marvel, Hamburgers de Sabor!" Once within the comforting bowl of orange seating, I'm astounded at what I find, or don't find. The contest is indeed underway, though the primary indication is the nine lonesome figures, plus a few coaches and umps, occupying the field. The place is reminiscent of the Oakland Coliseum during the years eccentric owner Charles O. Finley was running the A's like a rummage sale. One miserably foggy night against last-place Seattle, the club set an all-time record for the least number of paying patrons at a game. The team's broadcasts were handled briefly by a local college radio station. The roster included Dick "Wampum" Allen, Gary "Ragtime Band" Alexander, the openly gay center fielder Glenn Burke, and almost any other washed-up bargain Finley could pick up. Those A's had been the Karen Ann Quinlan of sports, a franchise on a respirator. But two respectable teams are playing on a balmy night in *béisbol*-mad Latin America—and there can't be more than a thousand people in the twenty-five-thousand capacity park. "Is this typical?" I ask Nino. He nods and tells me that the attendance is better "on the island," meaning outside the big city. But the league average is under three thousand per game, at least "until the playoffs and sometimes not even then." Those determine Puerto Rico's representative to the annual Caribbean World Series. Puerto Rico, the wealthiest and best-equipped participant, no longer hosts the series due to lack of fan support.

With the choice of seats before us, there's no need to claim space up in the press box. Nino insists on taking me there so he can be seen in the company of a writer from the North. His voice quivers and his chest swells as he introduces me to every beat writer hanging around to cover this snoozer. With their white embroidered *guayaberas* flopping out like protective aprons, these scribes look more like a team of barbers. The formica counters, covered with telex machines and stat sheets, are as streamlined and commodious as any back home. These glassed-in perches always feel sadly removed from the cheering crowds below, but with such a small crowd, the atmosphere is deathly quiet. I'm treated to a series of premature post-mortems. One writer cites a "Steinbrenner syndrome" among the owners. "They think they're bigger than the players. They trade at will, so that none of the local fans have anyone to identify with anymore." Others blame a lack of promotion. "In twenty-two years, I have never received a press release from any of the teams," says the host of a popular sports radio broadcast. "They take it for granted that people will come."

The empty stadium does offer one advantage. The lack of a crowd makes it easier to pick out the old-time players in the box seats behind the home-plate netting. "Leave it to Nino!" says Nino, leading me down the aisle. "I want you to meet a few friends of mine." They're all here because baseball, the sport that's not so tiring to play, is the sport its players never tire of. To walk away from the game, especially in countries where the game gives people all their wealth and community standing, is to turn your back on life. So old teammates are consigned to watch one another grow paunchier through the seasons of winter balm. On almost any night in San Juan, you can plunk yourself down in a row crammed with baseball legends eager to sign autographs or reminisce. Holding court are the survivors of Clemente's generation, the pioneers who endured discrimination and dislocation to pave the way for Puerto Rican acceptance in the big leagues. With a broad sweep of the arm and a foxy grin, Nino presents me to nearly every player I was hoping to meet on my trip.

"Hi there, Vic! . . . *Qué pasa*, Rubén?" Nino greets Vic Power, the power-hitting Cleveland Indian of the late fifties. Beside him, an intense and wiry Laurel to Power's mammoth, resplendent Hardy, is Rubén Gómez—known to local aficionados as el Divino Loco, the Divine Crazy—who pitched the first game in San Francisco's Candlestick Park. Next to him is Pédro Gonzales, one of the early Dominicans in the majors, here on a scouting trip, and on the aisle, grinning shyly, is the expatriated Cuban Orioles' star, Mike Cuellar. Leaning against the netting for a chat is Diego Seguí, now a pitching coach. So where's José Tartabull? Missing from this class reunion are the two men who dominated Puerto Rican ball's golden epoch: Clemente, excused to immortality, and Orlando Cepeda, self-exiled to Los Angeles after he served time for picking up a suitcase loaded with marijuana at the San Juan airport. "Cepeda was the one they really loved," one player tells me. "While Clemente seemed aloof, saving everything for the ballpark, sleeping fourteen hours a day, Peruchín was more extroverted, a man of the night, always partying. He was a home-run hitter and he had that rhythm within him, that beat."

I hardly know where to start tapping this mother lode of baseball lore. All I can do is grab a seat and ask for an explanation of why so many are empty. "When we first started playing," says Vic Power, "we used to get around fourteen, fifteen thousand every night. But it was different, because the team used to have Willie Mays and big-name guys. Plus now, we got a lot of entertainment, a lot of things goin' on at the same time." The Divine Crazy is bursting to chime in. "You want to know the reason why baseball's gone bad? In every Latin country, they have heroes. In Puerto Rico, we got no heroes now. You see, I can walk around anyplace and they say, 'Hello, Ruben, hello, *número veinte-dos*, hello, Divine Crazy, hello this, hello that.' Because I always play for the same team and people feel I belong to them. Before, people can say, 'I have Rubén, I have Clemente, whatever.' Now they come, they don't know who's playing. The players do good, they trade them. They don't live in the town, so the fans they can't ask him, 'Why did you do that? Why you swing at that pitch?' So the ballplayers don't talk to the fans, don't get them thinking, 'Oh my God, he talked to me, he's a human being like me.' In the Dominican, you see, they still have idols. Baseball is still number one. Because they see the ballplayers in their town. They see how once they were selling candies in the street, now they're rich. Tony Peña in the Dominican, when he retires, he's gonna be welcome over there. When Marichal retired, he had to leave the Dominican Republic. That's right. He couldn't stay there, the people boo him. Because he don't play. Clemente, too, they used to boo him. The first time he played was because I used to play the outfield, too, and I told the manager I was sick. I told him, 'You got a kid over there, play him.' But the players now, they think only of themselves. They don't realize that what comes up, it has to come down."

The supplanted generation usually voices such complaints about the upstarts following in their footsteps. In this case, the rapidity of the Latin players' advance, and of Puerto Rico's transformation, only heightens the discontinuity. Though Vic Power looks too jovial for sustained bitterness, he cannot help grousing, "Sometimes we have trouble with the Puerto Rican player because he don't hustle enough. They been paying them too much money. I mean, I played with guys like Ted Williams, Musial, Bob Feller, and they didn't get all that money. I wonder where that money was before! Oh, baby! My biggest salary in the major leagues was thirty-eight thousand dollars. Now the average Puerto Rican kid wants that for a signing bonus. The kid's mamma, she knows too much!"

Ironically, what's killing Latin pro ball is the success of its graduates. Now that the Latin player has gained a measure of "equal opportunity" at the top, he no longer wants to play at the bottom. Advances in treatment and pay for Latin players in the major leagues have worked against their own leagues. In the past, local heroes dutifully returned to represent their home teams, so that nearly all of the great Latin stars of the past actually had year-round careers for twenty seasons or more. Roberto Clemente was one of the first to protect his longevity by sitting out the winter season. Irate Puerto Rican fans sent rocks through the windows of his house. A player with today's multimillion-dollar contract has little incentive to risk injury by playing local ball. This has become a more obvious bone of contention in the Dominican Republic, where national idols like Mario Soto, Joaquín Andújar, and Pedro Guerrero no longer perform before home crowds.

It is less of an issue here because so few genuine stars are being developed. The obvious explanation, as Vic Power implies, is Puerto Rico's relative prosperity. Poverty has always bred ballplayers, not just in the Caribbean but in the ghettos and backwoods of the U.S., too. Puerto Rican youngsters now have many more educational and vocational opportunities. When they do commit to a career in baseball, they demand more money for their sacrifice. Scouts no longer comb the bushes here as they do in the Dominican Republic. In the meat market of baseball, the Puerto Rican *pelotero* just isn't enough of a bargain. Pound for pound, a Dominican or Venezuelan is cheaper and more highly motivated to succeed. This may be why Puerto Rico hasn't produced a genuine box-office draw in over a decade. In the press box, I'm told that this year's candidate for "the new Roberto" is Rubén Sierra of the Texas Rangers. But writers and fans have been through many candidates in their wait for the second coming of a baseball messiah.

At the same time, the quality of gringo talent is dropping. Each Latin team is allowed to import up to eight North Americans, who were once top-drawer major league or Negro League stars. With lowering attendance, the best Latin owners can afford are Single-A or Double-A prospects seeking more on-the-job training. The National and American leagues use the Caribbean leagues as their free testing ground—a relationship that's been formalized with a ban against hiring players with more than a hundred days' experience in the majors. Often, the better North Americans are brought down only for the last month, or weeks, of the winter season. They can earn up to $6,000 a month in Puerto Rico, while native players, no matter how good, never get more than $3,000—a disparity that widens in the other Latin countries.

All these factors work to lower the quality of local play, which must now compete for attention with the hundreds of major league games carried to the island by cable television. "Those games, after all, are a visual delight," one of the sportswriters admits. "So why should people come to a ballpark where they have to go into a stinking room to take a piss, where the food is not nearly as good as in the States?" Overexposed to the original, Puerto Ricans won't settle for imitations anymore. With attendance down, a self-defeating cycle is set in motion. The sad condition of baseball perfectly illustrates the predicament faced by any successful colony. Puerto Ricans have become spoiled by U.S.-manufactured goods and no longer value their own handicraft. The game thrives only in the hills, alongside whatever still passes for the indigenous. "Out on the island," says Vic Power, "that's where they still love their baseball!"

The whole row nods, including a conspicuously nonathletic fellow in business slacks and penny loafers, white oxford shirt unbuttoned halfway down his burgeoning gut. As soon as I've given him a glance, he thrusts out a chubby hand and introduces himself as Mister Castro. "But my friends call me Pochi," he explains in a tone that suggests I can consider myself one. Nino Escalera keeps winking, nodding, prodding me to pump questions at the living legends lined up like ducks in a pond, but I find myself in a conversation with this incessantly cheerful public relations man. His bulging eyes and pallid skin suggest an Iberian courtier. He incessantly wipes the sweat off, his metabolism unsuited to the tropical climes in which history has placed him. But Pochi is a lifelong *fanático*—an amateur chronicler of the game and the island.

"We were the very last to leave the empire, and we merely changed to another master." In half an inning, Pochi fills me in on Puerto Rico's long-standing loyalty to the Spanish crown. He reminds me, too, that Cuba shared a similar fate, and that Cubans and Puerto Ricans retain a special affinity. I remind him that billboards all over Cuba still read, "We must liberate Puerto Rico!" This Castro's not surprised, or impressed, by the campaigns of another Castro. "You know what they say about Cuba and Puerto Rico? They are two wings of the same bird." Does that make the Dominican Republic in between them a torso or a carcass? Pochi speaks of Puerto Rico's next-door neighbor as a dark pit. "Their economy's at least fifty years behind," he says, illustrating his point with stories of the recent mass drowning of Dominicans trying to land illegally on Puerto Rico's west shore. Shortly afterwards, another rowboat full of escapees was attacked by sharks. By recent estimates, at least a hundred and fifty thousand Dominicans live illegally in Puerto Rico. "We have our aliens, too, and our ghettos. The Dominicans stick to themselves because some Puerto Ricans are not always hospitable." Not Pochi. By the seventh-inning stretch, he's insisting that I spend New Year's Eve with him in Ponce. "The whole family together! The home-made delicacies! It will be a native Puerto Rican fiesta."

But what does the term "native" mean in these parts? Just what is this Puerto Rico? Officially a commonwealth, a protectorate, unofficially an anachronism or a cutting edge, a depopulated zone or a people factory or a marketing test group, a sixth borough of New York City, a strategic U.S. military installation, one huge fast-food franchise floating in the Atlantic? Why not a sovereign nation, if Grenada can be one, if Andorra can be one? Come to think of it, what is a Puerto Rican? I've arrived at a place in between, full of in-between people leading in-between lives. Staring at the vacant orange rows, I think the fans' current motto may have been voiced by Clemente himself, back in the early days when his broken English was still fair game for reporters. After bunting in the ninth inning of a tie game, he returned to the dugout to tell Pirate manager Danny Murtaugh, "Boss, me no feel like home run." It's depressing. I've come to Latin America in search of this throwback to more innocent times just as the times are eroding that innocence. Where Americanization is farthest advanced, the American game is most threatened. What the empire giveth, the empire taketh away! Or perhaps Nino Escalera has the answer when he sighs at game's end, "In life, there's only one Clemente."

WAKE UP, PUERTO RICO!

"**C**lemente, Clemente. I tell you, man, he was a different breed of cat. There are so many stories, just lend me your angle. I need a hook, brother, anything to get me rolling. . . ."

If I'm a complete blank, that's because it's six in the morning and we're cruising in fifth gear past the Condado's shuttered bodegas, the Dunkin' Donuts, the hotel monoliths. "In Puerto Rico," warned Vic Power, "you've got to go, go, go." It seems that I'll have no choice now that I've caught a ride with a whirlwind named Luis Rodríguez Mayoral. He was recommended to me as a board member of the Ciudad Deportiva, or Sports City, a recreational facility for poor youths conceived by Clemente and carried on in his memory. But sitting on the board of trustees, like keeping the Clemente flame, is only one more moonlighting gig for Luis. He's the first of many *fanáticos* I encounter who use their fierce attachment to baseball as a means for squeezing a living out of the stingy local economies. While paying the bills with a public relations job for Eastern Airlines, Luis writes a daily newspaper column, serves in various capacities for the local winter teams, organizes the major leagues' annual Day of the Latin Player. At the moment, he's on his way to host the sports segment on local television's version of the "Today" show. It's called "Despierta, Puerto Rico!"—that's "Wake Up, Puerto Rico!" He's roused me so that I can serve as this morning's guest.

"Clemente used to say that he was a better driver than Fangio," Luis continues, perhaps apropos of his own maneuvers. "That's Juan Manuel

50

Fangio, he was the greatest Latino driver. Yes, Clemente could drive like a madman sometimes. That was his way of taking off the pressure. In uniform, he was a poet, an artist, man. I think of him like a Picasso. Outside the white lines, as they say, he was just another guy with *muchos chistes*. Lots of jokes. You know, he used to play the organ. 'Cielito Lindo' and that shit. He was some character. I just thank God I met him before the higher power took him away. Some people thought he was aloof, because he built a wall around himself for self-protection. But to get along with him, all you had to be was sincere. He attacked everything he got involved in with this fanatical sincerity. A lot of people say he was a hard-ass, but he was very humble. He used to say that to be respected, you have to give respect. Like when he asked for his parents' blessings after the Series. A lot of guys would have been thinking about champagne and the broad that they had lined up for later. But he wasn't like that. He was a reference point where humanism is involved. . . ."

From the way Luis slumps low in the bucket seat of his black Mazda, I'm amazed he can see any reference points. "I remember, one time I backed into his car, you know, the Dodge Charger that they gave him for being MVP of the Series. I thought, shit, he is going to kill me! But he says, no problem, *es material*. You can always fix that. . . ."

Luis can steer me wherever he likes because he's promised to fix up a meeting for me with the esteemed Doña Vera, Clemente's widow. "*Seguro*, man," he assured me with a wink, though a sure thing's never quite so sure on this island. In baseball, as with everything else here, there are too many people fighting over the same few crumbs. The "good life" is a roster with a strict twenty-four man limit.

"Clemente believed, like you and I do, that we were living through a cycle of materialism. If he were alive today, he'd be worried about all this prostitution going down. In every sense of that word. *La balance*, the balance of *valores*. It's so fucked-up. He'd be speaking out on that, but not in a way to offend people. Clemente *era diplomático*. He admired Muhammad Ali, Gandhi, Kennedy. And especially Martin Luther King. He met him. We used to talk about this stuff all the time. Clemente could have been a politician. But not in the sense of going on an ego trip, where once they get elected, they forget about the people. . . ."

How does he know such sentiments delight me almost as much as being called *brother*? I have the feeling that Luis is a master at assessing visiting gringos and playing on their prevailing view of Latin America.

Around big-league scouts, I'll bet he does as good a job at rating his "brothers" like so much horseflesh. In the company of big-league executives, he could play the charming native guide, wiseassing all the way. With me, he can let down his politics. But not his hair. Under the brown fedora he affects, Luis is utterly bald. Without this prop, he appears more sober than his age, a whiter-than-white-bread civic leader. With his dome cloaked, he's the mischievous kid with chunky smile and mooning eyes. Luis may be pushing forty, but with me, he knows it's safe, even preferable, to reveal the unreformed ball fan cruising for action and autographs. Despite the Spanglish inserts he uses to their best effect, he makes me feel that we're two all-American bozos doing what we like to do best.

"You know, we're just bool-shitting, hombre. Like me and Roberto used to do. But what else is there? I mean, *sabes*, this is the real stuff. Right? Like, did I tell you that Roberto loved to shine his shoes. He was a snappy dresser, but, as we say, *conservador*. Always went out in a suit and tie. That's why I tell Latino players today, 'If you want to be remembered, *coño*, dress like Clemente.' You know, the genius of someone like Roberto was that he noticed the simple things. The things nobody else talked about, the things that get taken for granted, that's what he was curious about. He's like Chi Chi Rodríguez, another Carolina boy. Or Valenzuela. Those are the people who, as I like to say, have tasted the earthly glories. I mean, you can't study to be a ballplayer. And the Lord made him in such a way that he could attain great things. It's like anything in life. Joe Brown, the Pirates' G.M., once said, 'Clemente could have been the best doctor, the best lawyer.' Because he had that drive within him. *Tenía carisma*, as we say. Yet he could still remain proud of his roots, he could retain his identification with the struggler. You know, he was playing with tomato sauce cans and a broomstick when he got discovered. It was a rice salesman, Roberto Marín, who put Roberto on his first team, the Sello Rojo, that's a brand of rice. It's not difficult adjusting yourself to sleeping on a good bed or having air conditioning. What's hard is to mentally digest the good things in life. But so many Latin players, they get lost in that shit. Like when you want a woman just so others can see. When you take a woman with that intention, it's only one step away from drugs. I always say to the players, 'If you gotta bang a girl, bang her. But not in your room. It's basic self-respect. . . .'"

"To bang" is the most useful verb in his native tongue. Luis explains, "I'm not a sinner, but *sabes*, I don't blame anyone if they can't resist the opportunity for a good bang." The word has more connotations than the sexual. The point of the game is to "bang" somebody before he "bangs" you. "He banged him pretty hard," Luis will say of one sportswriter's relationship with a player. All social life here seems like a scramble among siblings, as cutthroat as it is incestuous—especially among a baseball crowd where everyone's played with everyone else, knocked them in the papers, hired or fired them, roomed with them, slept with each other's wives. "Oh, don't talk to him, he's a loco," Luis warns me about one player. When I tell him later that I found the same person fascinating, he'll change his tune. "I told you, man. He's a super guy. Maybe the elevator doesn't stop on the top floor, but super." In Puerto Rican fashion, even long-simmering grudges are posed, mere opportunities for drama. To bang or get banged: that keeps Luis in perpetual motion around San Juan, checking up on scores and clubhouse rumors as well as various street-corner denizens for whom he's a godfather, money-lender, *compadre*, shaman. The pace of banging is what makes him a Puerto Rican. "Look at all the people on this tiny island! And all the rest of us in the South Bronx and who knows where else. We've got the rhythm. *Sabes*, Puerto Ricans fuck more than any people on earth."

With that, Luis screeches the sports car to a halt, double-parks. "Hey, man, you wanna stop for an o.j.? Come on, fresh-squeezed. I'm buying." Luis leads me past the fly-swarmed counter of an outdoor fruit stand to a back patio covered with ribbed green plastic sheeting. He knows the waiters by name. He has a customary table, right beside the jukebox. "Marvin Gaye. Remember this one? *Mi favorita*. Roberto would have liked this place. If there had been opportunities for him to give ovations to the fans, he would have been number one in that sense. Because he said, the guy who pays for my salary, going back to his identification with the struggler, is the guy who works in a factory, the watchman, the taxi driver. Those are the guys who pay me, so I must have respect for them. And he felt great responsibility to be in top shape every game to give his best to the fans. A lot of people called him uppity, but he'd say, I can't do these things because if I don't sleep, and don't feel myself well, I won't be sincere toward the fans, and if I don't produce, they'll start booing me. *Ese*, he had great pride in being a Latino, a Puerto Rican, a Negro. A lot of people misinterpreted his seriousness, saying that he used to eat a lot of shit because he was Roberto Clemente the ballplayer. But it wasn't like that, man. He was a proud man, but it was the type of pride, believe me, he never downgraded people. He was just deeply proud on a personal basis of Clemente the ballplayer and his abilities, and proud of his roots. You like the house special? You want some papaya added? *Bueno.* Drink up, we better go."

The cobblestones of old San Juan slow down Luis enough for one more story. "Speaking of food, you know about the incident in San Diego? After a game, Roberto told Manny Sanguillén he was hungry. He went for a walk, bought fried chicken, fries, whatever. And coming back from the hotel he saw a car following him very slowly. And he got kind of panicky. Finally, the car got up to him and three Latinos with guns made him get into the car. They took him to an isolated place, I understand it was Balboa Park, and they put a gun in his mouth and said, 'Give me your belongings.' So he said okay, and they took the gun out of his mouth, but he'd heard them talking Spanish. So he told them, 'I'm a baseball player.' *'Yo soy pelotero.'* And the guys say, 'Who are you?' 'I'm Roberto Clemente.' 'Clemente?' And they wouldn't believe it. And Roberto showed them the 1960 All-Star ring—he never wore the Series ring from 1960 because the writers picked Dick Groat MVP and he was pissed off because he thought he was MVP. Then he showed them a major league ID. 'Oh, Señor Clemente, we're sorry, we'll take you back, *perdone eso!'* So they took him back to a few blocks from the hotel, more or less where they kidnapped him. And he thanked God and everything and started walking. Then he hears a horn, and looks back, and the guys are coming in reverse. And he thought, 'Oh my gosh, they're after me again!' But what they did was to return the brown bag with the chicken. And the fries."

Luis parks in a lot at the back of an office tower so new that its foundations hardly seem set. "Clemente led a charmed life. A short time before his death he told Vera that he had dreamed the night before about the funeral. And he mentioned to Vera the names of the friends that were there carrying the coffin. On October 1, 1972, the day after he got his three thousandth hit, Vera and I presented him with a trophy that contained a plot of earth from his beloved *barrio* San Antón. When Pancho Coimbre saw a photograph of that activity in my home a few months later, he told me 'That guy was dead right there.' It's something spiritual in the photo, there was sadness on his face, and there was something around the face—how you call it, in Spanish we call it *aureola*—like when you see pictures of Jesus Christ, there's like a light or something, a slight light, I'm gonna show you that photograph. In the Latin countries, there's a science called *espiritismo*. You know about this? Spiritualism. Like voodoo. *Exacto*. The roots are in Africa, right, and though I am not a master of that, since I was a kid I have been able to foresee things, feel things. Brand me as crazy, but I have a strong spirit, as they say. Don't be afraid of me, I'm down to earth, man, but you know it's something within me spiritually. And I used to receive vibrations from Roberto continuously and I'd tell the guy in Spanish, '*Tu eres espiritista.*' You're a spiritualist, why haven't you worked in that field? And he simply used to smile. He never said yes or no, he'd just hit me with that smile. Roberto had something peculiar about him, in that when you said something about him that was true, but he would not admit, he came back with that smile. Like when he used to say that he was so strong, he could take a nail and bend it when he was six years old. Then he'd give me that smile."

Commentator, columnist, publicist, community activist, coach, boolshitter extraordinaire—to the list of Luis Mayoral's credits, I must now add interpreter of the spirit world. Life in Latin America is indeed lived on several parallel levels. Luis leads me through a back door, into the basement maze of the TV station's electronic hardware. At the first editing room, we run into an elderly technician. "*Mira!* Look at the nice tits on this one!" Luis pinches the man's chest through his turtleneck. "You know what we call him? The world's only ugly Puerto Rican." In return, the staff greets bald Luis with *bombilla*, Spanish for lightbulb. They are the ones lit up by his presence. We pause before a video monitor to whip through some past interviews. Luis has to show me Luis in Dodger Stadium with Pedro Guerrero, at spring training with George Bell, in Nueva York with the "New Yorican" John Candelaria. "You know, when the Pirates wanted to sign Candelaria, Clemente told his father, '*Ese muchacho vale mucho.*' He's worth more. So his father held out for a bigger bonus. He was always on the side of the players. He was the first Latino who didn't just play and take the money. All the success you see here, this whole generation of ballplayers, it's all the product of the Clemente drive. . . ."

Luis is pushing the elevator button for the penthouse. "Wake Up, Puerto Rico!" is broadcast from a single corner of the swank and carpeted top floor, which serves as a studio by day and a ballroom at night. Uninterrupted windows offer a three-hundred-sixty degree view of San Juan's staggering growth: the balconied condos lining the shore from Condado to Isla Verde, the colonial outposts of Santurce and Río Piedras merged into one sooty mass, the industrial parks that have replaced the sugar plantations of Carolina, Clemente's hometown. Through smoked glass, it almost looks like prosperity. Our interview takes place opposite the bandstand, with the two of us in molded plastic chairs set against the Cinerama view. The show itself is more Latin intimate in scale. The staff of four includes a winking cameraman and a producer to fetch coffee. The video camera looks state-of-the-art, but the graphic that announces the sports segment is a collage of action shots snipped from magazines and pasted onto a buckled sheet of cardboard.

Luis recites yesterday's scores with a professorial seriousness I didn't think was in him. He introduces me as a distinguished *"periodista de béisbol."* In both his native tongues, he asks the standard questions about the purpose of my book, my projected travels, my attraction to Clemente, and, out of the blue, my admiration for the writer still considered the great North American Latinist, Ernesto Hemingway. "All American writers are influenced by what he has done," I answer in a sleepy daze. I'm not so groggy that I don't notice the direction in which Luis mistranslates my replies. When I say that most North Americans are as ignorant of Latin baseball as they are of Latin history, he tells his viewers that I believe "everyone should get to know each other better." When I tell him that Clemente was the first player to speak out on behalf of the Latin American poor, Luis appears to Hispanicize this as, "Clemente had more than a great throwing arm." In private, Luis had proudly called himself a "son of Martí and Bolívar." In public, he steers away from my palaver about the unity of the Americas. But I don't mind. I'm watching a master in that tightrope walk between crusader and hustler, rebel and shill. Luis seems to alternate between them almost by instinct, bool-shitting all the way. I just don't understand how he can get away with such blatant sanitizing before his largely bilingual audience. Perhaps they, too, are used to such inaccuracies.

Then I hear music, up and over. A lush romantic bolero from the forties, sung by some Latin lover. What does this taped theme have to do with sports? Before I can conjure up an answer, Luis is holding a conductor's baton that's materialized out of nowhere. "And now," he

56

announces, live and on camera, "as we ask of all our distinguished guests, the author will lead the orchestra." The baton is thrust in my hand. The camera awaits. I look up, trying to disguise my amazement at this absurd yet characteristically Latin touch. I begin to rock my hands back and forth, a sleepwalking Zubin Mehta. I sway my head in time to the strings and the congas. I am no visiting expert anymore, which is fine with me. And Luis is no longer a commentator. What is he at the moment? A prankster or a black priest? Just a buddy trying to give me a bang? I hope I'm not making a complete fool of myself. Before all Puerto Rico, I am trying to summon forth the spirits. I glance at Luis for approval. He is smiling the strangest smile. The music fades. He hits me with that Clemente smile.

DIVINE CRAZY

Where do you come face to face with divinity? At Howard Johnson's, San Juan branch—where the customers, not the scoops, come in twenty-eight flavors. El Divino Loco had suggested a breakfast meeting under the orange roof. He pulls into the orange garage at the appointed time. This Puerto Rican *inmortal* drives a wobbly-wheeled, semi-crumpled, twenty-year-old Fiat sedan. Like its owner, this tinkerer's pride shouldn't be out on the road, let alone revving so high. At sixty, Rubén Gómez exhibits not an ounce of fat or resignation. He's all legs in brown polyester slacks, a gangly kid sprinting from his car the same way he sprinted to the mound in the 1954 World Series.

"I played thirty-one years, winter and summer, sixty-two seasons of baseball. And look at me now! I'm ready to go. When ballplayers today say they're tired, they are liars. Have you ever heard a person after walking two or three thousand miles say, 'My arm is tired'? No way, because it's the legs that carry the weight. When you eat good food, sleep nice, train good, no way you gonna get tired. But they don't train the pitchers to go nine innings now. They let them walk to the mound and all that, they train physically and mentally slow to do something fast. Players who have the sore arm, that's in the brain. They wanna take it easy and steal the money from the owners. Players today, they want to come out of the ballgame. I used to say, 'Gimme the ball, gimme the ball!' The arm doesn't bother me. And I still train every day. I'm still at playing weight, a hundred and fifty-four pounds. I could play today."

Divine Crazy

A prematurely matronly waitress spots the Divine Crazy on his way to his favorite booth. She giggles and runs to the kitchen at the sight of this pin-up boy from her youth. The recognition brings a smile that's uncomfortable with modesty, a smile that intends to say, "Oh, you needn't!" but comes out like, "Please go on!" Beneath a Nixonian nose, his rounded, overlarge upper lip curls with bitterness to reveal a ferocious set of teeth. The Divine Crazy has teeth that won't let go of life.

"I was raised in a family where nobody went to bed later than ten o'clock. My father was an Englishman and he said everyone has to be at the dinner table at five o'clock. I'm gonna be sixty years old and I haven't changed. When you are raised in that way, when you have family, it's like you have a shield against anything bad that can come. 'Cause when you have so many people that you can look up to, you think two or three times before you do something. See how many people they end up in jail because they didn't stop to think! They're not criminals, but they didn't think, and then they're sorry, it's too late. When I manage, at the Santurce club, I used to fine the ballplayers three or four thousand dollars. Not fifty dollars like now. Because nobody wants to leave the money to the owner. You better believe it. It's like when children play, if it's their bat and ball and someone do something they don't like, they take it away. Children and grown-ups, they are the same. Think now of all the old people you see around, they're alone, they're still doing childish things. So you have to be careful. An' if you don't perform right, they put you in jail."

Across the table, Rubén Gómez stares hard with eyes too close together from squinting toward the strike zone, eyes that never let up. It's as though I'm an umpire and he's trying to get a break on a bad call. He presents his case over ham and eggs, against the clatter of dishes and a Beatles tune turned into a Muzak waltz. Though age-spotted, his long, mournful visage looks positively adolescent in its earnest concentration. Today, says the Divine Crazy's face, today's the day I turn over that new leaf!

"I first played in Bristol, Connecticut. Then they traded me to Canada because I hit the owner, right in the face. Because I had an argument with a ballplayer and they fine me and I know I was right. So I say to the owner, 'Give me the money.' When he doesn't, I waited 'til the ballclub left and went to his office and I took a bat. He was alone and I come with a bat and I say, 'I want my money or I kill you. I don't care what you do to me. You're not gonna steal my money.' Then I hit the bat on the desk, smashed everything. And he write the check. So he traded me to Canada, where they had all these ballplayers who want to make a new league, Sal Maglie and all those guys, so I play with a better calibre of ballplayer. I was bought by the Yankees in 1950, they sent me to Kansas City. They pitch me two games, I pitch shutouts, then they didn't pitch me for a month. And I told them, if you don't pitch me, I'm gonna go someplace else. So I called the Dominican Republic and I asked if they want me. You ask them about el Divino Loco at the airport in Santo Domingo. I set records there nobody will ever forget. Later on, when I sign again with the big-league club, I tell them you gotta pitch me this amount of games. If I don't win this many, you don't pay me. If I do it, you pay me. Years ago, all the ballplayers went through these things. A lot of them are afraid to talk about that. But I've been a tough person all my life. In New York, the press call me, 'The Butcher of the Caribbean.' Okay, one time I almost kill that Pittsburgh manager—what's his name?—that Danny Murtaugh. They get the bat out of my hands just in time. They put me in jail in the Dominican Republic. I threw at a guy, he come after me, so I hit him in the ear with my fist. The army put both of us in jail. But since I was playing for Trujillo's sister, she told the president to tell the Santiago army to let me out of jail. I was only in there about five minutes."

I don't know whether to believe anything this man tells me, but after a while, it doesn't really seem to matter. His erratic record in the majors included a few fine seasons as a starter before the downhill slide that got him released in 1962, more years in the minors that earned him a shot with the Phillies in 1967, another decade of obscurity in Puerto Rico, throwing for whoever would have him.

"We used to make our own gloves, when I started playing. I could make one for you now. You see, we take the tarpaulin they use to cover the trucks in the rain, that's hard, you know, and we cut it up one, two, three. We made a good ball from that tarpaulin, too, an' it had some kind of oil on it, so it last long. Every time we'd see a truck with no one around, we'd cut out a piece. We had a lot of fun, you know. In our town, there were the Alomars, you heard of them? Six brothers, they all became professionals. We had less bars, less nightclubs then, so we had more time to spend on sports. We do it every day, so the better we get. Baseball has changed since then, but it's the same game. Take a monkey who comes out of a tree, who takes a coconut. Maybe he rolls a coconut like that, and when somebody see him they say, 'Okay, now we're going to play bowling!' Okay, take a child, put him in the jungle, give him a ball. He's gonna use a stick, he's gonna swing through that ball. He has never played baseball."

In Howard Johnson's, the Divine Crazy talks philosophy. "Everything we do in life is a copy of something. Somebody come up with an idea, maybe there's no can openers, maybe he sees a native do like that to open a coconut, he makes a machine and makes a lot of money. It's a copy of somebody else. Very seldom is a person on his own. I remember one time I went with a girl on the beach. I make love to the girl. An' she want to wash herself, but not with salt water. I climb up just like that to knock off some coconuts. I'm scared, but I get to the top of the tree. I'm scared, but because I was with a girl, I climb up like a monkey, I bring the coconut down. If you ask me now for a thousand dollars to climb a coconut tree, I wouldn't dare. But I was young. For that girl, I did it. 'Cause she had no water to clean herself. That's the only time that I climb a coconut tree."

In his fight for dignity, Rubén Gómez keeps track of all the wins and losses. "I was in Texas once, spring training with the Giants. I stayed in a place that was so dirty, I had to put on the uniform again, to use as pajamas. That's the honest truth. The next day, we play ball, we go someplace, one o'clock the bus is supposed to leave. I didn't sleep, but I stayed in my room, until one-thirty. I'm a disciplined person but this time, I come at one-thirty. When I came in the bus, everyone starts like this, applauding, 'Oh, Rubén's decided to come! He's here now. Very good!' I say thank you for the applause but I'd like to say something before we get to the ballpark. And I call Willie Mays, Monte Irvin. I say, you guys come over here. 'You notice something different? We're colored, you guys are white. You see, every night you sleep like a decent person. These guys, they were raised in the States, I don't know how they were raised. I know how Rubén Gómez was raised, in a nice decent place, with a nice decent family, everybody's the same and I slept good. But last night, I slept like an animal. I overslept today half an hour and you smart, white son-of-a-bitches, you know, you come around and applaud because I broke a rule. I hope that in the next generation you're born again and come to this country as a colored person so you know what I'm talking about. Thank you.' And you know what happened? Leo

Durocher come up to the side afterwards and said, 'Rubén, that will never happen to you again as long as my name is Leo Durocher.' And the next year, we didn't stay in no place where nobody couldn't stay together.

"After that, we had a helluva ball club. We gotta stick together. We gotta love each other like human beings. If a manager fine you, you hate him, but if you learn from that, you gotta love him. Sometime I used to joke with the guys and say 'nigger'. I used to say to Willie Mays, 'Come on, you white or what?' We keep happy that way. I want them to know that I'm a human being, that I can joke, but I don't want anybody to joke with me like that. In my mind, we want to be better than the white guys, to be recognized as the top ballplayers in the world. I always used to tell Willie, 'Willie, you see those stars over there? We are those stars. We're gonna go there and we're gonna catch ourselves.' So never forget it. As long as you think that, you have life."

Rubén Gómez is talking cosmology, not baseball. And he's dead serious. "The press, they give Willie Mays a bad image. When you come to talk to Willie Mays, you gonna meet a person who never touch alcohol, a person who'd go on his day off and play in back of the school, against the wall. We used to play stickball on a day off, we used to pitch to each other, use a broomstick. That's the real Willie, you wanna see it, you go to the school, he's right there. And I discover that if the press didn't write about me, it was my own fault. You know why? Because every time the sportswriter come, I was naked, taking a bath. I never came out, I was always the last. They never ask me, but it's because I don't want them to interview me. Now I'm not gonna do that anymore. You gotta meet me personally and find out that I am a human person."

He uses the term like a title that must be bestowed. "I never argue with the umpires. I might say, 'You motherfuckin' son-of-a-bitch' but not so the people can see. One time, we lose a game in the eleventh inning on a home run that was foul and all I say to the umpire is, 'Sir, a human being has to live with his conscience, and I know you're not going to sleep for weeks and weeks because you made a mistake. Because the only person in this ballpark who thinks you're a human being is a blind man.' And the next day he apologize, he says he talk to his friends and they tell him that ball was foul. I tell him, 'That doesn't matter. But did you sleep last night? No, you didn't. I told you, that proves you are a human being. Because something happened that woke up the part of the brain that is sleeping. You didn't sleep one night and that one night is gonna take five years out of your life.'

"And I want to tell you about Mister Earl Weaver, I won eleven games and o for him. You know what he did then, Mister Weaver that big manager of the Baltimore Orioles? He said Rubén, since you're old, I'm not going to pitch you in the playoffs. Eleven-and-o with six shutouts, and he say those words to me! He lose the first two games, so he decide to pitch me and I say to him, 'I'm gonna show you what this old man Rubén Gómez can do.' And I pitched a shutout in Ponce before twenty thousand, twenty thousand and one that was my family. And he said, 'Rubén, I'm gonna manage in Baltimore and you're gonna have a place on my bench as a pitcher.' And I'm still waiting. Because he's a liar. Years later, when Frank Robinson comes to Puerto Rico to manage, I have the clipping, they ask Earl Weaver in Detroit, a girl I used to go out with from Detroit sent me the clipping, he said, 'If he can manage Rubén Gómez, he can manage any player in the world.' You know what that means to me? I never had any trouble with him, the only trouble I ever had was to tell him I'm gonna pitch a shutout to show you who Rubén Gómez is. I was fifty-two, and I pitch a shutout. You know what I did? 'Cause I tell you the good things about me, I want to tell you the bad things, too. When he become famous and he come to Puerto Rico and he come to meet me, when he extend his hand, I slap his hand and say, 'Get the fuck out of here, you son-of-a-bitch.' And that's the only thing I've done in life that I regret. And now, today, I apologize to him through you. Because human beings should forget."

The Divine Crazy is a tempest momentarily becalmed. He does not view himself as a walking short fuse, but as a gentleman forced into action by constant affronts. He goes on fighting because even the fights he wins are not worthy of him. What makes Rubén Gómez so divinely crazy is that he's always proudly pulling himself out of trouble he knows better than to have gotten into in the first place.

"I used to say to the ballplayers, if people boo you, you gotta give thanks to them. It's because you're worth something, you're good at something and they don't want you to do it no more or they're jealous. Those people who boo me, they're gonna pay for my food, for my clothes, for the study of my children. Don't get mad, do something to get one more person mad at you. In anything that you do in life, the thing is to have the ability to do the things that you like and the things that you don't like. I'm gonna give you an example. You don't wanna be here right now, talking to me, holding that thing in your hand. You wanna go to the beach, but for you to become the person you have to be, you are here. And that's the secret of success. Guys who don't do that are still walking up and down in the street. Nobody knows them.

"Last year I work with Correa, the kid in Texas. Mothers pay me to train their kids, but I run a small school of two or three ballplayers. If I take five or more, I would be stealing the money of the parents. First, I have to sit with them, talk with them, tell them jokes, strong, light, and medium. And I will look at each reaction of the faces and I will know how they've been raised and how I should treat them to get the most out of them. Like one time, I have a kid who can't hit with the men on base. He had this obsessed pattern, like he believed something. So I told his mother to bring that child half an hour ahead of time. I took him to a place and I showed him how to box. They brought me the child to teach him baseball and I teach him how to box. And it turned out his brother beat him, so now he can hit first. After a week of training, his mother come to me and say, 'I'm so happy because this is the first time he ever raise the hand to somebody. I want to know, Rubén, what you did with him?' And then sometimes, I will pray that it rains. You know why? Because when you are outside and the student has a ball in his hand, a part of his brain is used to move the ball up and down, in and out of the glove. When I teach, I'm a selfish person. I want a hundred-and-some percent of that brain.

"I would like to be the general manager now! I sold thirty thousand tickets in one day, at a city hall, to show this owner I can sell tickets. I sold the way I was taught by Aetna Life Insurance Company 'cause I took a course in Hartford, Connecticut. I sold the bus tickets to take them all the way from Guancos to San Juan and all the way back after the game. Now I'm studying securities. That's why I don't go that much to the ballpark, I want to make sure I pass that test. You don't need that much schooling, that much college to be a manager. You can always learn how to talk if you go to a banquet. Plus you can talk in English and Spanish. It's even better if you talk broken English, because then the ballplayer listen harder, he pay more attention. It takes more dedication from the ballplayer to the manager. And a Spanish manager is gonna be more open as a human being. White guys, they're afraid of their own race. We're not. We're more open because we're more healthy people. You can ask a player and he'll say, 'I love him.' Because a Spanish manager will go out of his way to please you, he'll take you to his home. A white guy doesn't want to be seen with a player, but we don't think like that.

"I don't care how many years I've played baseball, I don't care how much money I have won in my life. If I go in a restaurant, and I ask for a steak medium rare, if it comes well done, I eat it. I say lady, I ask for it medium rare, remember me the next time. She's not the one who cooked it, why should I give her hell, like a lot of people come to a restaurant to give hell to the people? I should go inside the kitchen an' kill the guy in the kitchen, huh? But I don't know if the guy in the kitchen is the one who make the mistake, too. I've learned a lot. I wish I could play ball with my sense of humor now. I'm more mature, but I'm more strict also. There's too much beauty about life to be angry. All I care is that now, in my own home, people they're still the same with me before I became Rubén Gómez, the athlete. I can go anyplace and they can say, 'Oh, God, Rubén hasn't changed—yet.' Before I was the athlete Rubén Gómez and now I come back to normal and I stay the same. And that's the beauty in life."

One of the waitresses has beckoned her friend from the kitchen at Howard Johnson's. Behind a post that separates the tables from the counter, they peek around, giggle. The old woman in her paper tiara calls flirtatiously to el Divino Loco.

"You know what she say? 'When your wife die, I want to be the first one on the list.' That's beautiful, eh? Everywhere I go, it's like this. Twenty years ago I stay here with the ballclub, and she remembers. And I try to treat her the same as if she was a ballplayer. Because God says anything that comes up, must go down. They say also that Puerto Rico's getting too Americanized. But we'll never lose our culture, we'll never lose our Latin blood, we're not all gonna stop talking Spanish. No way. That's our whole heritage right there. But politics, they say that, so they can get money, go someplace, be a senator. But Puerto Rico is gonna keep that Latin feeling. Of course, we'll get more, we want more Americanized things. The person who's satisfied, he should be left behind. I don't care if it's my own family, if they don't want to improve. You gotta keep the old things, old traditions. But we're gonna move up. That's why that star is still there and I'm gonna start reaching for that star. And when I stop it's because God says, 'That's enough, Rubén. You dead now.' "

THE LAND
WITHOUT HEROES

Serendipity. That's the only organizing principle I can attach to this island's perpetual-motion machine. People roll around like ball bearings until they eventually carom into everyone they need to meet. The trouble is that I'm still trying to line up formal appointments. At least I've transferred to lodgings where there's a phone in the lobby, as well as a ceiling fan and an amiable expatriated Ohioan *patrón*. This new guest house is in the shadow of a twenty-story, butterfly-shaped luxury hotel. I sneak over there for a poolside breakfast buffet complete with papayas, mangoes, and busboys who look like Mafia hit men. The staff here seems unusually sullen. I can't blame them: To get served here, I need show no room key, just my white skin. Yet the hotel cashier fails to warn me she only honors the traveler's checks of paying guests. When I appeal to an assistant manager at a desk in the lobby, this bored lobby Lothario suggests the casino. Inside this ocean-front glass cage lined with one-armed bandits, they're willing to take dollars in any form. I consider killing the afternoon at the nickel machines, but I'm uncomfortable lingering amidst the Versailles mirrors, flocked wallpaper, and racial unease. Everything hits me wrong about the Hotel Dupont Plaza.

As I return to my guest house for a swim, Nino Escalera's white Buick is out front. He's just shoving the transmission from park to drive when he notices me waving for attention. "Get in," Nino says, lowering the electric window like a friendly kidnapper. "You wanted to see the Sports City, right?"

The Land Without Heroes

The scout explains that Carolina, Clemente's hometown and the site of the facilities built in his honor, is right on his way home. We're immediately trapped in the early-afternoon exodus of this New Year's Eve holiday. Nino waits quietly, almost contentedly, on an interminable boulevard crammed with cheap appliance stores, corset shops, a hideous jumble of hissing signs and chipped tile facades. "Puerto Rico is doing good." That's how he views the traffic jam. "Puerto Rico is getting to be nothing like Puerto Rico."

Neither is Carolina, which begins somewhere past the airport. Here, Clemente's father Melchor had been a majordomo in a sugar mill, his mother Luisa Walker a cleaning lady. Roberto, one of their seven children, had to work three years lugging milk cans to save enough money for a bicycle. Now the mill smokestacks of the cane plantations are gone, replaced by half-vacant industrial parks and shopping malls. Carolina is just another grubby, centerless suburb. I suppose there must be a town church someplace. I don't know how Nino locates the plot where Clemente was born. The family house itself has been torn down and replaced with a rusting doorless shell of a Chevy sitting in tropical weeds. There's no plaque mounted on it. I hear a family argument through the open door of the one-room clapboard cabin built against the back fence. Poverty is still easy to find in Carolina, though it's no longer the endemic, slaving-in-the-fields variety. "We still got plenty of poor kids without any shoes," Vic Power tells me. "Some of that stuff Clemente was taking to Nicaragua, he could have left it here."

But Clemente left his hometown something. Before his death, in the years when, as Luis Mayoral put it, "the grass was getting greener," Clemente began talking about a Sports City whose playing fields would be free to all Puerto Ricans. Clemente envisioned it as a "utopian thing," in Mayoral's words. "He didn't want to create world-class athletes but to keep sports within the picture of the family, to keep kids from the temptations of the materialistic world." It took his death to put the plan in motion. "People would tell him they were going to help, but when winter came, they never did." The Sports City is now funded through an annual telethon and exhibition game between two visiting major league clubs. I expect an Olympic village cut down to Puerto Rican size, or at least a Boys' Club on a grand scale. Instead, the Ciudad Deportiva Roberto Clemente gives me more of a shock than the malls of Carolina. From afar, it's a void of brown lawn, a swampy interruption in the sprawl

67

of sooty *rancheros*. Where the scale of San Juan's new highways is grandly North American, here the pace of development is thoroughly Third World. Where Carolina is a paradigm of "the new Puerto Rico," the Sports City looks to be a victim of pre-boom ways. The whole operation could be fit in a single corner of any California country club.

The only thing that convinces me we're heading down the right driveway is a statue of Clemente dividing the lanes at the main entrance. I'm not surprised when I learn that this ghastly representation is the work of a Dominican exile who used to specialize in busts of Generalissimo Trujillo. A Little Leaguer, cowering at the sculpture's base, clutches at the cleats of his stern, bat-wielding idol. A bronze demi-Zeus in a Pittsburgh Pirates uniform just isn't convincing. In one of the untended fields that stretch away on all sides, an appliance distributor has sponsored a modest signpost that reads, in Spanish, "Roberto—now that your dream is being realized, all Puerto Rico is with you." The sign's backdrop is a donut shop and a Texaco station. Nino points proudly at the lone concrete shell on the way to the parking lot, announcing, "This is the museum of Roberto's life." When I ask him to stop so I can look inside, he tells me the rooms are still empty.

Over and again, the old-time ballplayers complain, "The Ciudad Deportiva has been very slow . . . we do what we can, but the politicians have taken over . . . until a few years ago, they didn't even have a water fountain. . . ." Exactly fourteen years after Clemente's death, I count four diamonds, two basketball courts, one outdoor pool, all supervised from a small clubhouse in a construction-site trailer. Inside, Nino introduces me to the one person around, who turns out to be the man in charge, Pedro Barez Rosario. He seems pleased that I've turned up on this holiday afternoon to provide him with some official duties. On a stroll around the premises, I'm shown the newly completed swimming pool, first on the island equipped with wheelchair ramps. A golf course is being planned, and an ambitious program of sports therapy for problem students is being coordinated with the San Juan public schools. Still, Rosario's delivery is more upbeat than the facts he presents. The two hundred thirty-three acres on which the park sits were donated by the Puerto Rican government, along with a million dollars' seed funding. Rosario says it took far more than that million to reclaim and condition the land. "This place was like the Everglades."

Every available fence-post and dugout bench is plastered with the logos of Gillette and other U.S. company sponsors, yet Rosario complains, "All the corporations love to be associated with the Sports City, but they don't give much. You call Pepsi-Cola and they tell you, 'Oh yes, Roberto Clemente was a great man.' Then they send a check for ten dollars. And when you go to the government, you have to fill out twenty-five pages to get a few dollars. If only we had a new government. . . ." Before I know it, the director isn't talking about the Sports City at all, but delineating for me the names of all the various political parties on the island, complete with their respective stands on the only issue that counts: statehood versus eventual autonomy. When I ask his position, Rosario admits, "I am one of those who feels we should be prepared to become a republic, whatever the outcome of the debate." Amidst the batting cages and shaving cream ads, he dares utter the word "independence."

Back at the office, I remind him that my visit has special meaning because it's taking place on the exact anniversary of Clemente's death. "Ay, that's right! Today is the day. Every year, you will find Doña Vera at Piñones." I know Doña Vera is the title bestowed on his boss, Clemente's widow Vera Savala. When I ask Rosario if Doña Vera would mind if I accompanied her to this beach near where Clemente's plane fell, the director tells me, "I don't think so, but she's probably down there right now. You should try and find her right away!"

Serendipity points the way, but one glance at Nino tells me he won't cooperate. He's already late for his family celebration. "And I wanted you to meet my wife. . . ." This probably isn't the first time he's been shunted aside by bigger stories and better players. By the time we're in the car, he's converted his resentment into gallant resignation. "I understand, you got a job to do. I try to get you close as I can, then you have to take the bus." He takes me nearly two-thirds of the way back against the prevailing traffic, into the face of a blinding sun. Nino's annoyance vanishes as soon as I tell him he'll get an acknowledgment in my book. He drops me across from the last motels facing the ocean, in front of San Juan's Club Gallístico, a stucco mound with an awning and elaborate tiered entrance that looks more like a posh nightclub than a cockfighting ring. The bus turnabout a half-block down marks the end of the line for the megalopolis. I set out and soon realize I'm heading out onto an elongated sand bar. On one side, there's the fenced-off marsh around the airport runways, on the other, unbroken beach. The only structures along the road are boarded-up cervecerías big as tobacco sheds. This must be a popular strip on weekends, but I'm the only one trudging along. Oblivious to the calendar or the late-afternoon heat, I have leapt the bounds of logic. I'm out of synch with my environment in that unexpected, maddening, and exhilarating way only the traveler can be. And these are the moments to savor: those three uphill miles I forgot to calculate, that local holiday—be it Ramadan, Juárez's birthday, or National Laceworkers' Week—which turns my chosen attraction into a ghost town. Now I'm a lone spectre haunting the waves, a panting version of Clemente's phantom. Maybe he's up there somewhere, having a catch in his home whites with Tris Speaker and Rogers Hornsby and Shoeless Joe. Maybe when I get back, I'll sign on with the Pacific Ghost League.

I can't figure out if I've entered or left the section of highway that's called Piñones. I'm right under the planes alighting at San Juan International, so I must be somewhere in the vicinity of Mrs. Clemente. Now I wish I'd pinned down Señor Rosario as to the particulars of Doña Vera's widow's walk. After the crash, she went wading out into these rough, rock-strewn seas in search of some clues of Roberto. For days, she stood by the seashore. At each rocky promontory where I imagine she might be continuing the vigil, I follow dirt paths out to their limits. I trespass across seaside backyards full of goats and gutted station wagons. I slog across vast curves of dune hemmed by postcard-perfect rows of royal palm. I don't really want to barge my way into a private ceremony or stick my micro-cassette recorder in anyone's face. I'm relieved I never find Doña Vera.

Instead, the overpowering lushness of the Caribbean landscape lies before me, all for me. For the first time in Puerto Rico, I feel like I've actually traveled someplace, even if this view is not necessarily distinct from a thousand other windswept pirate coves. Close beside the mechanical formations of blue landing lights and runway patterns, the island reverts to its primeval state. Here nature seems to be turned up a notch. The wind scalds, the sands sting, the leaves don't rustle but chatter. The edge of my sight waffles from so much blue, so many refracted rays. Man hardly disturbs the view. From tar-paper shacks, barefoot boys peddle cigarettes. Behind roadhouses that offer chicken-on-the spit, dazed chickens and sullen teenagers wander through the laundry lines and mud paths of ragged settlements. Amidst the miraculous abundance that was here to begin with, there's no evidence of any economic miracle. Just too many palms, and too little to do.

The Land Without Heroes

In the natural camouflage of this habitat lives the creature known as "Caribbean man." For all the stereotypes of the happy, maracas-shaking native or the swivel-hipped hustler or the straw-hatted laborer, what does anyone really know about the guy? His culture is one of the most vibrant on earth, yet except for a few oral histories, scholarly tracts on life expectancy and cane-cutters' revolts, one of the least observed, catalogued, championed. Just before my departure, a friend showed me one of those appointment books put out for the benefit of some United Nations charity. A picturesque glossy print faced each week, fifty-two variations of ruddy-cheeked peasants weaving baskets, hearty Ektachrome fishermen repairing their nets. Before flipping through this miscellany of mankind, I bet that there was not a single photograph snapped in a Caribbean nation. I wish I'd bet more: My friend and I found Eskimos, we found Yemenites, Mozambicans, Solomon Islanders, cave-dwellers, Zulus, Lapps. Haiti, Guadeloupe, Cuba, Trinidad, Jamaica, and Antigua went unrepresented. None of our continental cohabitants made it into the class picture. We fail to see them not because they are too few, but because they are situated too snugly against the belly of power. They have been lost in the shadow we cast.

Overhead, the jets roar off with their loads of sun-sated tourists, following the flight path Clemente never completed. The arrivals and departures seem stacked so close—how do that many people fit onto this oblong pill floating in the Atlantic? At Piñones, I'm suddenly aware of how the sea must shape values on so meagre a landfall. Never mind if Puerto Ricans still favor a diet of beans over fish, as though still trying to pretend they're in Europe, or anywhere else. Here, the sea engulfs everyone. At the end of Clemente's greatest exertions, his fiendish concentration on swings and throws, the only thing that awaited him were these lapping tides. No wonder he had no trouble holding on to his humility, despite "tasting the earthly glories." From these waters, Clemente learned the lesson voiced by José Martí, another spokesman of the Caribbean poor, that "all the world's glories are contained in a single kernel of corn."

It doesn't seem out of character for the man to have made his final slide here. What remains inexplicable about the death of so controlled, so precise an athlete is that he was not calling the signals. Why, oh why, did the Great One trust in any engine but his own? Fourteen years later, conjecture still swirls around the island. "You hear that he was running away to screw a woman," Luis Mayoral enumerates, "that he was running away *from* a woman, that he was carrying off bags of money, that he was trying to keep from paying his taxes, all types of bool-shit." But was Clemente the good Samaritan trying to go beyond signing autographs? The conscious internationalist doing his duty? The egoist snared by his own pride? Or another bystander caught up in Latin America's slaughter of innocents?

The authorized version of events begins three weeks earlier with Roberto's trip to Nicaragua as manager of the Puerto Rican National Amateur team. In a visit to a Masaya hospital, Roberto was so moved by a legless boy that he promised to send false limbs the boy's family could not afford. As the story goes, the memory of this boy haunted Roberto and inspired him to throw his full energies into the relief effort when the earthquake struck just ten days later. "See, Nicaragua, they were right back like we were at the beginning," says Vic Power, who accompanied Clemente as a coach. "A lot of kids with no clothes, no shoes. And he was a very sentimental man, too. He liked kids, he had three kids. He worry a lot about people."

A second version places direct responsibility for Clemente's death on political repression. Rumors abound that Roberto felt he had to be on that plane because Nicaraguan strongman Anastasio Somoza's corrupt National Guard had siphoned off the first two shipments of medical supplies. "He heard the militia was stealing things," Luis Mayoral claims. "And he got really pissed off." It is repeated that Somoza and Clemente spoke by telephone on the day of the crash. If they did, the conversation did not reassure Clemente enough to dissuade him from seeing the next delivery through for himself. The Nicaraguans venerate Clemente as yet another casualty of their revolution. Some offer another motive. Apparently, Clemente had barred several Nicaraguan sports reporters from a team meeting. As a result, the papers branded him *"un negro malcriado,"* an uppity Negro. Vic Power upholds this chronology: "I was with him three week before he died. He feel a little bad about the press in Nicaragua, because they say something, they criticize him. They say that he thought he owned baseball. An' being that he was a proud man, he tried to go back there an' show those people he was better than that."

None of the above explains a gesture characteristically Latin in its impulsiveness, its extravagant senselessness. "A man who is, shall we say, the chairman of the board, does not have to leave his family and his home a few hours before the New Year," Luis Mayoral argues. "He can always send someone else." But Clemente, who was happiest giving batting tips to Matty Alou or free chiropractic treatments to the afflicted of his neighborhood, did not think in terms of "someone else." Both the adoring and the envious attest, "The man wanted to leave a big mark and this was his way to do it." Luis Mayoral is not the only one to see a hefty element of fatalism in Clemente's takeoff in an untested aircraft at night during a heavy storm. "They told him that plane was bad," insists Vic Power. "It didn't start around two or three times. It was overloaded and he still wanted to go in that thing! Oh baby! The weather was bad, raining and thunder and everything. An' he still wanna go! You know, maybe that was the destiny."

Luis Mayoral goes further. "I'm positive that if he'd chosen, this would have been the way he'd have wanted to end the script. Basically, he chose to make the transition the way he did. I'm not saying he knew the plane was fucked up. He wasn't stupid. He extracted the supreme sacrifice looking for a better tomorrow. And what did he get in return? Immortality." To Luis, "Clemente's death is proof that there is a divine plan. There has to be a supreme force, call it God or Buddha or whatever, that handles us as it wishes."

Such is logic's final resort in a culture of tragedy, born out of subjugation and forged through sacrifice. From the Aztecs to the death squads, Moctezuma to Che Guevara, Latin America has anointed its pantheon with blood. The more preventable the blood-letting, it seems, the better. Why should Latin American baseball be exempt? For Clemente, death was an extravagant gesture worthy of the finest "hot dog," a final inelegant but effective lunge at an outside curveball! Adios Unforgettable One, a.k.a. Bob, called "that dirty P.R.," called the malingerer and the captain, who looked like a trimmer, more smoldering Belafonte, who thought he was a better *pelotero* than any white man and usually was, who kept track of every man for and agin' him, who gave me one more reason to make it around another turn, one more excuse to show up for another season, who died as he lived, unable to resist championing America's brown-skinned victims. Clemente the trouble-maker, the pain-in-the-neck, Clemente the fabled hypochondriac about whom fans joked, "Just think how good he'd play if he ever got well!" Clemente with small catastrophes behind him and the big one ahead, Clemente preening in polyester britches, Clemente riding out another self-made storm of bad press, Clemente with a glare that could topple skyscrapers! Clemente and all that righteous anger spread thin across three thousand hits!

Having failed to locate Clemente's grieving party, I can at least do a little on my own. Sinking to my knees in the sand, I stage my own memorial. From the farthest spit of beach, I can look back at the entire sweep of San Juan's high-rise progress. A billow of smoke rises above hotel row like an immense torn parachute. From this distance, it doesn't register that another New Year's Eve cataclysm has befallen Puerto Rico or that I may have been saved by timing that can only be termed serendipitous. On the beach at Piñones, I don't exactly get religion. But I do admit, aloud, against the hissing of palm fronds fanned by the wind, that I once had a hero—and that Clemente will remain my hero, in spite of all the naysayers I may encounter. Now what I've been hearing since my arrival hits me with full impact. No one has any heroes anymore, and that's why baseball is dying, as the soul of Puerto Rico is dying. This is all part of the new sophistication here. No one is going to be anyone's fool anymore, believe anyone's promises, accept that, amidst all the pollution of values, anyone might be a shade less corrupt than anyone else. In this place, it's become dangerously old hat to expect anything from anyone—from politicians or astronauts, movie stars or martyrs, even from yourself. So where do I find that Hispanic capacity for outlandish dreams and fearless gestures? What human signposts can point my way in this land without heroes? I realize I'm discounting what might be termed the heroism of daily life. Undoubtedly, Latin Americans are the reigning masters at that. But a nation needs examples to place on its plaza pedestals, somebody to swing a bat in the name of "the people who suffer." If this island is going to become a nation at all, if it wants to stay whole, it will need as many heroes as it can get. Hundreds of heroes, *por favor*, until everyone feels heroic. Everyone an unforgettable one! Everyone a divine crazy!

FELIZ AÑO NUEVO

I've come as far as I can from San Juan's air-conditioned lobbies, too far for the wail of sirens or fire-trucks. I have no way of guessing that a fire broke out in the very casino where I cashed my traveler's check. My cab's halfway back to town before the transistor wedged against the dashboard broadcasts, "Dupont Plaza." Police cordons block the way to my mildewed cabana. Crowds of onlookers have claimed the best scenic viewpoint directly across from the hotel's sumptuous driveway. A black cloud clings to one flank of balconies like an external elevator shaft. A sign for the first-floor "Chow Dynasty" restaurant flickers hypnotically through the flames. Police helicopters swoop in close to the roof and extend rope ladders toward guests who've made it onto the roof. From the street, nothing about their body language suggests these people are doing anything but enjoying the penthouse bar. Their cries have no chance against the pressurized blasts from the fire-truck nozzles. A dozen hoses can't quench this monster's thirst. The smoke forms a thousand-foot spiral. The choppers make pass after pass, but none of that mars the waning of a perfect beach day. This just doesn't seem like the worst hotel arson in American history, like a hundred and six people are losing their lives.

The closer you are to disaster, the less you feel it. Either you're trapped within the calamity's ferocious momentum, or you've escaped—the more cataclysmic the event, the less frequently do these extremes connect. Certainly, I never feel the presence of death though my cheesy guest

75

house happens to be right next door. I figure the whole thing will be over in half an hour and decide to go for a swim. I don't know how I ever get onto the beach. By the end of my dip, there are cops stationed at every point of shore access. I simply change and waddle barefoot down the alley on the far side of the hotel and I've got the whole huge sandbox to myself. Floating away in the Gulf Stream, I've probably got the best view in the house of the rescue effort. I'm reminded of Kafka's famous diary entry, "Germany declares war on France. Swimming in the afternoon."

I can't help thinking that this couldn't have happened to a nicer hotel. The Dupont Plaza struck me somewhere to the left of gauche, an ugly venue for the uncomfortable coexistence of the indolent and the insolent. Still, bad taste isn't a capital offense. And my Norteamericano assumption that the fire is the fault of slipshod hotel administration or safety violations soon proves naive. Before the slightest evidence comes in, every Puerto Rican I encounter, taxi driver or ballplayer, *independista* or monarchist, is certain the fire is the doing of the nefarious Teamsters, the *tronquistas*. Everyone in town talks like they've been party to the breakdown of protracted negotiations over a new labor contract for the hotel. And everybody is privy to both the union's and management's reputations. No one gets away with anything here, especially anything malicious. In such a context, nothing can be accidental. The most random events turn symbolic, the most foolish acts accrue to the credit or discredit of all. Whatever mischief their compatriots are up to, Puerto Ricans react as if they're in it together.

By the time I've rinsed the sand from my toes, everyone on the island seems to be heading toward the fire. I hope the shift in weight doesn't cause the whole place to capsize. Until now, I haven't been aware how many people are crammed into these 3,435 square miles, or how much they share the Latin weakness for military regalia, brass buttons, and shiny boots. There must be at least twenty different genera of cop guarding the scene of the crime. Every young tough who ever felt like strutting in epaulets now has his chance to be a hero, or to look like one. The profusion of khaki makes good visuals for the television crews that arrive in triplicate. Unloaded from rows of mini-vans, the latest hardware helps a dozen channels capture the same flames, the same burnt-toast facade.

While the whole population's coming this way, I'm off in the opposite direction. What reportorial instincts! The "big story" never seems so revealing to me as the continuum of little ones—and Pochi Castro, the affable public relations man I met behind home plate, has insisted that I come with him to Ponce for that "authentic Puerto Rican New Year's Eve." At first, I balk at a two-hour drive in each direction on such a night, but Pochi reminds me, "My family is expecting you! My parents, my cousins. Who knows, even a few pretty girls! You must share the warmth!" That sounds like a slogan I've heard somewhere, but I don't want to hurt his feelings. Besides, I'm a sucker for the word authenticity.

At least I'll get a glimpse of the rest of the island. By the time Pochi's sedan swoops down a designated ramp that's still open to nonemergency vehicles, it's nearly dark. And he hasn't told me that the evening's activities begin with an hour stop to pick up his wife and daughter in the far reaches of suburbia. The Castros' two-bedroom, one-bath *casita* seems the sales brochure's perfect setting for the prosperous Latino lifestyle of the future. A Toyota in every garage, a pineapple in every pot. Over the prefab mantel hangs a black-velvet portrait of John F. Kennedy, while the textured stucco walls are dotted with beaten metal crosses. Pochi's wife must finish her makeup—no small enterprise—so I sip ginger ale and alternate between watching bulletins on the death count from the fire and playing with Pochi's little girl, chubby as her father and just as winning, stumbling about in a white petticoat. Pochi's wife is equally angelic in a strapless party dress. He introduces her as his "high school sweetheart," and they seem to have lost none of their affection for one another—though Pochi couldn't have been this chain-smoking, double-chinned character when they met. But the man's appeal is in his innocent enthusiasm for everything from baseball to Puerto Rican history to stray gringos like me. In the box seats, I figured Pochi for a diehard booster of the *gente*, a nationalist through and through. Now I see him as an unquestioning participant in a barely formed middle class that's pinned all its hopes on the Stars 'n' Stripes.

We all ride to his father's house, following the north–south highway that serves as the island's gleaming new spine. Occasionally, I can gauge the topography by the lights of mountain villages floating past. Pochi prefers a political debate to pass the time. "They don't have freeways like this in Cuba!" he boasts, trying to bait me. When I express my admiration for many of the accomplishments of that other island-dweller named Castro, Pochi brands me a "naive child of privilege." His tone is jolly, but he's clearly been itching to make such an observation since the moment we met. I try to steer him away from ideologies. "Never mind freeways. Wouldn't you like to live in a place where the ballgames are free?" Pochi shoots back, "And what about the poets?" Funny, I thought I was the writer and he was the fan. Many in Pochi's business circle are Cuban exiles, but that's not the only reason our discussion revolves around the Cuban model. In the Caribbean, the tiniest ripples in Cuba are felt as tidal waves. At each of the revolution's successes, a thousand militants rise up in emulation; with each of its failures, a thousand refugees arrive to spread the poison of disillusionment. Puerto Rico, like Miami, is full of such bitter types. Yet when Pochi congratulates himself for "subscribing to freedom," I'm tempted to reply, "Gee, I prefer servitude myself." Pochi's wife and daughter have fallen asleep in the back seat and I think they've got the right idea. There's no point in continuing this car game. Pochi and I are using the same words but speaking a different language. To one of us, freedom means self-realization, opportunity, security; to the other, freedom is responsibility to the group, the risky business of acting on behalf of shared needs. Each of us subscribes to one of the two truths afoot in the world. When I argue that the materialism now overtaking Puerto Rico cannot make man happy, Pochi points out that were it not for such material advantages, I would not have been able to travel here to advance my theories. How can I dispute that? For a society, as for an individual, acquisition comes before contrition. Pochi pooh-poohs me by patting the dashboard of his new car.

We arrive in a neighborhood exactly like the one we've left: single-story white stucco houses with one palm tree and fenced-in lawn allotted to each. Tonight the iron security gate to the Castro house stands open, an invitation to chaos. Various generations of Pochi's clan are wandering through the house and adjoining garage, where a freezer big enough for a butchered bear is filled with *cervezas*. Out in the concrete square of backyard, a circle of portly aunts and uncles sit in folding metal chairs. They chat quietly, hands at their sides, awaiting midnight. I meet Pochi's brother and sister, who resemble him in their dark curls, fish eyes, and premature stoutness. Even Pochi's new brother-in-law, a former Navy ensign from New Jersey, qualifies for admission to the clan with double-chin and an ever-damp expanse of chest. All the more room for tattoos! The assembled *familia* strikes me as a group portrait by Botero, the painter who satirized the Colombian elite by creating a gallery of blimpish, doleful, moon-faced types, a legless universe in which every creature tends toward the state of a padded ball.

Pochi's father and uncle are the exceptions: wiry, red-haired, and ascetic. They are near twins in their un-Spanishness. One introduces himself as Frank, the other as Eddie. Their English is unaccented, except for a hint of New York nasality. They've been Yankee fans since childhood. "DiMaggio, Rizzuto, Red Ruffing. Those were the days!" Yet they did not spend them in the Bronx. They have worked all their lives at the Union Carbide plant in Ponce. Hometown loyalty also finds expression through baseball. Frank and Eddie are champions of Poncero Frank Coimbre, who lives nearby. Did I know, one uncle asks, that Satchel Paige ranked Coimbre along with the fabled black catcher Joshua Gibson as the toughest hitters he had ever faced? As for Roberto Clemente, Pochi's father concludes, "He was a decent ballplayer, but hardly the best." His backbiting escalates when I tell him I've been guided around the ballparks by Luis Mayoral, also from Ponce. "Oh, yes, he makes a good living off Clemente's memory." Everyone knows everyone and nobody can escape the snipings of envy.

I'm relieved to meet their father, another Union Carbide man, an archetypal merry granddad with bushy white mustache. Grandma is another story. In her kerchief and patchwork skirt, she could head the Hatfields or the McCoys. When Pochi concludes his introduction by whispering that I'm an admirer of Fidel, this scrawny lady with jutting jaw welcomes me with a blast of cusses about that "traitorous son-of-a-she-wolf!" Fortunately, she spends most of the night supervising the *cocina.* Munchies are laid out on the narrow kitchen counters in disposable silver-foil trays. I identify a chunk of pork roasted long enough to slide off various unidentified bones, more fatty meat wrapped in banana leaves, rice and beans, bread loaves laced with sugar and fruits, several sticky coconut pudding creations. These traditional delicacies appear to have been set out to please the ancestral gods, for the same reason Poles in Chicago continue to choke down duck's blood soup. Puerto Ricans are just as assimilated as any immigrant group on the U.S. mainland. They've managed somehow to lose their native culture without ever having to leave their turf. "Why can't we eat regular?" one of the Castro teenagers asks grandma. "Puerto Rican food is too greasy." When Pochi and his siblings begin pulling out various instruments, I figure this is where the "authentic Puerto Rican culture" comes in. In

79

the backyard, he and his brother strum guitars while their sister accompanies them with a Casio electronic keyboard cradled in her ample lap. But a Christmas carol in Spanish is followed by the Beatles' "Nowhere Man." None of the elders join the choir. Pochi's father whispers, "All those children, and not one musician in the bunch!"

At midnight, everyone rises to embrace one another. They're kind enough to include this intruder in every last nuzzle and buss on the cheek. But I'm feeling more and more the outsider, whether from the heat or the residue of pork fat on my lips or the ballad of the baby Jesus played like the ballad of the Green Berets. It's strange to be sitting so calmly in the balm on a December night I associate with forced rounds through snow-clogged streets. Pochi recognizes my homesickness and implores me to phone California on the house. I forget that I'm merely in another U.S. area code. My friends back home are just laying on the sauteed calamari and Spanish bubbly. After making my resolutions— vowing never to search for authenticity, which is about as productive as searching for love—I head toward the screened-in back porch, where the younger generation of the Castro family has been keeping to themselves all night. They're glued to a year-end cavalcade of rock videos. It's not exactly indigenous fare, not even Guy Lombardo, but I, too, take refuge in Sting and Wham!

Pochi's wife does the honors on the ride back while my host sleeps off the exertions of wine and song. By the time I'm delivered back to the off-ramp where the evening started, dawn glows tumescent over the Condado. I sneak back to my hotel like some reprieved Cinderella. To return my glass slipper, I have to circle police barriers, tiptoe over tangled hoses and satellite link-ups, slip through a chink in a wall of ambulances. I'm astounded at how many folks are out promenading past the Dupont Plaza. The fire's all over, the search for culprits underway. Nothing remains but the charred, flame-shaped stain that rises ten stories up the hotel tower like the work of a giant candle held too close. Were it not for the barely detectable eeriness born of sudden desertion, a full complement of guests could still be inside, sleeping off the piña coladas.

I manage a few hours' sleep, before I'm roused by the soundtrack of Godzilla meets Times Square meets Armageddon. The constant drone of traffic down the strip was hardly tranquil under normal conditions, but now every hot-rodder in San Juan comes inching through, honking horns that play commercial jingles or salsa riffs. Oh, what a feeling! Ay, *qué sentimiento!* Gaggles of teenage girls lean out the windows of souped-up hulks loaded down with *familia,* or poke up through the sun roofs, waving to the crowds like beauty queens. The pageant goes nonstop through the days and nights ahead. These resplendent riders head straight for the big emergency in order to ward off the smaller ones. In the embers, they look for themselves. Some have brought binoculars.

Plowing through the crush of disaster hounds, I can no longer tell rich from poor, wrong from right, ugly Americans from ugly Puerto Ricans. I don't think a contest in conspicuous—and undiscerning—consumption is what José Martí or Simón Bolívar had in mind when they spoke of "the unity of the Americas." They could not have envisioned the polyglot bicultural man cruising here. For I, too, make the rounds, zombie-like, from McDonald's to Taco Bell to Walgreen's candy counter to Baskin-Robbins. Contemplating my imminent escape to less fortunate realms, I find myself trying to store up on junk food like a chipmunk. Is the only advantage of protectorate status the availability of Milky Ways, the plenitude of Duracell batteries, a glut of organic shampoos? Taking refuge in my guest house, I stare in a stupor at the Cotton Bowl and the Rose Parade. How else do I know that this is the day I'm supposed to turn a new leaf except by the presence of the corn-fed Cornhuskers and the steroid-inflated Wolverines? Beamed into this lobby's exaggerated version of the tropics, the procession of padded warriors seems even more irrelevant than usual. Except for the tube, everything in sight is made of white wicker. Ceiling fans whirr overhead, not because anyone needs them, but to suggest a Bogart flick. Fronds wiggle seductively in the window, just masking the bumper-to-bumper mayhem beyond. No wonder Sydney Greenstreet has fled.

While I watch Asian-American cheerleaders in bobby socks vault toward the heavens, bedraggled Dupont survivors traipse through in search of a pay phone. A series of teenage girls reassure anxious relatives in luscious New Yorkese, "Uncle Mel? It's Sheila. Yeah, it's me. Every-one's okay. Yeah, Poppa took his heart pills. We was lucky to be on the right flo'! Was it in the pay-pahs? Really? Front page?" From my seat beside the television, I follow the drama which now envelopes the proprietor of our guest house. He's a Milquetoast fellow who's moved here to escape the nine-to-five in some Midwest five-and-ten. Despite his surfer shirt, he still looks unconvincing as a native innkeeper. He's getting his moment of celebrity now that a wire service quoted him as having predicted the fire. He has to explain to one panting TV crew after another that every hotelier on the strip knew the Dupont's labor unrest would lead to trouble.

Once the national championship game's underway, I find that his Puerto Rican help knows more than I do about the odds on Penn State. Football is gaining popularity here, though I can't envision a stream of Puerto Ricans following in the big-foot footsteps of linemen from Guam, another of our protectorates. Still, football is doing its best to supplant baseball as the sport of empire. The game perfectly reflects modern conquest: mechanized, drowning in euphemistic terminology, and above all, anonymous. The pilots who pushed buttons over Vietnam never saw their targets. The cornerback doesn't look in the face of a wide receiver until he's felled him with a vicious hit. If sport is sex, sublimated male aggression, then football is bondage and dominance while baseball is just tentative foreplay. And what's the sporting equivalent of the rape of nations? *Feliz año nuevo!* What a way to start the year! The crash of televised half-time cymbals mingles with the incessant horn-blasting. It hardly seems possible that I've come here in pursuit of something so understated, so without drumbeats.

RED LIGHTS
ARE FOR EVERYONE

"**O**h, baby! There you are!"

I'm amazed that Vic Power recognizes me coming down the lower reserved aisle.

"What's going on tonight? I had trouble getting into the park." In fact, all six lanes into the lot were so clogged that I had to get out of my taxi and walk. Now I'm baffled to find the stands as empty as always. That makes Vic Power even easier to spot: the most massive form claiming a box seat.

"Cyndi Lauper concert next door," he explains. "Everyone goes to see her."

"Oh, I thought everybody liked baseball all of a sudden."

"That's right. They like baseball, but they like Cyndi better. Oh, baby! I wonder why." Vic Power rears back with a laugh that absolves the universe. "But we came to see the ballgame while Cyndi is so close to us! I guess we don't care that much about her. Yeah, that's right. We devoted to the ballgame."

Victor Pellot Power has been devoted almost since his birth in 1931. Groomed as an outfielder, with the stature of a classic first baseman, he was that rare player who could nimbly handle all the infield positions—and did so during his twelve-year tenure in the majors. Despite his girth, he possessed the quick, responsive hands and feet of a much smaller man. Of a ballerina, it's been said. There are those who claim that he fielded his position as well as any man in the history of the game. Their

83

proof is Power's eight first baseman's Gold Glove Awards. Signed by Tom Grathwaite, the New York scout who also discovered Mickey Mantle, he was supposed to become the Yankees' first black player. According to rumor, Power was bypassed in favor of mild-mannered Elston Howard, perhaps because he was outspoken, perhaps because he was Latin. Traded to the lowly A's, then Cleveland, Power labored for teams that always ended up playing second-fiddle to the Bronx Bombers. In the winter leagues, too, he was overshadowed by the two dominant figures of Puerto Rican ball, Clemente and Cepeda. Still, that makes him the third-best native player of the modern era.

The fans on either side of us treat him like one of the guys. Leaning back with their feet up for the nine innings' haul, they turn their attention toward Vic's formidable presence only because he's this rooting section's head chatterbox. If the area behind home plate were an African village, then he'd be its chieftain. A gentle, benevolent ruler, Power holds court in the heat, exuding evaporations of aftershave to mark his territory. He sweats off his round, bald dome, shakes with laughter from the very center of his formidable round presence. Since his playing years, he's gotten big enough to take up two seats. Now he's the local representative of the California Angels. Removing and replacing his bifocals each time he scribbles on his pitching chart, Power looks very much like the serious scout. He's definitely one serious talker. He carries on three or four conversations in two languages, concluding them all with the cry, "Oh, baby!" The byplay is only foreplay leading up to a climax of humor he can squeeze out of life's stingiest moments.

"It looks like San Juan is your town," I tell him.

"No, I born in Arecibo, on the north side of Puerto Rico, around one-hour drive. When I was sixteen, I signed pro baseball with Caguas, that's right in the center of the island. I grew up there, I went to school there, I played baseball there. My father died when I was thirteen years old. He worked in the sugar cane factory, where they make sugar. My mother used to sew, make dresses. She died fourteen years ago. She used to be my best friend and my best fan. ·Went to all the games. Beautiful! After my father died, she never remarried. She just worked, worked, until I became sixteen and started working so I can support my family. I'm very proud of what I was making in the Puerto Rican League. It wasn't that much, it was two hundred fifty dollars a month, but that was '47. I support my mother and brothers. The rich kids in Puerto Rico, they don't play baseball. They go study, they become lawyer and doctor. The poor kid have to play baseball to get some money."

"Was it hard for you when you first came to the States?"

"Yes. It was very hard for me because when I start, I start in Canada, an' over there, you know, is French. Then when I come to the States, I have trouble, 'specially my accent. My accent was very bad. I can't pronounce too well. I remember they interview me one time. The guy asked me what I think about an American League pitcher, an' I try to say, you know, 'some other pitcher' an' it sound like I say 'son-of-a-bitch' an' they stop the program and everything. Because my accent was very bad. Now I'm not better, but you can understand me." He laughs. "I'm doing better, Yeah!"

"I heard Clemente got angry when the reporters printed his mistakes."

"Yeah, well, he was a very proud man and he didn't like nobody making fun of him. But I had some bad experiences when I was in the States, before I got adjusted to the system."

"What kind of experiences?"

"Well, like racial experiences. Like when I first went over there, I tried to eat in the restaurant an' the lady told me, 'Sorry, we don't serve Negroes.' I tol' her, I don't wanna eat Negro, I want some rice and beans.' You know, I didn't really want no Negro. I knew what she means."

"Did you ever have problems with teammates?"

"Yes, well, teammates they always like me. They always like me, but I always thought they were pretty cold. For example, when I used to be in spring training, we cannot eat in a white restaurant. But then I have to travel in the same bus with the guys, an' they stop on the road so they can go eating. An' I can't go in. But they never brought me a sandwich or a hamburger! I just stayed in the bus waiting and after they ate, they came in, nobody brought me nothing. An' they were my friends. An' we played together. But they were very cold."

"Did you ever say anything? Rubén Gómez told me about a speech he once gave. . . ."

"No! I just get adjusted to the system. But one time Gary Bird—Gary Bird was one of our pitchers when I was in Cleveland —an' I told him, since Cleveland moved the spring training to Arizona, and I knew he was living in Texas, I told him since I was driving to spring training, I was going to go through Texas. I was going to visit him. An' he told me, 'You do that, Vic. But remember, you gotta go in through my kitchen.' But then I told him, 'Listen, Gary, if you come to Puerto Rico, you can come in my living room! You don't have no trouble!'

"Then later on, I ask him, 'Gary, why the white people don't like the colored guys here in the States?' He hesitate for a moment. And he tol' me, 'Vic, it's been like that for a hundred years an' we gonna keep it like that.' An' you know, he was my roommate. An' I get the message, it's the way they are. But he's still my friend. An' we played together for four years in Cleveland. But he tol' me the real truth.

"You know, I had some trouble in the South, when they caught me, for what they call over there *jaywalking*. Jaywalking is when you walk in the street with a light. An' the policeman took me to a judge, a white judge, he wanna put me in jail. He ask me how I plead, 'Guilty or innocent?' 'I tol' him, 'Mister Judge, I innocent.' He ask me, 'Why you innocent?' An' I say, 'Well, listen, I'm a Puerto Rican. I came here to the South, I don't know nothing about the South. I was in the street, I try to get in a restaurant, I see a sign that say For Whites Only. I try to get in a bar an' the bar say For Whites Only. I keep walking an' try to get in a movie house an' they say For Whites Only. Then I walk to the end of the sidewalk an' I see a bunch of white people an' they went by when the green light was on. Then I stop. An' when the red light was on, I pass. An' the policeman caught me. I thought that the red light was for colored only!'

"Well, the judge told me, 'Listen, I'm gonna let you go. But remember, the red light is for white, colored, everyone!' " There are laughs all around.

"Where did this happen?"

"That was in the South, in West Palm Beach in Florida. It's changed now. It changed a little bit after Kennedy, because after Kennedy we got all those laws, you know, an' you can go in a hotel, you can go in a restaurant, an' everything. It's much better now. But I got a lot of respect for all those colored players like Willie Mays, Henry Aaron. I don't have to mention Jackie Robinson, because you know what happened to him. Now it's nice, all the colored guys playing over there, they're gettin' a million dollars and everybody's fine. But then we hear that Dwight Gooden, he have some trouble in the States, and we don't know exactly what he did, what happened. It's a funny situation. . . ."

"You mean the police were picking on a black guy?"

"Yes, like when I was in Cleveland, I remember one time I went to the corner where they got a stop sign. I stop. I look to the left, I look to the right, then I pass. Then the policeman stop me an' he ask, 'Why you didn't stop on the corner?' When I tried to explain, he tol' me, 'Don't argue with me!' When he ask me who I was, I said, 'I'm Vic Power. I'm the Cleveland Indians first baseman.' An' he say, 'Routine investigation.' Then he let me go. But I'm pretty sure I stop on that corner. You know, I was driving a Cadillac. Sometimes those policemen they don't like to see a Negro guy driving a Cadillac around downtown."

"Did you ever get into fights on the field?"

"Oh yes, I got a million of them! When I first went to the major leagues, they were throwing bean balls. An' we don't use no helmets or nothin'. Oh, baby! I have to fight every day to survive. I have some bad experiences. Like right now in Puerto Rico, there's a man working as a pitching coach for the Arecibo club, his name is Bill Monbouquette, an' he was pitching in Boston when he throw three times right behind me. I told the umpire, 'You wanna talk to him or you want me to tell him?' An' when I start walking to Monbouquette, he start running all through the Boston park. My first two years in the major leagues, they used to throw at me. Later on when I start those fights, it was easier. I remember Casey Stengel used to tell those guys on the Yankee bench, 'Leave him alone. Don't wake him up! Let him sleep!' 'Cause when they wake me up, I do a lot of things.

"Like you know, I gotta record where I stole home plate twice in one ballgame, playing with Cleveland against Detroit. We were losing eight-to-seven, an' I stole and tied the game eight-and-eight, later I stole to win it nine-to-eight. That became a major league record. An' the press asked me a lot of questions, they ask me, 'How you do that, especially when Rocky Colavito was hitting, when the year before he hit forty-two home runs. An' I ask the sportswriter, 'How many times at bat?' He told me, 'Six hundred times.' So I tol' him, the law of averages said that he wasn't going to hit a home run in that time. But later on, another guy come an' ask, 'How you do it? You not supposed to be fast, you a fat man, you a big man, you not supposed to steal base!' He asked a silly question. So I tol' him, you know, 'If it was daytime, they could have caught me. But it was a night game. Nobody saw me coming in." More laughs. "In baseball, you have to fight back or the whole league start throwing at you. You have to let them respect you."

87

"Did you ever think about giving up and coming home?"

"No, never. An' that's what I teach the kids, the kids that are going now to the States. I tell them all the time: You have to adjust yourself to the system. They're not gonna kill you. That's what I tol' Joaquín Andujar, when he had all that trouble in the World Series. I was there, I hope he took my message. I tol' him what I told you tonight. 'Joaquín, you gotta get adjusted to the system. Forget about the umpire, forget about the other guy, just get adjusted. If you do that, you're not gonna have trouble.' Right now, you are in Puerto Rico. It is different than in the States. It has different rules. But if you get adjusted to the system, you not gonna have no trouble."

"Is there racism in Puerto Rico?"

"They have it, but it's different than in the States. Here, they have a lot of private clubs and a lot of private things. And if you check them, they don't have Negroes in the club. They're just for whites only. The government, most of the top guys, they white. An' you look in the stands right now, eighty or ninety percent of the people they white. The colored people, they stay away. An' I'm aware of that, because I go everywhere. I go to the hotels an' I check and see. You go to the bank, and ninety-nine percent of the people working in the bank, they all white. You got to church, ninety-nine percent of the church people, they all white. You know, I can see. I'm not blind. But that's the system. Stay quiet, you don't have no trouble." The crowd roars at a double play.

"Now I been working with kids seven up to twenty-one, I wanna keep them out of the trouble we have in the streets, like drugs. This kid pitching right here, I start working with him when he was nine years old. That's Juan Nieves. He pitch for Milwaukee last year an' he won eleven games. I got him a scholarship to the Avon High School in Connecticut. Around thirty percent of the kids playing in the Puerto Rican league right now, they have come from my clinic. Most of those kids in Puerto Rico, they come from a very poor family an' the only way they can become somebody, is either way, if they play pro baseball or get a scholarship so they can study. When we get some kids that don't have the talent to play pro baseball, but they got the talent to play college baseball, we make all the arrangements an' send them over there."

"Does it cost more to sign them these days?"

"Well, in Puerto Rico, we having a big trouble now because they have signed two or three kids, like this kid pitching, Juan Nieves, they give him a hundred fifty thousand dollars. Now everyone in Puerto Rico want that money. Most of those kids, they want big bonus. I've been trying to tell them, you have to sign. Then you have to produce. If you do good, they gonna pay you."

"Is there a limit on how many you can sign?"

"Well, we don't exactly have a limit. I mean, 'cause we might get a Ted Williams, Stan Musial, Bob Feller. You never know." He laughs. "A Roberto Clemente!"

"How fast are these guys throwing?"

"Well, this kid, he been throwin' ninety-three miles an hour, an' Nieves been ninety-one average." He repeats for a fan, "Sí, noventa y uno."

"How do you know?"

"I gotta gun." It's hidden from me in the next aisle down, a bright yellow model that looks like a blow-dryer. "I can read it."

"I thought you were some kind of genius."

"No, no! I'm talking to you, but I'm checking. I know what's going on."

"What's the first thing you look for in a player?"

"Legs. He gotta be fast and he gotta have a good arm. Because you can't teach that. The other things, you can teach him. You can teach him how to hit, how to field. But they have to go fast, fast legs, good arm."

"And do you ever scout the Dominican? Have you been to San Pedro de Macorís?"

"San Pedro right now is the top city in the world to develop ballplayers. Guerrero, all those guys come from San Pedro. I've been asking everybody, what they do over there, what they eat? So I can bring the secret to Puerto Rico. They got something we call here in Puerto Rico, mofongo. In Santo Domingo, it's called magú. An' I think that's the secret. That's made of banana. They get the green banana, they boil it, they mash it, they put some meat. An' that's all the Dominican Republic guy eat, an' most of the poor guys here in Puerto Rico eat. Maybe that's the secret thing that develop the ballplayers. We're gonna bring that to the States so we can develop some ballplayers down there." The whole section laughs.

"I heard that Clemente used to eat a dozen eggs mixed with grape juice in a blender."

"Yeah, he used to do that. Make him strong. Maybe that's the secret. I managed Clemente in Caguas, and we went out together. We had some girls, we went out. And when we went out, he drink. I mean, he wasn't a drunkard. But he did what all human beings do. And sometimes when people write things about him, they become fanatic. I don't know if it's true, but they say Lincoln never say a lie. I don't know if that's true. . . ."

"Lincoln what?"

"He never say a lie. Or Washington. Washington was the one? Washington never lie, yeah. Maybe it's true, I don't know. We're not gonna check the history." Vic laughs. "But human beings, they drink sometimes, they go out sometimes. You have to do things like that sometimes."

"You mean people make Clemente a saint because he died?"

"Well, he died for a good cause because he was bringing things to Nicaragua."

"I'm planning to go there. . . ."

"Oh, yeah? I wonder how things are doing down there. Yeah, they like baseball because they don't have nothing else to do. But it's not well organized. I think one of the big guys there, the president of the league, the government there put him in jail or something, I don't know. Too bad. I haven't been around Latin America lately because of all the trouble, but before that I been in Guatemala, Colombia, Nicaragua, Panama. I went to Cuba. I stayed there fourteen days. An' one thing I like about Cuba, I don't see no drunk people, I don't see no thieves, I don't see no prostitution, nobody fighting in the street. I conduct baseball clinics all through there, but when they're having all that trouble, we just stay away. We don't want no trouble. They got some trouble down there with the American government, you know. Some of those guys kidnapping Americans, or something. We can call them crazy guys. In Santo Domingo, the people, they better. Puerto Rico? Ehhhh! You never know. You saw what happened over there in that hotel? Oh, baby! Like I say, there are some ugly Americans. But we can find some bad Puerto Ricans, too. . . ."

In time to a last burst of laughter, Juan Nieves completes his shutout. Vic Power packs up his Juggs gun and clicks his attaché case. Under the grandstand, we run into a minuscule old woman wrapped in a gray shawl who gives "Señor Power" all the credit for the success of her fastballing son "Juanchi." Though his home's out in the suburbs, Vic offers me a ride back into town. He even invites me to join him in the morning for a scouting trip to the mountain village that features "the most beautiful women on the island. Oh, baby!" Unfortunately, Cyndi Lauper's show in the Roberto Clemente Coliseum next door has also just let out. The parking lot is flooded with Latino teeny-boppers whose sad and willowy Spanish eyes look even more plaintive ringed in thick strokes of punk mascara. Black curls have been dyed even blacker, shorn in lopsided patterns, or braided to look bratty. It's a contest to see who can be as disheveled as Cyndi, but a certain peasant grace and lassitude sabotages the "in look." Amidst today's grubby, bohemian hordes, I see yesterday's white-gloved beauty queens.

Vic Power starts his Olds 88, a model as wide-bodied as he is. But there's no point. We're in gridlock for an hour. Eventually, he quits burning gas and the two of us stand on either side of the car with doors flung open, leaning against the hood and scanning for movement up ahead. It's strange to see a man of Vic Power's size immobilized. "Oh, baby!" He's stalled no matter how many times he moans his trademarked cry. None of the next generation even pauses in recognition before the legend who tells me, "I think that I'm obliged to give those kids in Puerto Rico my spirit. So that maybe it can be different for the future guy."

JOSÉ CAN YOU SEE?

I wake up resolved to go scouting with Vic Power. I've had it with "lots of blah, blah, blah," as Power puts it. "Puerto Ricans making speeches. Oh, baby!" No more memorializing. Let's see tomorrow's Clementes! But Luis Mayoral is coming to fetch me for the annual ceremony in Carolina and I don't want to ditch him without an explanation. He zips up through the cordon of police, electric as ever at seven on a Sunday morning. "Go ahead, brother! Vic's a good guy. He'll show you the *verdad*. Truly. What our culture is really made of, *sabes*. You can't write your story unless you get out on the island." In San Juan everyone refers to "the island," as though the rest of Puerto Rico is somewhere east of Borneo. I notice that those who keep urging me to head out never seem to get there themselves. When I phone Vic, his sleepy wife informs me that the scout has already hit the road. I have no choice but to follow Luis. I, too, am stuck: on the island but never in it.

A striped tent big enough to house a provincial circus has been pitched in the Sports City's parking lot. But not even half the seats inside are filled. Ballplayers don't like to bestir themselves this early and many of Clemente's former teammates have warned, "That ceremony is for the politicians." Actually, most of those in attendance seem to be small-time notaries public, insurance men, and shopkeepers, nearly all members of the San Juan Lions clubs who sponsor and dominate the annual event. Local officers proudly sport the gaudy yellow vests of their chapters. A number have also dusted off insignias, medals, and tricornered caps to prove they're veterans of foreign wars. *Our* wars, I have to remind myself.

The rest of the audience consists of needy children bused in for the occasion. The Lions, too, are engaged in what one calls "redeeming our youth." I meet a number of reformed delinquents, residents of a halfway house for drug users and gang members. Their ill-fitting Sunday suits seem to be on loan, their bearing strikes me as a little too upright, their respectfulness too rehearsed. Later, when their sponsors aren't looking, they ask to inspect my elaborate Japanese jogger's watch. They're impressed by all the digital readouts, but analog-illiterate when it comes to telling time. Boardinghouse tables run the length of the tent, laden with Christmas toys and stuffed rabbits. For the younger orphans who sit still through the palaver, the reward is a rubber dump truck or a stuffed Garfield the Cat, that gringo of the animal kingdom.

A handful of aging couples wander in from the adjoining neighborhood. Limousines bring the duly appointed representatives of church and state, a television crew sticking close. The Clemente family arrives last. Luis points out Ricky, the son who's shown the greatest aptitude for baseball. Ricky's older siblings, Luis and Roberto Junior, had made a stab at organized ball "only to honor their name." Ricky looks like your average high school senior, showing a mouthful of orthodonture every time he smiles. But there's an unaffected modesty and a stiff-spined invincibility in the way he wears his three-piece suit. I can hardly believe the woman beside him is the one I've been trying to locate all week. My image of Clemente's widow Vera was frozen in 1972. Countless photos had shown a sultry local beauty with sculpted cheekbones, arched eyebrows, and incongruous blond wig, escorted from the funeral services by Willie Stargell and other grieving Pirate teammates. Like her husband, Vera Clemente projected a mix of brooding spirituality and finely tuned animality. Now she's swelled to the proportions of an operatic diva—though in a floor-length gown trimmed with white lace, she reminds me more of the lead soprano in a gospel choir. Later, I hear that she leans heavily on chocolates for consolation. It seems fitting that she has taken on the size to match her community stature. This sweet Carolina girl is not only the boss lady of the Sports City but Puerto Rico's equivalent of Coretta Scott King. To her has fallen the role of community pillar, the fate of "spokesperson." Exhibiting a charm that's half-innate, half-stoic, it's easy to see how Mrs. Clemente has become Doña Vera.

The speakers' podium is flanked by an immense Stars 'n' Stripes, wilting on its stand, and an easel that holds a portrait of Clemente in Pirates' cap. The rightfielder's eyes are cast skyward in a visionary gaze chillingly like the one plastered on a deified Che Guevara. The opening round of song reveals the crowd's tripartite loyalties: the International Lions' hymn, the Puerto Rican anthem *"Mi Borinquen,"* and last, "America the Beautiful." And why not the one that begins, "José, can you see?" That's the punchline of the old chestnut about a Mexican attending his first ballgame who misconstrues Francis Scott Key's inquiry into his adopted country's concern for the quality of his seat. The joke is the Hispanic variant of every immigrant group's befuddled first encounter with the American way. That such an encounter should take place at a baseball game is hardly coincidental. Given the ethnic makeup of the teams standing for our anthem, the opening line should be changed to "José, can you play?" Considering the nation's ongoing myopia toward our Latin neighbors, that most American of questions ought to be, "Oh say, can you see José?" But I've never misconstrued "the bombs bursting in air." Since the Vietnam War, I've never risen for the Star-Spangled Banner, not even in the bleachers. Let the Lions identify with the "purple mountains' majesty." I do not join their thickly accented, "Land of the Peel-grims' pride."

The oratory lasts for hours. A long-winded pastor manages to work into the benediction that he's a *fanático* of the Detroit Tigers. A couple of bankers extol the virtues of community and charity exemplified by Clemente. Luis Mayoral's contribution is more personal, basically a sanitized version of his standard rap. Under this tent, he doesn't mention *espiritismo* or Clemente's *internacionalismo*, the "identification with the struggler" or banging someone before he bangs you. He plays his audience the way Clemente played a carom off the fence. With a tremble in his throat, I hear him confess, *"Me hace falta Roberto Clemente."* I miss—more accurately, I lack—Roberto Clemente. By the time a representative of the governor reaches his keynote remarks, my attention has drifted. Fourteen years earlier, Clemente's death actually caused the inauguration of a new governor to be postponed. And Governor Rafael Hernández Colón had begun his address by declaring, "Puerto Rico has lost one of its great glories." Now my ears perk up at a familiar theme. "To unite its political, racial, and social differences," the representative declares, "Puerto Rico needs heroes." So what else is new?

José Can You See?

The guest speaker this year is Clemente's former roommate, Panamanian catcher Manny Sanguillén. I remember him as the freest swinger in the tradition of Latin free swingers, the baddest "bad ball" hitter. "You can't walk your way off an island," is what they say in the Dominican Republic to explain why Latin players rarely have the patience to wait for four balls. Sanguillén used the heaviest and longest bat in the majors to reach out for pitches most hitters let go. With his dimpled cheeks, bouncing gait, and gap-toothed grin, he lent joie de vivre to every game. In a tight-fitting suit and gold wrist bracelet, with his blond Miami wife and beige Manny Junior in tow, he looks quite the respectable business type. But he still flashes the smile that once led Clemente to remark that he would be the most popular player in the world if only he looked like Sanguillén.

"Roberto used to say that in his heart he loved everyone, even if it didn't show on his face," Sanguillen tells me after the ceremony. "He taught me everything. When I first came to the big leagues and saw a suit I liked, Roberto went out and bought me five of them. He bought me a monkey, too, and named it Manny. He was always straight with people. On our way to the seventh game of the '71 World Series, he predicted he'd hit that winning home run off Cuellar. I remember, the taxi driver was running down Clemente, saying he was a complainer and all that. The poor guy didn't realize who was in the back seat. But Roberto gave him a hundred-dollar tip and then he autographed the bill so the driver would know who it was coming from. He never said anything to hurt anyone, only to improve them. He was toughest on himself—if he made an error, he took two hundred flies the next day. Because of him, I was the first Latin player to catch all seven games in a Series. I never played ball until I went to Bible school when I was nineteen."

What did he do before that? "I was a killer," Sanguillén answers, then waits just long enough to flash his fluorescent grin that I begin to believe him. Maybe he was like one of the sullen reformatory students filing back onto their Greyhound, maybe baseball really was his rehabilitation. But I doubt it. Despite what every high school gym coach might say, sport does not build character, but reveals it. And Manny has character to spare. I wonder if he thinks his mentor would have felt comfortable among this pious crew. When a tropical storm moves in, suddenly threatening to blow the tent off its stakes, drowning the day's cant, I feel Clemente is taking his revenge.

Milling about until the rain passes, I'm approached by one weary Lion after another. All have an urgent need to apprise me of numerous abortive attempts to settle in the States. None of their conversation is about Roberto Clemente. The subject on everyone's lips is the Dupont Plaza fire and "those sons of she-bitches, the *tronquistas*." These watch-dogs of the status quo don't mean to, but they confirm the force packed by a single act of terror. In Puerto Rico, where the struggle isn't over territory or even money, everything turns on image—a point not lost on the *independistas*, who, despite being jailed in large numbers on vague conspiracy charges, occasionally reach out and bomb U.S. banks and military installations. The Dupont incident threatens more than economic loss to the men here, more than a simple loss of face. They are the ones who've staked their lives on the proposition that their island is just another American state, with problems, divisions, and social under-currents no different from the others. Nothing that a little more invest-ment capital couldn't solve. Yet this illusion of stability can be shaken by a single arson. With one burst of flame, the world is given notice that there are still plenty of left-behinds in the great shopping spree. Worse still, the fire revives a notion of Puerto Ricans as hotheads and trouble-makers, prone to violence like their accursed island neighbors.

"The difference is that here, the system is soft," one old gent explains. "Over there, in Cuba, it's to be or not to be." To be *what*, he doesn't specify—but the other Lions all nod. They can't speak the dreaded C-word. Their lips pledge undying loyalty to the American standard of living, but their eyes tell me something different. They are the baggy, retreating eyes of men who've been robbed of hope, stripped of dignity. These loyal soldiers in their fraternal regalia may be more financially comfortable than any men of their age I've met here, but they are the first to take their continuing tenure on the island as a defeat. "All we want," says one of these heroic Lions, "is to sleep quiet in the arms of our Uncle Sammy."

A caravan of black Cadillacs assembles underneath Clemente's bronze form. I'm about to follow them toward a luncheon at the Carolina Lions' den, an afternoon of dominoes and empanadas in the lair, when Luis sneaks up and whispers, "Stick around. I may have a surprise for you." Today, the Sports City looks considerably more like a going concern, its diamonds packed with *equipos locales*, whose uniforms are brand-new, with each teenager's name embroidered on the back. On a gate-legged table in the shade of a patio attached to the main bathrooms, Luis sets out a small microphone and transmitter and starts interviewing every loiterer in sight. I don't know whether he's being broadcast any further than the confines of the complex. Luis is a one-man station, a thousand kilowatts at least. He introduces me to a tall, Anglo-looking pitching instructor who's running a clinic for high schoolers. He immediately volunteers that he's an ex–major leaguer. When I ask his name, he whips out a stack from his uniform's back pocket. These aren't business cards, they're his Topps baseball card, circa 1961: "Rudy Hernández, p, Senators." On a far diamond, a staff member patiently hits grounders toward toddlers stumbling about in their first uniforms. This old coach, covering his beer gut with a T-shirt bearing the icon of Clemente, guides his charges so lovingly through their first awkward stabs and stoops that I can't take my eyes off him. He teaches baseball the way some master sitarist passes down ragas.

Luis calls, "Oye, my man! Doña Vera is coming!" I'm humbled that she's willing to talk with me on this anniversary. Nothing in Mrs. Clemente's manner suggests that this may be her millionth interview. Her smile is gracious and she makes no effort to stifle a high-pitched, schoolgirlish cackle that reminds everyone within hearing range that she's just regular folks. "Oh my, I'm afraid there's nowhere comfortable for us to go!" After glancing around, we settle on a covered dugout bench alongside the one unutilized diamond. She sits with hands neatly folded, breaking her sanguine pose to sweep back the fine strands of brown hair that blow onto her forehead. The wind carries the robust, restorative clatter of bat upon ball.

Doña Vera talks with pride about the past fourteen years: the efforts to keep the Sports City going, the rapid development of Puerto Rico, the unending number of leagues, ballparks, streets, community centers, and hospitals named for Roberto. "The years pass," she says, "but I know the people don't forget him." This is the official widow speaking, yet when I press for more private reminiscences, she offers them without hesitation. With her, there are no boundaries between public and private. She tells me how Roberto first spied her from his car as she was walking toward a Carolina drugstore. It was, as Doña Vera puts it, a case of "love at first eye." That very night, Roberto told his mother that he had met the woman he was going to marry—but Doña Vera did all she could to slow him down. "I make him suffer so much, oh my God!" Giggling all the way, she describes how she enforced a traditional courtship. Her tone suggests that she now finds her hard-to-get behavior both ridiculous and quaint—as though she, too, were a kind of relic of the old Puerto Rico. "My family was raised like in the old times, we have to ask permission to go from here to the corner." She did not agree to date Roberto for weeks, and when she did, she had to be chaperoned.

She had no idea that he was a famous baseball player—only that "they had a big welcome for him in Carolina, that he was doing something good, but I didn't know the details"—at least not until she saw the commotion when he met her for lunch at the bank where she worked. Eventually, he persuaded Vera and her entourage to come and see him perform at the ballpark. Of course, the game was rained out! But Roberto showed his characteristic perseverance and the two were engaged by the next All-Star break, married by the end of the season. "Everything was so fast!"

Their matrimonial life wasn't always blissful. Roberto had "two personalities," on and off the field. When he had a bad day, she had to wait for him to start talking. He was always complaining about the treatment of Latin players. "They make a good play, the press don't mention them. They do something bad, they put it on the first page!" Her husband was hardly the typical one-dimensional jock. He played the organ and the harmonica, worked in plaster and ceramics, made lamps and all sorts of handicrafts. He wrote poetry—to his children, in celebration of a ranch he'd been able to buy. Due to this own chronic back problems, he became "a chiropractor without a license. Sometimes at one o'clock in the morning, he'd have people in the house, getting a treatment. You know, he was something special.

"He knows people from the president all the way down, but he preferred, the few months of the year when he was here, to be with the people that grew up with him." As he grew wealthier, Clemente worried that his neighborhood *compas* were afraid to see him. He spoke of moving to a smaller house where visitors would feel more comfortable. "That was the way he talk. That was the way he think." Whenever he traveled, Clemente liked to leave the tourist areas to talk to people on the street about their condition. Doña Vera reveals something new about the events leading up to his death. "When we went to Nicaragua, he said, 'I like it here, because it's like Puerto Rico was before, many years before.'

It was country-like, the view and everything, like when they have the sugar plantations in Puerto Rico."

Rooted in Clemente's impulse to rescue Nicaragua was nostalgia for a Puerto Rico which he sensed was fast disappearing. I don't know why I expect to hear anything more definitive. Those in the middle of history offer eloquence, but rarely their true motivations. Speculating about her husband's sense of his own destiny, Mrs. Clemente sounds pretty much like a hardboiled tabloid pundit: "He always said, 'The day I retire, nobody will know it.' He wanted to leave the remembrance that he was on the top. And that happened in a different way."

Now she tells the story once more. After fourteen years, she can tell it as though it's someone else's story. She confirms that Roberto accompanied the relief supplies out of concern over corruption. "After the first shipment, they didn't want them to touch nothing once it arrived in Managua, just leave it and go back to Puerto Rico. So our man had to tell them, 'If we go back, we'll take all the supplies with us, and we'll tell Mister Roberto Clemente, who's in charge of this campaign.' And once the soldiers hear the name Roberto Clemente, they called Somoza's son, Tachito. And he signed a permission for them to move all those supplies to Masaya, in two trucks, you see. Then we sent the second flight, three flights. Then Roberto was leaving on the fourth one. The owner was a young fellow, who came to us at the airport, give us a card, and said if we need a plane to take supplies there, he was available. Then Roberto ask me, and I said, you know, if you think it should be done, I let him decide."

Doña Vera isn't giggling anymore, but her tone is not designed to elicit pity. "And this plane looks better than the other one from the outside. And we didn't know it was bad. That next week, four of us were planning to go to Masaya, and to Managua, to the distribution center. And the flight we lost, where Roberto died, we were sending some emergency equipment for operations, like those tubes for tracheotomy and some other things they needed for emergency in the hospital. And they said that the children there were dying of hunger. Then we got a kind of milk for babies, all that food was lost in that flight." She allows herself to dwell on the loss of formula. "There were five men, including Roberto. The only body they recovered was the pilot because it was tied up in the seat. That was something terrible."

"And this all started because of the young boy without legs he'd seen in Masaya?"

"Yes. They didn't have a pediatric wing or nothing there, all the patients were together, in very bad condition. . . ."

Before she can finish, one of the smallest boys in the Sports City stumbles in our direction, looking for the water fountain, clutching his first baseball bat. The circle is completed.

"*Hola! Cómo está?*" She softens at the sight of the boy. "*Ay, qué lindo! Qué lindo!* Nice bat, eh? *Disfrute.*" That means enjoy it. "Okay? Adios!" It doesn't take much for Doña Vera to soften.

"I tell you," she confides, "we were married for eight years. I was very happy, I get to know him very good. Sometimes him and myself thinking the same time, the same thing. I have so many good remembrances. Except I had to fly from Pittsburgh to Puerto Rico for the children to be born here, then go back. He wanted them to be born here, to be Puerto Rican. I insisted to stay there when our youngest was born because that trip was so long. He said no, no, no! I want him to be born where we born, it doesn't matter how much we spend, it doesn't matter nothing, I want him born where we born." How out-of-date the gesture seems!

"He was very proud to be Puerto Rican always. And every time he win a trophy or something there, he feel very proud but not personally, for Puerto Rico. Everything he won, the three thousand hits, the batting championships, the Gold Gloves, he think first on the island."

I leave Doña Vera feeling I'm finally on the island, too.

CENTER FIELD
JARDÍN CENTRAL
Dominican Republic

"The turtle can't dance because it has no waist."

—Dominican children's song

EPIPHANY IN SANTO DOMINGO

It's the night of Epiphany in Santo Domingo. A processional makes its way through the fetid back alleys as it has every January since they started getting fetid four hundred and ninety-one years ago. The crush of true believers bears on high three plywood wise men, complete with prop scepters and beards of white cotton. It's a long way to Bethlehem and there are seas of Christendom to cross. "On the day of the Three Kings," Tony Pérez tells me, "all the children would ask for a ball, a glove, and bat." If only the Baby Jeeze had made a similar request! He, too, might have been blessed with a long-term contract. Signed his autographs Jesus Alou!

I've arrived quite by accident on the day that marks the end of the holiday season. And already I'm having my own epiphany. What response other than transcendent elation can I have at the sight of baseball caps on every customs official who manhandles my backpack, thumbs through my boxer shorts? Welcome to the country disguised as a tryout camp, where play-by-plays are broadcast on buses, where children take their cuts in every cane field with sugar stalks for bats, where shortstops outnumber scholars or honest politicians! Are you planning to stay for extra innings?

"*Te gusta el béisbol?*" I ask my first cabbie, knowing his reply will take me all the way into town. Among his favorite *jugadores*, he lists Pedro Guerrero of the Dodgers, who grins on billboards throughout the land promoting Presidente beer; then "Cesarín," affectionate shorthand for the Reds' César Gerónimo, who's no Indian chief but my favorite union boss, having just replaced Rico Carty as the spokesman for the Dominican *Federación de Peloteros*; and Felipe Rojas Alou, the final vowel pronounced here less like igloo and more hello. *"Jesus y Mateo tambien,"* the driver reminds me of the other Alou brothers. How could he know that Matty Alou was the name engraved on my boyhood mitt? Or that the three names are engraved in every bleacher bum's memory as the only siblings to play in the same outfield. The Alous were the property of the Giants, who, thanks to a scout with undue influence over Generalissimo Rafael Trujillo, once cornered the market on Dominican players like United Fruit did with bananas.

I celebrate my own epiphany when the driver mutters, "Manuel Mota." Not diminished to diminutive Manny in these parts. How can I possibly explain the process of identification which made that scrawny, dark exotic one of my favorite summer friends? Mota, baseball's all-time best pinch-hitter, struck me as the quintessential Latin player: underrated and underplayed, faceless, originless, a Zen master at bunting, the All-Seeing One of the seeing-eye single! I counted myself the sole devotee of the cult of Motaism, a creed whose commandments were, "Humility is the better part of a batting average! Whatever you do in life, always make contact! Get the bat off your shoulders, kid! Choke up on reality! Keep your third eye on the ball!" Reactivated at forty-four, Manny Mota was so ageless that he could, as Tommy Lasorda said, "roll out of bed Christmas morning and get a base hit." Maybe because he was doing just that in Santo Domingo.

The driver's next listing from his personal roster sounds to me like "King Wallah." King Wallah, King Wallah . . . I flip frantically through my encyclopedia of rosters, stats, apocrypha. "Sí, King Wallah!" Does he mean Dave Kingman, a.k.a. King Kong? Or could he mean Babe Ruth, pronounced in these parts like the candy bar, the Sultan of Swat? *El Sultán de Macho?* "No, King Wallah, *tercera base.*" That clue makes me realize he means Tim Wallach, the Expos' third baseman who led the winter leagues here one year in home runs—a feat that's enough to grant him the status of an *inmortal.* I have another cut-rate epiphany when the driver nods at my successful identification, waits with me in satisfied silence for King Wallah's imaginary swat to land. Is it that I'm thrilled at this latest evidence that a pleasure so private as baseball can also be so widely shared? Or is it just that I'm finding the world in its place? Like a home-run ball, we travel not to discover, but to confirm.

Epiphany to realize that so much of traveling is taken up getting through the obvious (like name, rank, serial number) while the absurd (like risking dehydration to visit the holy shrine of some religion you never heard of) usually gets taken on faith. A greater epiphany arises in Santo Domingo because the startle-at-first-sight of lands previously mis-imagined is better than love, or at least more revealing. First arcade of palms lining the bumpy causeway from airport to town is like a curtain that never quite rises to reveal Caribbean breakers glinting in lunar footlights; first oven heat through rolled-down windows; first thatched jukejoints hawking *pollos al carbón*; first kids frying plantains over fires set in discarded oil drums; first fortune-tellers shrouded in kerchiefs, barefoot on the road to nowhere with guavas in their aprons; first peasants with machetes dangling obscenely from their belts, first shudder at the power of a machete, so rarely unleashed; first pickup truck beds stuffed to the point of capsize with tied-on layers of cotton rag; first army units making unreported movements in the night. The sight of more automatic weapons in ten minutes than I've seen in my life.

My epiphany's to be found in whatever we can retain from these magic moments before the grotesque turns commonplace. For sanity's sake, I'll soon turn this Hieronymus Bosch canvas into a Norman Rockwell in which I can comfortably operate. That's Gerónimo Bosch, as in the San Gerónimo Hotel and Casino where I'm headed, perhaps named after César Gerónimo. As in Juan Bosch, the gray-headed, egg-headed reform-ist who was the first democratically elected president after the Trujillo dictatorship, the only democratically elected president ever. Booted out by the military, he became the first beckoned back by a popular revolt of "Constitutionalists" which might have succeeded if Lyndon Johnson hadn't dispatched forty-two thousand Marines. Citing a "Communist threat," L.B.J. never did make the place safe for democracy—just for big-league scouts like the legendary Epifanio Guerrero. Another epiphany!

Even then, Dominican history was inextricably linked to baseball. The first people in the outside world to learn of the '65 uprising were the Western Union operators at San Francisco's Candlestick Park wiring inning-by-inning results to the Dominican every time Juan Marichal pitched. The ball scores didn't get through—that's how everyone knew that the government radio station had been seized. "What I yearned for most of all, and I believe this to be true of the majority of my countrymen," Marichal would later write, "was a stable, democratic form of government. But with troops in the streets and people being hurt and killed, it gives you a strange feeling to talk political abstractions when you are thousands of miles away, playing baseball for a living." Epiphany to realize that I'm entering the site of the last U.S. invasion in this hemisphere before Grenada. To carry an American passport in the Americas is to follow a trail cleared by the Marines. What a set of groundskeepers!

The highway funnels through a *barrio* sunken in mud, smoldering piles of garbage ash anointing the sidewalks patroled by packs of scrawny hounds. This outlying neighborhood produced the bravest fighters, I recall from the slew of reporters' eyewitness accounts of the "Dominican crisis." Our crisis, not theirs, since when has the Dominican ever *not* been in crisis? Twenty thousand Dominicans died in the fighting, and in the years following the invasion, an estimated three thousand dissidents were exiled, jailed, or disappeared. The Dominican Revolutionary Party, which we'd sought to keep from power, became the establishment party— and showed just as little capacity as its predecessors for getting the nation out of hock. Its last leader, Salvador Jorge Blanco, was under investigation for corruption and its previous chief of state committed suicide in office rather than face scandal.

"Abajo Bosch! Viva Balaguer!" The familiar players of two decades are brushed in gory tempera drippings on Santo Domingo's walls. "Qué Viva Wessin y Wessin!" How quickly the armories emptied back in '65! The plaza we're skirting may be the one where the rebellious army officers dumped truckloads of artillery and ammo and beckoned the populace to come and get it. No pamphlets or public service announcements on their use or target. How those guns were scooped up like Christmas candy! "The truth," concluded a United Nations report, "is that when thousands of frustrated men and women attempted to get hold of a rifle in order to shoot in the streets of Santo Domingo, there were communists among them; there were Catholics; there were reformers; there were reactionaries; but the democrats, and above all the needy, predominated." From the looks of it, the needy are still needing, still predominating.

Epiphany on the bridge over the Río Ozama, an evil name for this deep-carved gulch trickling ooze from jungle highlands. Before 1492, everything in sight lay within the territory of the lady Cacique Catalina.

Epiphany in Santo Domingo

Then one of Columbus's advance scouts fell in love with her, poor girl. Upon the scout's urging, the city of Nueva Isabela was laid out on the Ozama's east bank. In 1502, Bartolomeo Columbus ordered the town moved to the far side to quarantine a malaria epidemic—and had Catalina hung from her heels. The devout fellow renamed the place Santo Domingo after his own Genovese cobbler father, Domenico. And there it is, St. Dominic, Saint-Domingue, all aflicker! So small for a place so storied, so coveted! Streetlights wobble on the hillside like hundreds of Japanese lanterns, run off the same generator about to give out. No skyscraper middle, no downtown clumping, just scabrous arms of port cranes ready to unburden the stray ship, one set of smokestacks for the city's electric plant, and upriver, an embankment of shanties sliding, sliding toward sea level. The low, wet sky is uncannily yellow, trapping every particle of light and turning it sweaty. A city in the tropics at night is a pitched tent that's lost its mosquito netting. And it's by night that those cities look their best.

The bridge leads into the first of many grandiose rotaries that spin like potters' wheels around the statuary of play soldiers on play horses so beloved by Latin American civic planners. Beyond downtown, these boulevards fan, leading to oases of money, outposts of Chase Manhattan and Goodyear. Old ladies gamely wave wilting bouquets of violets at the passing traffic. The cavernous *mercado* is closed but gives off the permanent scent of mango, palm oil, and poultry wastes. Shuttered shop windows are crammed with blenders and Rubbermaid basins. I recognize the single narrow chasm between heavy, grillwork-laden art-nouveau department stores as el Conde, the nation's five-block Fifth Avenue. Those few Dominicans able to spend money on luxury goods are said to *dar un Condazo*. At this hub, there are actually several functional stoplights. I better keep from blinking or I'll miss this center of a nation. Epiphany is an inaccurate term for the eyeball-wrenching required to appreciate this place. Santo Domingo teaches that a change in scale is more important than in consciousness. Add six feet to our bedroom ceilings and we'll all feel like kings. Add six feet to the stadium fences, and there'll be no more home runs.

Old Santo Domingo is a honeycomb of cobblestone nuzzled between two fortresses. One is the headquarters for the ever-menacing remnants of Trujillo's military presence, guarded by peasant boys in puttees; the other is the original Spanish arsenal whose puny single turret on a bluff is now defended by persistent guides. Lined with rough-hewn doors and thick bolts, the curved lanes seem hermetically sealed off from current-day indignities. The Santo Domingo which the Spaniards built has the air, if not the look, of today's suburban satellites. The Americas' first Levittown, with twenty-four-hour security. This was a planned community, austere in white stone, causing Governor de Oviedo to boast "that as touching the buildings, there is no city in Spain, not even Barcelona, so much to be preferred as San Domingo."

Somewhere in here is the first cathedral of the New World, containing the tomb of Columbus, whose alleged remains were carted back and forth so many times between here and Havana and Spain that nobody's sure whose bones are inside the crypt. The victim of a bureaucratic tangle typical of the empire he founded! Bones never do much for me anyhow. I have my mini-epiphany when, in the evening balm out front, I spot stickball players using the trunks of spindly palms for bases, the four meagre sides of the cobblestone plaza for base lines. Just an epidemic away are the ruins of the Americas' first hospital. Where's the plaque commemorating the first syphilis sore? The Alcazar, residence of the incompetent Diego Columbus, sits on a bluff by the river, a Moorish cigar box set between solitary, rubber-necked palms on a regal lawn. It doesn't seem right that any of these conceits of masonry should still be standing. These streets exist as hallucinatory after-images of a civility that had no chance. A century after these foundations were laid, Sir Francis Drake would be razing the city, and all the inhabitants would flee inland to escape raiding pirates. Though the conquest that began here spread with astonishing rapidity all the way to Patagonia, the continent proved too big, the vision of what should be done with it too narrow.

Beside the berths where galleons loaded with gold once set out for their return to Sevilla, the Santo Domingo Chamber of Commerce plans new docks to lure Love Boat cruise lines. In the English-language *Santo Domingo News*, stories of development loans and beach resort construction are sandwiched between ads for acupuncturists and racquetball clubs, pizzerias and Chinese restaurants like La Gran Muralla—another way to spell the Great Wall. Today's road map to empire tells me this palm-lined seaside promenade is the Avenida George Washington, which leads into the Avenida Franklin Roosevelt. Granted, it must be tough to find local *presidentes* to name anything after, since most were ousted by coups or resigned in scandal, but no city up North would offer such

Epiphany in Santo Domingo

unvarnished homage to our democratic figures, our *caudillos* without epaulets. We still want to think of our exalted *líderes* as just plain folks—perhaps the ultimate Yankee conceit. Now we're crossing the Avenida John F. Kennedy. And where's the Avenida Bowie Kuhn? So good to get away!

Is it still Epiphany in Santo Domingo? After checking into my hotel, I reach the waterfront Malecón in time for a more pagan fiesta. Along this palm-fringed sweep are most of the country's restaurants, serving fish on trellised patios; discos lit with pink neon, some outrageously, ludicrously elegant with long awnings, doormen in top hats; the leading hotel-and-casino credit-card enclaves. Amidst breaks in the gutted embankment, trailer stands of impromptu barbecuers outdo one another with grandiose names like "el Universario" and "el Extraterrestre." In the shadow of Sheratons, the local citizenry slinks about, souvenir hawkers and money changers, panderers and amputees, leggy showgirls and off-duty croupiers loosening their bow-ties.

Everywhere, teams of waifs wash windshields at stop signs and peel oranges. These appear to be the country's two leading growth industries. The kids are called *tigritos*: the little tigers, cubs of the nation. In some other land, the savvy ones could point the way to every brothel or *generales'* haunt. Here, they keep tabs on every training camp of *las ligas grandes*. And who are all these gnomes in shiny spats and helmets so big they slip over their eyes, guarding the waves with rifles twice their size? Beware the quiet places, like quiet people, look out for the ones with no brochures, who go about their rounds without too much fuss. Countries that rarely make splashy headlines are the tight-lipped stalkers among nations, pent-up, psychotic. Vents of protest, the occasional primal scream, are needed to keep the body politic humming. In Latin America especially, a show of spilled blood is a sign of national health.

Generalissimo Trujillo was traveling along this same seaside rampway from an assignation with a mistress when his black Chevy Bel-Air was surrounded outside of town and ambushed by subordinates. The exalted ex–plantation thug died pumping lead, his last cry not *"Et tu, Brute!"* but the favored Caribbean expletive, *"Coño!"* This CIA-approved tyrannicide ended the thirty-year reign of Latin America's state-of-the-art dictator. The people ran into these streets singing a newly composed merengue, "They've killed the Goat on the highway and won't let me see. . . ."

Not so much farther down the coast is the stretch once called "the swimming pool." Troublemakers of all ilks were fed there to waiting sharks. The murders were paid for with funds from the Dominican treasury allocated for "birdseed." Some more miles along is the Casa de Caoba, Trujillo's all-mahogany ranch retreat, lying gutted, unattended, stacked with livestock trophies and Boy Scout caps. Gone are the owner's nine thousand ties, two thousand suits, three hundred fifty uniforms. Thirty years ago, I would have been arriving in a place called Ciudad Trujillo—renamed by the puppet legislature out of "popular demand" while Trujillo was out of the country.

From 1930 to 1962, the country existed in a virtual quarantine enforced by Trujillo, of whom F.D.R. reputedly said, "He may be a bastard, but at least he's *our* bastard." While Trujillo worked with North American interests, this exalted poor boy claimed personal ownership of sugar mills, copper mines, the trucking industry, private customs payments, insurance policies, dairy farms, slaughterhouses, flour and match monopolies, the only shoe factory in a country where walking barefoot was outlawed, the peanut oil plant, the beer brewery, the racetrack, and, of course, a ball team. The man who powdered his face to look white turned the island into a private fiefdom for sundry charmboat relations like his brother Petán, who ran the fruit monopoly and was known as "Pipi" or "pimp"; his sister Nieves Luisa, a reformed prostitute; sister Japonesa, who ran the lottery concession; brother Héctor, called *el Negro* as the darkest of this nouveau-Aryan gang; his playboy son Ramfis, made a colonel at age three; daughter Flor de Oro, whom poets extolled as *"una flor exquisamente exquisito."* At a time when most of Flor's compatriots earned under two hundred dollars a year, the train of her wedding dress was a hundred forty feet of ermine. When she took a Brazilian businessman as her fourth husband, Trujillo made Portuguese compulsory in all schools. To boost farming productivity, he ordered cows milked to music. When a landowner complained at a dinner party about the annoying presence of Haitian squatters on her estate, Trujillo had twenty-five thousand of them slaughtered—and paid Haiti twenty-nine dollars a head as reparation.

There was always epiphany, there was always baseball. Trujillo, the great anti-Red, self-proclaimed First Anticommunist of the Americas, was a lifelong "red man." Those are the colors of Santo Domingo's Escogido club—meaning those "chosen" to challenge long-time rival

Epiphany in Santo Domingo

Licey—which was owned by Trujillo's son-in-law. One of Trujillo's sisters used to roam the streets of Santo Domingo taking up collections in a straw basket for the Escogido players' payroll. Trujillo preferred to hoard the best prospects for his *fuerzas armadas* squad, and imported the top Negro League stars to stock his own team. He may or may not have ordered Satchel Paige to pitch a shutout or face a firing squad. Ponies and polo were more to Trujillo's refined taste. Yet among his few lasting public works are the country's four ballparks which he modeled after the Baltimore Orioles' spring training stadium in Miami. These are the only monuments to Trujillo's beneficent reign which the vengeful mobs left standing.

"In this house," the signs once read, "Trujillo is *el jefe.*" At the ballpark, I'll find the graffito, "In this latrine, Trujillo is *el jefe.*" And the symbol of liberation is the Mercedes-Benz. "We've got more than any city in the world," my cabbie boasted. Obviously, he's never been to Teheran or Bahrain. And Hong Kong has more in a single parking garage. Everywhere, I hear that the country's future is secure with "a good man" at the helm. In a divisive election that nearly led to civil war, Dominicans turned back to pro-American two-time president Joaquín Balaguer. Author of more than a hundred books of history and poetry, Balaguer is the perfect combination scholar-statesman so often bred by the Latin American elite. Despite his role as a minister in the final years of the Trujillo regime, the octogenarian Balaguer has somehow maintained a reputation of personal honesty. During earlier reigns he hunted and jailed his enemies ruthlessly, but people now speak of him as their beloved pet dinosaur. Presiding over a nation so dominated by throngs of young people in motion, whose national symbol is the vigorous ballplayer, whose national song is the wildly exuberant merengue, he seems the living personification of an out-of-date, out-of-solutions oligarchy. When the sightless Balaguer gives a speech, an adjutant in full regalia moves the microphone to within range of *el presidente's* ever-moving mouth and platitudes. After decades of thievery in high places, Dominicans feel safer with a thief who can't see too far. Here the blind actually lead the blind.

What sort of republic is this anyway? A pimpocracy, from the looks of it. The long-legged café au lait gals appear briefly on the boulevards, precious commodities taxied from cabaret boîtes to hotel room assignations. They spontaneously offer themselves, blowing playful Dinah Shore kisses. "Mañana," I answer to all beseechments. By mañana, I will have learned to say no. In Santo Domingo, the line between prostitution and true love is as thin as the pair of stockings that will buy *un puro amor*. Forty percent of the married men in this country have children by women other than their wives. When do they accomplish this? If these creatures of the *noche tropical* are really so sensual, then why the endless sublimation of cruising the same blocks in their passionmobiles or parking with doors open so the radio can blare? What gives with this town?

Epiphany dinner at midnight, and I'm among thousands. Order the sea bass, on the menu as *mero escabeche*. Sounds like a second baseman for the '62 Mets. Too hot to be tempted by the revolving trays of antipasto on a cart at the Vesuvio Uno. In Santo Domingo, the preferred food is Italian. And the waiters are all from Jackson Heights. "I live on Queens Boulevard for fourteen years. Why I come back? Don't ask, caballero. Ask a lady!" These fellows squirm to get out of their starched collars and into a conversation. The maître d' himself turns a blind eye when bleeding-heart diners respond to the pleas of *tigritos* begging through the hedges. He's probably witnessed this siphoning a thousand times over. I place into the small, dirty hands that reach through the foliage whatever I can sneak from my continually replenished basket. Let them eat garlic bread!

Or squander it in the casinos. This is not Reno, with its steak-and-eggs breakfasts, kiddie parlors, false cheer. These are places to lose in. The dealers look like secret agents. The managers head off for secretive transactions in the men's room. The full-length mirrors show smooth-talking gents and paunchy society ladies, a profligate elite working as hard as it can to show wealth is as irrelevant to them as it is to most of their countrymen. I plunk down at the blackjack table next to some ballplayers. Mark Grant, Giants' prospect, is betting low. Tony Phillips, Oakland's utility infielder, is hardly the slick sort, but prefers open-toed sandals, a necklace of trade beads, and a T-shirt. "I love these people because I've had to struggle for everything, too," he confesses. "This is where I spend whatever I make." He looks like a contented man when he loses it all on a single hand.

Can it still be Epiphany now that the baby Jesus and his unshaven guests have been stowed away for next year and a more pagan fiesta's being staged against the lapping Caribbean for backdrop? Throngs of

Epiphany in Santo Domingo

teenagers crowd around a half-dozen bandstands to worship the distinctive national sound called merengue, a tangy treat whipped up by *conjuntos* gyrating in time. Trim chorus lines seem locked in a contest to make this hard-driving Hispanic polka more up-tempo, more frantic. The horns trill so fast they begin to sound like train whistles, plaintive and furious. The piano that sets the basic chords imitates a team of horses at a gallop. Bird-calls and whistles punctuate the increasingly insistent beat. The sleepy conga man in hipster goatee taps out an ancient S.O.S. on a double-skinned tom-tom with tape-wrapped, sure-footed hands. The highest priest adds a dash of spine-tingling by scraping the *guayo*, an instrument derived from a shredder for yucca root that looks like a huge cheese grater.

In the oral-based culture of the Caribbean, some beats sound warnings, some celebrate triumphs, some echo with the longing for lost kingdoms. This music is an invitation to the moment: a call to live harder and love more wildly and go out in a blaze, squandering what little you've got, including passion, embellishing and embroidering every gesture, finding some new comical, crazy variant in life's insistent melody. Just as Puerto Ricans and Cubans look down on Dominicans as loud, uncouth country cousins, so merengue has been viewed as the Latin music for hicks. Though Dominicans are ethnically more African than any of their island neighbors, their *merengazo* beat is not as polyrhythmic as salsa or so-called Afro-Cuban music. By dint of its utter sincerity, madcap turns, and infectious hilarity, the music has overpowered more sophisticated island rhythms. Even in New York, merengue is suddenly all the rage—signaling, like the baseball boom, the Dominican Republic's belated acceptance into the Caribbean community. It's an awfully urgent beat for such a sleepy place, but the perfect sound for a country both so blessed and looted. In no other music on earth does the happiness sound so sad or the sadness so happy.

To an all-girl rendition of Wilfrido Vargas's "*Soy Un Hombre Divertido*"—roughly translated as "I'm a party kind of guy!"—I review the numbers I've culled from United Nations status reports, State Department warnings, and scalding Marxist tracts. Like a true *béisbolista*, I need to know the relevant averages and percentages, compile my own back-of-the-bubble-gum "stats." The numbers on the Republica Dominicana must be scanned in rhythm, absorbed in time with the congas. Life expectancy, a mere 55.4 years. *Ay, ay, yay!* Infant mortality, over a

113

hundred per thousand as of 1970. *Cómo?* Only one-fourth of those who reach childhood make it past secondary school. *Díme!* As of 1970, annual gross income averaged just over a thousand dollars per capita. *Ugh!* Out of 660,000 rural workers, only 154,000 collected regular wages. *Caliente!* A cane cutter working the 1935 harvest earned a daily wage of fifty cents—and for only half a year, at that. By 1971, real wages still fluctuated between seventy and ninety cents a day. *Agua, agua!* Sixty percent of the labor force is chronically unemployed. Between 1969 and 1978, real wages dropped from $80 a month to $54. The "free zones" established to encourage foreign investment boast the lowest wage rates in the Caribbean. Transnational corporations such as Falconbridge exported a total of $400 million in nickel between 1978 and 1981 alone, but paid taxes of only $2 million to $3 million a year. Gulf + Western's operations were virtually tax-free. Meanwhile the budget deficit rose from $93 million to $331 million, the trade deficit from $184 million to $537 million. *Oye!* The numbers only benumb us, further clog the stat sheet. But these figures add up to the most remarkable number of all: some fifty players in the big leagues, some two hundred in the minor league pipeline. Play ball! *Por qué no?* There's nothing to report, only nuances to scavenge. The game's all over: rich bested poor 17–3, strong blanked weak 22–0. Dance to the dance of epiphanies!

I seek refuge at the San Geronimo. But the television in my room does nothing when I turn it on. An inspection reveals that there's no electrical cord attached. The thing's just a prop to be set down on a night table. In this capital of crowing roosters, the veneer of modernism doesn't just peel away but buckles up in great chunks. Is a television a television at all if it doesn't turn on? The bellhop brings a replacement and I discover the hotel gets more channels than I do back home. Cable is the newest conqueror of the Caribbean, and where pirates once roamed, the inhabitants pirate signals at will. The satellite dish has brought all these islands closer to the electronic bosom of the mainland. How can the Dominicans watch our situation comedies set against backdrops of abundance without feeling their situation's closer to tragedy? What do they make of the weather in Chicago, the sports scores from Atlanta, football's weekly injury count, the hype leading up to the Super Bowl "Super Domingo"? There are no Super Sundays in Santo Domingo.

Epiphany in Santo Domingo

The more confused I am, the more I feel at home. And how do I explain that I experience travel's truly epiphanous joy lying spread-eagled in my boxer shorts on a moth-eaten bedspread, flipping the dial back and forth between a local interview with Juan Bosch and a Home Box Office rerun of *Billy Jack*? In a shabby studio, the wizened former president and spurned savior looks noble as ever, and far too professorial to give the generals a taste of their own medicine, too in love with the sound of his perfect articulation as he rambles on about the destiny of the Dominican people. How pallid in word and image does *el* ex-*presidente* seem, how pointless all his spent breath beside the swift certitude of a Bruce Lee kung-fu kick, a Charles Bronson spree of revenge! The movies on this hookup have been exported because they're too brutal for the home market's consumption. The decapitated heads of opium war lords and lopped-off breasts of the sexy heroine are left to drip on screen, Mongol hordes and Mexican *bandidos* and everything that threatens the American way of justice get machine-gunned into fleshy bits. Flip. The professorial prez lectures on about the true meaning of sovereignty. Flip. A punch in the nuts loses nothing through dubbing. Flip. Juan would put a stop to all this ballplaying nonsense if he ever returned to power. Flip. Chuck Norris, blond and certain, breaks dark skulls with the side of his palm.

"America is many and yet it is one," said Juan Bosch. "Everything that has happened in one American country has happened in all the others." Penultimate epiphany in Santo Domingo. I close my eyes and suddenly see all of this as an old-fashioned county fair tug-of-war. Our power, their dependence. Their beauty, our cunning. Two squads cheered on by local bathing beauties, periodically resupplied with kegs of *cerveza*. Why is it, then, that it's so hard to see the rope?

Travel is the way global issues get personal. Heat rash, malaise, malaria, monotony, rotten diet, paranoia, dysentery, illiteracy—when it happens to you, you must deal with it. The question is one of boundaries, to use the latest gringo psychobabble. I'm most content when I've lost track of where I leave off and some country in the throes of agony begins. Is that the Amazon in my angry veins? El Salvador's migraine or mine? If that palace is my grandiosity, then where do I sign up for the three o'clock tour? Is that my bad breath aimed back at me in the form of open sewage ditches? That must be me asking for a handout. I am my own food riot. And if I have trouble falling asleep, that's because, after five hundred years, this nation is only just waking.

Epiphany's over in Santo Domingo. In the beginning, there was Santo Domingo. At the end, there will be Santo Domingo. But for the duration, give us anything but! While we still take breath, give us a fighting chance! Get me out of here, *mamacita*!

TO DIE
IN SAN PEDRO

The beach palms are giving way to fields choking with cane in flower. Higher than an elephant's eye and dense as dreadlocks, the stalks' silvery tails blot the horizon. An hour's drive east of the capital is the realm of *azúcar*, the sweet shit. "From Santo Domingo sugar," went a sixteenth-century saying, "were built the fairest palaces of Spain." From the offspring of brawny sugar workers, playing in company-sponsored leagues, have come the best ballplayers. Around a bend in the coastal highway, just past a roadside Coco Frio stand, partially obscured by a banana grove, a newly posted billboard announces, "Welcome to San Pedro de Marcorís. The City Which Has Given the Most Major Leaguers to the World."

Más peloteros—there is no disputing this local boast. With dozens of citizens on U.S. team rosters or on the way up the pipeline, this provincial port of eighty thousand definitely has the Americas' most men in spikes per capita. At least eight shortstops from the same Little League have gone on to the bigs—including Rafael Ramírez, Julio Franco, Alfredo Griffin, Tony Fernández, Rafael Santana, José Uribe, Nelson Norman, Mariano Duncan. The large number of workers drawn to the canefields from Aruba, Curaçao, and other West Indian islands explains the preponderance of English last names—as well as the San Pedrans' larger-than-average heft. "San Pedro is like a prize apple tree," Tony Pérez has said. "Every apple you pick is gonna be good." Stop at any bodega in town, and you'll find someone who claims kinship with Jorge

117

Bell, the first Dominican MVP, the Dodgers' Pedro Guerrero, or the volatile Joaquín Andújar. The menu of a pizzeria on the main road into town features the Rico Burger and the Carty Burger—named after the first of San Pedro's big leaguers. A generation of immigrants has taken up the Carty line of work the way villagers from Canton have gone into laundromats.

As I cruise in my rental car past the harbor's crumbling balustrades, the tin shanties in the banana groves, I can hardly believe this Macorís, as those in the know call it, was once a cultural showplace of the Caribbean, with an opera hall where Jenny Lind sang. Or that this region was once such a hotbed of political ferment that Trujillo had to burn down the bridge which connected the town with the rest of the island. The radio offers a popular merengue of the moment with the English lyric, "Sippin' on my guava, watchin' the sun go down. That's all I need, in San Pedro de Macorís." All that remains is a single plaza, a gaudy cathedral, a seafront promenade, a dock piled with sugar sacks, a medical school supported by an Arab millionaire, and a modest "free zone" where foreign companies are encouraged to make use of the local cheap labor. Rotting garbage dots the curbs and row after row of batten cottages crowd the unpaved alleys.

But look closely and you'll find one growth industry. Underneath the grimy smokestacks of the Ingenio Porvenir—the "mill of the future"— are two diamonds. Behind the university are three more. The Estadio Tetelo Vargas functions as a community, and daycare, center. When the winter league teams aren't using the park, tryouts and rookie games are staged every day of the year. In the lots outside, barefoot kids sharpen their skills using sticks and rocks. Though it's just past ten in the morning, the cap vendors are laying their multicolored stock along the sidewalk before the ticket booths. Six hours before game time, the *tigritos* have assembled to glimpse arriving players, run errands for team officials, or simply extinguish another day without work.

Dominican children don't stand in line for autographs. They clamor for something to put an autograph on. "When a baby boy is born in the Dominican," I'm told by Ralph Avila, a long-time scout for the Dodgers, "the first gift that friends and relatives will buy him, if they can afford it, if they really want to be good to him, is a mitt. And later on, a bat. But even those who don't get such gifts will go out into the fields, mark out a diamond, and play with a stick or broken stalk of sugar cane for a bat.

They will make gloves out of newspaper and cardboard. They will use an orange, a melon, a papaya for a ball." Point a camera toward any trash-strewn lot in San Pedro de Macorís and every kid in sight strikes the same pose. They lock their knees in a professional stance, grip tightly an imaginary club.

All roads in this republic lead to baseball—no matter how rutted or circuitous, no matter how many times you get stopped. I'm finding that the local rental cars come with a busted headlight or other defect just noticeable enough to insure a cat-and-mouse affair with one or another of this country's *fuerzas armadas*, very armed forces. These up-to-date highwaymen do their robbing in a variety of uniforms. They write out their tickets very slowly so you've plenty of opportunity to dissuade them. They like to linger over the word *tribunal* until you can almost hear the sharpening of a guillotine blade. Then they inquire whether you might have some whiskey in the back seat, just a *botellita*. It's not that there's any law against booze in the car, it's just that they like whiskey very much. There's even a stand down the road where you can buy some for them. They will be happy to guide you there. At this point, "No *entiendo*" is not good enough. The only workable strategy to avoid coughing up a bribe every hundred miles or so is claiming to be a roving right fielder. Even coming from a conspicuously unmuscular Yankee, the magic word is *pelotero*. Me with ballclub, *señor*.

It's been this way ever since two enterprising Cuban brothers established touring baseball clubs as early as the 1890s. The Marines soon followed to further indoctrinate the populace. U.S. forces invaded six times, including the eight-year occupation begun in 1916, about which, due to military censorship, the people of the United States knew nothing until 1920. "From their stay in the Dominican Republic," a U.S. government report later concluded about one of our six earlier occupations, "the Marines learned valuable lessons in counterinsurgency, or what was called then the conduct of 'small wars.'" The stay began with some excuse about quelling local anarchy or protecting U.S. citizens and with the same edict. "For the present and until further notice," began U.S. Executive Order No. 12 of 1916, "no elections will be held in the Republic of Santo Domingo."

When the Marines landed near Puerto Plata that year, destroying the town hospital with a bombardment from the gunboat *Dubuque*, the locals seized the U.S. consul as a hostage. His Dominican captor said later that "it would have broken my heart to shoot such a cheerful old gentleman." The citizenry simply changed the words of a popular merengue: "Now Puerto Plata has what it never had before, Americans on shore and more of them out in the bay. I don't love you anymore, I don't love you anymore." Yet even before such direct intervention, this fragile republic was in the habit of offering itself to the highest bidder. "San Domingo" broke free of Spain only when it was conquered by neighboring Haiti. Soon after the revolt that established the Dominican Republic, the country actually appealed to be reabsorbed into the Spanish empire. Reeling from one protector to another, the Dominican attempted to become formally annexed to the United States. A Senate bill in 1871 missed passage by a single vote. In the end, racial suspicions won the day over greed. Much as they wanted to expand American economic markets, the good senators recoiled from the spectre of "ten or twelve tropical states" with dark-skinned voters who were, according to one Republican, "confessedly in the lowest state of poverty, and must remain so forever, because they will not work."

The U.S. settled for controlling the island through proxy presidents like Jacinto ("Mozo") Peynado. "He can't be Peynado (combed) because he's bald," joked those he ruled. "He can't be Mozo (a lad) because he's old. He can't be Jacinto (hyacinth) because he smells bad." Changes in power were frequent, but as one North American historian wrote in 1905, "In Santo Domingo, a revolution does not mean any difference in political principles or anything of that sort. It means that a certain number of 'citizens' plot together in order to seize the government and get the offices and emoluments that are incidental thereto." Sixty years passed before a Dominican leader first signified "his intention to voluntarily retire at the end of his term." In the meantime, as one history of the period commented, "Santo Domingo's worst periods of disorder have never been able to subdue the enthusiasm of foreign investors." In the days when there were plenty of brochures, land speculators beckoned with claims that, "The man who will work can be comfortable within ten years. In this land, flowers bloom at Christmas and catarrhs are unknown. In short, it is a white man's country!"

While the U.S. established more direct rule over neighboring Puerto Rico, its approach to the Dominican Republic has mostly been one of unbenign neglect—not so much avarice as ambivalence. Ulysses S. Grant was the first of many presidents to propose a U.S. naval base at

Bahía de Samaná, a natural harbor at the island's east end and one of the most strategic sites for guarding Caribbean sea lanes. Yet Samaná remains undeveloped and open for bidding to this day. For thirty years, Trujillo served as both bidder and auctioneer. In the years since Trujillo's assassination, Gulf + Western Corporation chairman Hiram Bluthorn made it his pet project to acquire as much of the island as possible. After Bluthorn's death, the conglomerate threw the local economy into further disarray by divesting itself of most holdings. The ensuing influx of Japanese investors may yet turn the island into the outpost of Oriental commerce which Columbus thought he was contacting. The Dominican's been a kind of sweet girl next door—a lover spurned because she's been a little too easy to get. Only the development of baseball talent has attracted and held the interest of Big Daddy.

Yet how unaffected by changes in regime is the countryside outside San Pedro. I'm as far as I can be from Santo Domingo, where the rich spin roulette wheels, the landless scrounge, and the ones in between clerk at Chase Manhattan. The real stuff is here among the roosters and the stolid old gents in straw hats and the ladies on the porches in their Sunday lace dresses. Though a player may be listed as hailing from San Pedro, he's most likely to have been raised in a surrounding company town like Consuelo, built around the most productive *ingenio de azúcar,* or sugar mill, in the country. "Consuelo is a bit like Pittsburgh," says native Nelson Norman, who played for the Pirates, "only the mills are not steel but sugar." And the black smokestacks pour out sorghum soot. A maze of dirt streets encircles the black flanks of the plant and its surrounding freight yards. Ox-carts wobble under unwieldy loads of cane. A single moviehouse, painted aquamarine, provides entertainment. The marquee outside the modest tabernacle next door announces, "*Cristo Viene!*" Goat meat hangs from racks in open stalls. Yet the names of the mills are pure poetry here: Ingenio Amistad, Ingenio La Esperanza, La Caridad. They're as lilting as such places are killing.

Like all the country's road signs, the placards marking the dusty lanes advertise Montecarlos, the Dominican cigarette whose red-and-white package is an exact copy of Marlboros. "This sidewalk brought to you by. . . ." What a country, where the government can't even afford to sponsor its own streets. Money calls the shots, where it can be found— but at least everyone knows this. The line between commercialism and real life is frequently crossed during ballgame broadcasts as cartoon figures appear on the tube to plug booze and smokes between every ball and strike. The radio announcers, too, mix their play-by-plays with pitches of another kind. "That swing's as smooth as Bohemia beer. The hitter's as sweet as Bermudez rum. . . ." The hucksterism's so blatant it's nearly innocent.

How can people wearing Sergio Valente jeans and tuning in Walkmen continue to live here? By now, I shouldn't be surprised by the slick dudes in Afro-sheened hair wearing Mets T-shirts. The economies of many villages like Consuelo are fueled with monthly checks sent home by most of the three hundred thousand Dominicans now working in New York City. "With the exception of going to church," concludes some academic research into this so-called Dominican diaspora, "the public activity most often engaged in is the attending of New York Mets baseball games." According to this same study, up to half the folks buried in island cemeteries have done stints in Nueva York. Dominican gravediggers say, "They always come back, one way or another."

The ballplayers always shuttle back and forth, too, though their skills earn them enough to leave the mud and the heat forever. From the *pueblo* to the penthouse, from the hovels to the Hilton. How do my favorite Americans make this most American of transitions? The stories are many and always exaggerated: A Hispanic rookie ordered ham 'n' eggs for two years because he couldn't pronounce anything else; in a more recent variant, the Giants' José Uribe lived on Chicken McNuggets. From such abrupt leaps in environment people once went mad, like some of the sailors who wandered off the boats from here back to Spain as lunatics. The past spring I had watched one son of San Pedro negotiate the jarring transition from his hometown's shaded plazas traversed by horse-and-buggy to the endless franchised boulevard tentacles of Phoenix, from the perpetual summer of his island home to a false desert spring.

We tend to think of the ballplayer's life as an uncomplicated one, a simple matter of keeping his nose clean and uniform dirty. Yet Joaquín Andújar arrived at the Oakland A's camp ten days late due to "visa problems"—the euphemism ballclubs always drag out when they can't explain a Latin player's tardiness. He came without family, agent, or even a lease on an apartment. He had to face a new employer, new teammates, new sportswriters eager to devour him, a ten-day suspension for a World Series tantrum aimed at umpire Don Denkinger, and, just as camp got underway, a possible suspension and heavy fine from baseball commissioner Peter Ueberroth for prior drug use. He brought with him a reputation as baseball's premier hot dog, the game's *número uno* head case. Opposing players called him "Walking Underwear," or worse still, Jack. They knew that riled this man who disdains blending in. "I have a beautiful name," he told the press outside the A's locker room. "Maybe that's why they pick on me. They cannot forget my beautiful name." He introduced himself by admitting, "I've been called so many things that I forget them. All I know is that my number is forty-seven, my name is Joaquín Andújar."

Surrounded by microphones and furiously jotting reporters, he offered jokes instead of gripes, homilies instead of bitterness. "Baseball is no different from the army," he said of his trade. "You go where they send you, even Vietnam, Alaska." He seemed eager to take a leadership role in a clubhouse that now boasted enough Hispanics to require a "Se Habla Español" sign. The team included the suave, swivel-kneed Alfredo Griffin, a lifelong pal from the Dominican who lived "half a second away." Though Andújar confirmed that he'd changed the color of his self-designed mansion from Cardinal red to a neutral blue, he denied any motive other than that "the paint got old." About his former teammates, he said "I give you a million dollars if you find one of my teammates who does not think I'm a good guy."

In the Andujarian schema, there are no bad guys, only those who err in good faith. The umpire Denkinger was now "my friend. He make a mistake, I make a mistake." Joaquín did not aspire to be perfect, only to be Joaquín. "Everybody is human. Everybody makes mistakes. Name me somebody who never makes a mistake." Under more pressure than most men could handle, this supposed nut case looked like a tough nut to crack. At close range, he was revealed as the one article that professional baseball sorely needs yet seems increasingly unwilling to tolerate: a human being.

Which may explain why controversy has dogged Andújar from Cincinnati to Houston to St. Louis to Oakland. Yet Joaquín always acts surprised by the fuss created around him. Through drug charges and suspensions, he is forever the kid caught with his hand in the cookie jar, the misunderstood philanthropist. All he asks in return is the forgiveness that he seems most willing to grant others. Though his last manager, Whitey Herzog, promised "never to trade him in a thousand years" only weeks before shipping him to Oakland, Andújar insisted, "He is my daddy" and continued to buy him boxes of Dominican cigars. "But don't print how much they cost. They come from my heart." For his newest manager, he promised, "My heart and my arm." The look in Andújar's eyes reminded anyone watching that he was not playing for himself alone.

Even in the overdone boot camp atmosphere of spring training, Joaquín went his own way. He stood out as the player who made the least effort in team calisthenics, stretching exercises, and tae kwon do poses. He wasn't unwilling to work, just to take orders. Often he would trot off later in the day to a second diamond for hours of relentless practice on his pickoff moves. The pitcher's discipline is self-imposed, especially this pitcher's. And when word spread that Andújar would apologize to umpire Denkinger at their first meeting since the World Series incident, more reporters huddled around this home plate summit than had been present at rounds two and three of Reagan-Gorbachev. But Andújar wanted any making-up to be a personal matter. While the press waited for the pitcher's public contrition, he paced the dugout. Satisfying both his mischievous nature and the macho image required by his Dominican mates, Andújar joked, "Apologize? Maybe I keeck his ass!"

Watching Andújar being interviewed for Phoenix Spanish-language television, I had seen a different man: relaxed, articulate, simpatico. In his native tongue, he did not have to hide behind coy Stengelisms. With a muttered *"bueno,"* he was off on lengthy orations in which he appraised the *"aficionados de* Andújar" of his goals and hopes for the coming season, then thanked the *fanáticos* in a half-dozen countries for their support. *Fanático* is so much more than fan—and *orgulloso*, the word he used to describe his feeling at joining Oakland, gets diminished when translated as "proud." After this interview, Joaquín did not scurry off, but autographed several balls for the reporter's children, gave the reporter his room number, and agreed to have dinner with the entire crew.

"About growing up in the Dominican Republic," Joaquín Andújar has said, "I can tell you that I love the Dominican Republic and I love twice as much my hometown of San Pedro de Macorís. I was born and raised there and I have all of my friends there who are very modest and I will never forget them. One of my wishes is to die in San Pedro de Macorís." To die in San Pedro! His battery-mate would never be caught wishing to die in West Covina. But then West Covina could never be as encrusted as this place with so much history and folklore and superstition and tribal wisdom and collective storytelling and music and customs and magic. On a dusty truck route near San Pedro's industrial zone, I get lost trying to find the side-by-side mansions built by Andújar and Griffin. Finally, I realize I've been driving right past them. Built smack against the busy road, surrounded by empty lots strewn with trash, the two houses sit like marbleized, nearly windowless bunkers, vaults for the loot baseball has bought. A boy in shorts guards an iron gate topped with a giant letter A.

Unable to find a hotel around San Pedro's one shaded plaza, I spot a sign for Punto Garza, a clump of oceanfront condos off the rutted coastal highway. The place is a typical Third World resort struggling to approximate some brochure's idea of luxury. Just ignore the lizards in the showers. The whitewashed cinderblock foundations are rotting, the pool leaking, the outdoor bar unattended, the walkways muddied. Old men in hilariously baggy uniforms stroll the grounds with rifles slung over their shoulders, providing just enough security to scare away customers. I park next to a silver Olds 88 with "St. Louis Cardinals—World Champions" embossed around the license plate. A tough local mama lets the rooms from a dank office which doubles as a *tiendita* stocked with Popsicles, fried pork rinds, and Pampers. As we bargain lightheartedly over rates, I notice a powerful man dozing off on a chair in the corner. He wears the standard local garb of swimsuit, rubber sandals, unbuttoned Hawaiian shirt and wraparound sunglasses. "Before I give you the key," asks the boss lady, "don't you want to shake hands with *el gran lanzador dominicano?*" There may have been other great Dominican pitchers, but in this *oficina*, in this precinct of his birth, there are no rivals. He rouses himself slowly. Clearly, Joaquín Andújar wants to be left alone to savor both his anonymity and his glory. Here is the face I'd seen that prior spring: the hook nose, close-cropped hair, sculpted cheekbones, skin of Caribbean café au lait, familiar from World Series close-ups, intimidating runners back to first base.

"Hello, Joaquín. We're a long way from Ho Ho Kam Park. . . ." This brings a smile, though I can't tell if he remembers me. If I'd had the kind of season he's just had, I wouldn't want to be bothered. But he greets me dutifully, prepared to make baseball small talk.

"In the Dominican," he tells me, "everyone they are treated the same. . . . Of course, I love my country. Everyone love their country. . . . It was tough in the beginning. I was only sixteen when I first play in Canada. I speak no English. Some French. *Un petit peu.* When I go

125

there, I forget my wife, my home, everything. I think only baseball. . . . What do my parents do? They do nothing, I support them. I am the only son. . . . No, America is not different from what I imagine. I seen it all on TV. . . . Like we say, 'It's not hard to get used to a soft bed. It's no problem adjusting to three meals a day.' . . . The reason we get so many ballplayers? Because in my home, there is only baseball. I have my own little league, three hundred kids. I get up every day at seven A.M. to teach them. But no one writes that. . . . All the time you see them, little kids playing in the streets with no shoes on their feet."

And had he been one of those kids? "Yes, sir," Joaquín Andújar answers, staring back. His eyes confront me now, moist, doe-like, light brown with a hint of pirate cove green, full of pride and hurt, ready to cry or wince with laughter at the least provocation. In his look is a pleading for respect that he cannot hide. There is also dismay at having to bother with another intruder who can never understand. You can see it all when you look into the eyes of Joaquín Andújar. That's why it's best to look closely. Savor the presence of number forty-seven while you can. He is only passing through on the way home to Macorís.

NEVER GET THIS CLOSE
TO ANYTHING
YOU LOVE

$\mathbf{F}$ollow a ball team for as much as one road trip and you'll find they spend less time perfecting their prowess than they do robing and disrobing. Two-thirds of being a ballplayer is looking the part and this quotidian impersonation is no less strictly ritualized than the rest of the game. The cramped stalls and bare benches of Dominican locker rooms turn big-league when it comes to each upcoming contest's undress rehearsal. Every performer's aim is to toss aside self-consciousness as one would a dirty towel. Patting guts, scraping groins, exploring for hemorrhoids, sniffing dirty socks, realigning scrota—before one's brethren, one must be entirely comfortable with all functions common to this animal. To that end, ballplayers do things in front of each other that they would not necessarily do in front of themselves. They do not need mirrors, they have each other. The more teammates spit, saunter, fart, the more they'll get comfortable at home plate. Playing with one's self is preliminary to "playing within one's self" and that's the key move in this game. (Think of the great ones: Ted Fucking Williams, Petey Neanderthal Rose, Nasty Ty Cobb, the Gluttonous Babe.) Baseball is the one sport that demands that you be just who you are and strut it.

These self-made myths cannot take form until the uniforms they've been issued are made un-uniform, altered, reconcocted, sabotaged. They don battle dress with the grim deliberation born of the infantryman's thousand superstitions. Players placate unknown martial gods by replicating particularized combinations of jock-cup, cut-off long johns, torn undershirts, knee socks. Some insist on knickers so tight they look sprayed-on, and wear them to just below the knees. Others let them droop as far down as possible and turn the stirrups sideways to hide or show the most of white socks known as sanitaries. Every bill of the cap is creased differently. Ballplayers are not enamored of clean lines but of raggedy details; these are not the sort of recruits who puff out their chests in a reviewing line, or even pass inspection. No yes-men in this platoon, just maybe-men who chew tobacco while mulling over the situation. This least militarized of team sports does not attract team players. Because when all the clubhouse chatter dies down, the acts common to this sport must be undertaken in merciless isolation. The main discipline required of combatants is that they shield themselves in more eccentricities than can be crammed on a bubble-gum card. The armor of style that finds fruition in a hitching swing or sidearm relay begins with the length of sock, the number of wristbands per forearm.

Is it for this glimpse of manhood reverting to boyhood then apehood that I've fought my way past the mob of clamoring *tigrito* kids? Or charmed the grizzled equipment manager with my broad smile and white skin? Won a final wink of approval from the baby-faced, unautocratic manager everyone calls el Chilote? Where armed guards patrol condominiums like doormen and rifle-bearing sentinels snooze before every *cambio*, one does not ask, one takes. Every man can go as far as his bluff takes him. Here, privilege is guarded with guns and titles because there's so little of it to go around. Where every shoeshine boy and priest, every army colonel and country cousin eventually gets access, there's no call for proper IDs. My password is *"Periodista!"* I'm checked for the sincerity of my interest, and the proof is that I've made the trip. Here, credentials don't count as much as *cojones*. Those are the balls you don't play games with.

For the next ten days, I'll fly along with the Aguilas Cibaeñas, "Eagles of the Cibao." As they criss-cross the island to complete a playoff series against San Pedro's Estrellas del Oriente, "Eastern Stars," I won't let this ballclub out of my sight. Loosely affiliated with "los Pirates de Peetsboorgh," they've long been the Brooklyn Bums of the Dominican league. As the representatives of Santiago de los Caballeros, capital of the Cibao region first plundered by Columbus, this franchise has always played second fiddle to the wealthier teams representing Santo Domingo. During the Trujillo years, a victory for the inland upstarts was always taken as a political blow against the regime. But underdogs lose all symbolic status when you can watch them stoop, emerge from toilet stalls, take their time hoisting up pants, waddle hog-tied by their underwear. Have I been let in on the proceedings to offer an eyewitness account of Omar Moreno taking a dump?

I don't need a program to distinguish the players, just a quick scan of elastic. The roll call is written in block print with magic marker: PEÑA, DILONE, MARVELL WYNNE, HOSTETLER. The names that make a magical incantation for a continent's kids are emblazoned across the cummerbunds of jock ballast. The writing helps the equipment manager keep track of all the oft-dirtied laundry, but may also be there in case the players forget just who they've become. At short range, the most striking aspect of ballplayers is that they don't look like they're ballplayers. These campers could have been chosen at random off the street: a balding and knock-kneed assortment of loan sharks and tummlers. Baseball requires no special inheritance of size or bulk, just a tenacious normality. As one pitcher asked another during spring calisthenics, "Who do they think we are, ath-e-letes?"

Only two here stand out as members of the species *homo jockulus*. Ted Power and Cecilio Guante are a matched set: with massive tendons and disproportionately swelled chests, great craniums, necks that are more like welds in flesh, feet nearly webbed. They share a playful ease with their hugeness. Bearish Teddy, early of the Dodgers, lately of the Royals, might have been raised guzzling ten gallons of milk a day; now he's switched to beer he swills down like lemonade. He's quite the dandy with Gay Nineties mustache complementing rueful blue eyes and tight blond curls. Guante, early of the Pirates, lately of the Yankees and the Rangers, preens on tiptoes, a Grecian messenger sculpted out of ebony with arched purple pear halves of buttocks, hairless thighs so developed their musculature builds into flexing triangles. Because they are both over six-six, the two bullpen pals can shout their taunts and teases over the heads of teammates. "Guante, you sick motherfucker. . . . Guante, you're nothing but a sidearming cocksucker." Power's name speaks for itself and Guante means glove, a great name for a *pelotero*. "Catch some of this, Guante," says Power, stripping down. "Suck my underwear, Guante." Guante grins and answers, "I no hungry, Ted." Power throws his boxers in the other pitcher's face. "Eat my shorts!" Guante tosses them back like a hot potato. "No gringo food for me. But maybe you like *comida*

dominicana. Hokay, Ted?" As Power and Guante chuckle, their uncir-
cumcised rubber trunks, more miracles of the glandular system, sway
and knock against inner thighs. Their humor is as tight as their muscles,
their laughter monstrous. They're the sort of players who'll never quite
make it. Their fastballs come too easily, their strength is so predictable
that it turns to weakness. Were the dinosaurs as carefree as Cecilio and
Ted? The earth shudders with each step they take on their way to the
showers.

The head counselor here is a local boy made good, *el capitán* Tony
Peña. The scuttlebutt suggests that Peña has failed to fulfill his potential
as the most promising catcher of his generation because he insists on
coming to work every day of both summer and winter seasons. A catcher
has only so many squats in him, but so far Tony has refused all
suggestions to ration his. He acts like a man who cannot conceive that
he'll ever tire. To spite all his critics, he's created a new receptorial stance
that looks like the work of some contortionist swami. He spreads his legs
apart in full split so his mitt-target is as low in the strike zone as mankind
can get. Sitting shirtless on the edge of the massage table while a wizened
old trainer rubs his neck, Tony drowses, his Fu Manchu affectation
droops, his coffee-colored torso turns shockingly flabby and his jaw works
tenderly on a big chaw that fails utterly to eradicate his inherent
gentleness. But he is always the first Eagle out the dim clubhouse chute.
Warming up, Tony Peña is burning hot.

"You throw the ball like you wanted to be a pitcher."

"No way, man. No pitch, always catch." He raises his brown hand and
slices it through the air. "Always, always."

"How do you do it? I mean, how many games have you caught this
year? Two hundred?"

"I don't count, man. I go out an' play every one hard. I gotta play this
game hard because I love it."

"Do you play harder here in Santiago?"

"No, man, no way. I play the same in Pittsburgh, in Chicago,
anyplace. I only know one way to play this game. Hard."

The pursuit of excellence, *sin traducción.* This has to be the line he
always hands to reporters, but I don't mind buying it. With Tony Peña,
there's no difference between interview and conversation, professional
and personal. Slapping my knee, he rises to stretch himself from the
dugout's concrete overhang, a rambunctious koala in shin-guards "I

dunno, man. Maybe I crazy. . . ." Another divine crazy. "I jus' love to play this game. I play all the time, same way, hard and crazy, because I love it!"

Sweet baseball, that will-o'-the-wisp, that obscure object of desire. Even those closest to the game continue to adore it, maybe because they can never quite fathom it all. "You gotta be crazy!" Tony P. is no longer talking to me, but screaming for the benefit of teammates who've sauntered over to catch his act. He is using this interview to rev them up for the trials ahead. He is ranting now, instantly hoarse. "You gotta be crazy! You hear? Crazy! You gotta play like a crazy man!" His employers will pay Tony Peña just under a million for his next stint of craziness.

With equal fire, Peña leads his crew in a round of "Flip," "Fleep" to the locals. This game of hot potato with the ball is the Dominican way of warming up the ol' hand-eye cathexes. Each time the ball hits the turf, the last to touch it is eliminated, until the confrontation tightens to two. "Fleep" is a variant of some schoolyard game played across the States but here national legends play it all out for blood and bragging rights. Within this powwow circle where nothing counts but the quickness of a man's wrist and the sharpness of his tongue, this club ceases to be a grab-bag aggregate of Dominican vets on the slide trying to pick up a bit more cash, up-and-coming smalltown legends, apprentice shortstops learning their leather trade, Norteamericano minor leaguers who want to showcase their dedication to the teams that own them, and bullpen catchers happy to be along for the ride, however bumpy. Gathered round for one season, my team, any team, is a point of intersecting fates.

Take Bárbaro Garbey, chief instigator of *l'affaire* Garbey, a case unique in the geopolitics of baseball. The Barbarous One has the distinction of being the only Cuban from the mass exodus of Mariel harbor to sign on with a big-league team. Like other *marielitos*, Garbey is still haunted by a criminal reputation. Fidel Castro allowed this star player to go on his waiver list because Garbey was charged with fixing Cuban games. In his infinite wisdom, Commissioner Bowie Kuhn cleared Garbey to resume his belated career. After all, reasoned the Commish, Garbey's crimes were against Commie ball and therefore forgivable, if not downright blue-blooded. As his reward, Garbey will have a brief role for the Tigers in the 1984 World Series. But does that justify his fishing-boat ride into exile? Did he have second thoughts about the land of freedom once condemned to Triple-A Evansville, or the punishing pep talks of parole

officer Sparky Anderson? Rumors fly around the clubhouse that Fidel's
been placing scurrilous items about Garbey in the papers back home,
just to get back at the only post-revolution Cuban who has made it to the
Yanqui leagues.

No wonder Garbey plays and carries himself like a man under sentence. Even among his island neighbors, he's the Eagle who keeps his
distance from the flock. Maybe this is Cuban cool, maybe detachment.
Maybe he knows more about the insecurities of this profession than the
rest, who are themselves pretty damn tobacco-spittin' insecure. Maybe
Bárbaro just doesn't give a shit anymore. He plays third base like a
catatonic, then reaches for a cigarette as fast as he can each time he trots
off the field. He does not speak to his teammates and hardly lets go a
tight grip on a pair of black batting gloves. Dark and frail, Garbey has
the kind of eyes that dart constantly, though they show almost no white.
He smiles when some buzzard of a *campesino* sneaks down from the
stands to infiltrate the bench, search out Garbey and give him the power-
shake. "I am also from Santiago," the old man declares in a Cuban lilt.
I can almost hear the spring of cold-war tension inside Bárbaro pop. His
smile is slow, innocent, devastating. *"Santiago es muy lindo,"* murmurs
the old man in the chewed-up straw hat. Bárbaro Garbey nods, takes
another drag, returns to staring down at the dark chasms between the
tobacco-stained boards of dugout planking.

How fleeting our views of these summer visitors and how inaccurate!
I'd always thought of Miguel Dilone as the classic Latin ne'er-do-much:
an undersized, pigeon-toed speed merchant good only for late-inning
pinch running and the occasional bunt. In the Dominican, he is the
Aguilas' sober elder—and this year's reigning *campeón del bateo*, that's
batting champ. In a league where power hitters are rare, he has been one
of the leading singles hitters of the decade. But the years don't count, the
at-bats are for nothing, the long-term contracts up North and the trophies
are for naught. Miguel Dilone paces the dugout, bat in hand, stopping
here and there to assume his stance, bounce the knees and relax them,
break wrists, then meet the imaginary pitch, eyes shut, stroke in slow
motion, again and again. Like all the stickballers out in the street itching
to get in the game, Miguel Dilone acts like he's never gotten his ups and
won't ever get enough to get the moves down. He is still trying to get the
thing right.

What a comfort to learn that Omar Moreno still loses his mitt between innings! After all these years with the Pirates and others, this seasoned pro must pause to recall where he flung it just the way I do in my Sunday morning softball league, then conduct a chagrined, furtive search for the leather by which he makes his living. Dewy-eyed, pigeon-toed, high-waisted Omar! During the 1981 World Series, the cameras focused on his button-nosed Dominican wife, yelping "Come on, sweetie!" The trouble with Omar Moreno is that he really is a sweetie, and so is Omar Junior, called little O.J., who follows his dad in a size-two Yankee uniform and looks just as comfortable in it, just as cocky and long-legged as his *papi*! What a lethargic embodiment of grace! What an unfluctuating Arabian Panamanian temperament! His glove goes astray, but he doesn't.

During the first playoff game, I sidle up along the bench to a bashful kid with a light-toned, open face and César Romero mustache. He looks slighter than the rest, his resolve needs bulking out. He seems comfortable, even relieved, that he won't play tonight. Probably some poor backwoods recruit just hanging on so he can send his twelve siblings the three-hundred-peso minimum. I start to struggle with my Spanish, but he answers in perfect English, befitting a fellow who introduces himself as Stanley. Es-stanley in these parts. A name for a butler, not a *pelotero*. Butler-polite, he suggests, "If you want to know about Dominican baseball, you should talk to my father." It's his last name that's truly exceptional: Javier. Julián Javier, the bespectacled second baseman who was one of the first and most beloved Dominican big leaguers. I'd seen a pro wrestling sideshow televised to the nation from Estadio Julián Javier in his Cibao hometown of San Francisco de Macorís. So the first name must be a homage to a Polish teammate of Dad's on the St. Louis Cardinals named Stan the Man Musial. "My father never pushed me to be a ballplayer," says the boy. But they all say that. And I can't help thinking that Es-stanley was meant to have a cameo role on the "Love Boat" as some surburban blonde's solicitous love interest. Will this charming *chico* grow up into Es-stanley *el hombre*? Decode his DNA into bloop hits? Even after he's made the majors with my own Oakland A's and won the batting crown in the Dominican league, he practically bows before the wide-eyed boy scouts who want his autograph. "*Yo soy Es-stanley,*" he introduces himself, though all of them already know about him and his progenitor. I have not yet seen Stan Javier hit, but I have a feeling he must be overmatched.

CENTER FIELD/JARDÍN CENTRAL

And what do I say to the unmasked Marvell Wynne when he plops himself down beside me after scoring a go-ahead run? That this lithe prospect with the perfect baseball name goes from second to home faster than a skittish pony? That he reminds me more of Willie Mays than any other player I've ever sat next to? Biting his lip so that he won't grin too cockily, Marvell knows that he's onto something good. But I soon sense that Marvell's but a scared kid from the South Side of Chicago with little to fall back on if his speed fails him. From the way his wary eyes linger lovingly on his new roster of Hispanic soulmates, he's gained a lot more than baserunning savvy from his first exposure to lands where, suddenly, he has so many brothers of so many shades, so many new and vibrant dilutions of blackness. I take Marvell's subtle unloosening and multiply it a hundred times for the Negro League stars who escaped from rigid segregationist modes to this culture's raucous blurring of all distinctions. Winter ball must have been near to heaven for blacks of that generation. In their Caribbean brethren, these men must have recognized themselves and discovered that Africans are everywhere in the Americas. A lifetime's defenses are dropping, notch by notch, with each of Marvell's streaks home.

Then there's the caged Aguila: screwy Pascual Pérez. I only know he's a member of this team because he's the local star featured on the cover of the team yearbook. A two-page cartoon spread illustrates the infamous episode that earned him the nickname "I-85." That's the number of the wrong freeway Pérez drove down, causing him to arrive two hours late for a start with the Atlanta Braves. This time, he's been detoured by the Santo Domingo police. Thanks to a cocaine bust, the star pitcher of the Atlanta Braves is spending the season in the Santiago city jail that's just down the block from the team's swank sleeping quarters at the Camino Real Hotel. Rumors swirl that Pascualito was set up because he was fooling around with a girlfriend of a certain *jefe de policía*. Otherwise, why would the Dominican authorities go out of their way to nab one of their boasting points? But one never knows about "I-85." On the mound, he turns himself into a bouncing, glove-thumping, hippity-hopping mass of directed energies. Off the field, Pascualito always finds a way to get lost.

Chuck Cary's a different breed of cat: bred in suburban prosperity, sophisticated beyond his laconic ballplayer pose. "I don't know if I can make it in this game, because I just don't have that drive to make it. I know there's lots of other things I could do. This isn't my life. I've got alternatives." This inquisitive Berkeley grad actually wants to know, "What kinda government have they got here anyhow? Is it free or is it like Russia's?" He's been on this tropical boot camp longer than I have. "It's free," I tell him. "Free to do anything the army and the landowners and the American corporations want to do." Chuck Cary doesn't even swallow hard. "They had some trouble down here in '65, didn't they?" And I'm off, explaining about Juan Bosch and how the Marines were sent in to put down a popular revolt. Chuck's legs are folded, his gigantic, freckled lefthander's forearm at rest on his knees, his mitt ready beside his tranquil blondness. Nothing rattles him: not a good shelling by the bottom of the order, not the truth. He spits from his chaw and mumbles, "Good ol' Marines."

Child vendors race through, selling thimblefuls of sweetened espresso poured from thermoses into dixie cups. But one night a tyke hawks something else. "You wan' good pussy?" he asks Chuck. The coffee peddler is swooped up unto Chuck's Norteamericano knee, transformed into a kid playing horsey. "You got good pussy for me, José? *Verdad? Verdad?*" The little guy giggles. His front teeth are still coming in. "Yeah, man, *mucho* good pussy!" But Chuck wants to know how old she is. "Very j-oung pussy, man. Seven years old!" the boy boasts, before the pitcher lifts him off his uniformed knee and swings him high above the bench, gripping the seams of the kid's raggedy shorts like he's going to throw a slider.

Other unauthorized stadium vagrants roam the benches scrounging used mitts, gloves, jocks, scraps of torn undershirt. Anything that can be hawked or used. Dave Hostetler sniffs his long time, trusty batting glove, which a couple of raging *tigritos* are trying to pry off his hand. "You really want this?" A hand's sweat, in time, smells no different than a crotch's. The musk of ten thousand tight grips of the bat has turned scatological. "Poo-eee!" Hostetler's bloodhound snout droops in the netted pocket between thumb and forefinger. "Yucky-poo! You don't really want this?" The boys nod. If they could, they would collect his excretions in a jar.

Most of the time, Big Hoss is in agony. Six-foot four of Grade A prime *primera basista* reduced to tears as he trots in from his warm-ups. No more, he whines after another futile wave at three curveballs. *No más.* Two seasons back, he announced his arrival in the bigs with homer after

135

homer, until the pitchers got one step ahead of him. Maybe he got a step ahead of himself. Now the Texas Rangers have benched him in favor of yet another country-bred giant. He's volunteered for this winter duty to show he wants his job back. Right before Christmas, his wife delivered their first child. Hoss only got to see his daughter once. And this seemingly indestructible kid misses his wife something terrible. Lord, how he prays for a swift return. Modest and religious, he takes no comfort in the Dominican's pagan madhouse. He can't stomach another bus ride all the way across the island, back and forth over those damned rutted shitpile Dominican roads. Why can't these people learn how to pave a goddamned road anyhow? On top of that, he never gets a call, not from his wife, not from the umps. Stinking telephones, goddamned sightless natives. At midnight, alone at a table in the semiplush goddamned rooftop restaurant where the players always eat, Hoss is still muttering to himself. On the field, he's uppercutting at air in desperation. His stats won't look good to the Rangers, who keep badmouthing him and would like to unload his contract anyhow. He can't get over how they badmouth you at contract time and then expect you to come back the next season and give your all. It's un-Christian the way these teams act. He doesn't get general managers. He's too naive for a sport that's a business or a country that's a whorehouse. In another year, he'll be a note in the margins of the record book. Another phenom who faded quick as he flashed. Big Hoss, who likes to call himself a dumb jock, seems to be the only one who's figured out that this tropical ball ain't what it's cracked up to be.

The dugout is the worst place to watch a ballgame. The reinforced concrete bunker permits little awareness of the thousands cheering or razzing or munching or squirming. The game from the dugout has nothing to do with the game from the box seats. From ground level, the diamond is seen in cross-section: a single flat stratum of mica chips. The game is a progression of groaning knee-bends, a slow-motion aerobic workout with hunks of sculpted wood as props. The action is reduced to a series of dust clouds raised by the rough and impudent skitter of something hard and stinging and unrepentant. The flinging of ball from mound to plate and then around the horn, the spraying of hits, appears to be nothing more than a white sphere bobbing on a string. Fly balls lose their loft and grandiose arc. The crowd tells you if a catch is made in right and left fields' peripheral corners. From the dugout, too, baseball

136

moves with grim and silent rotation, sending off its on-deck hitters with extra determination, welcoming them back as they mutter to themselves, shoulders sagging. The contest is a procession as ordered and predictable as a square dance, only less fun. The contestants are eager he-men at a county fair trying to win kewpie dolls for their best girls, coming home with booby prizes.

Atop these dugouts, though, there is dancing. The overhangs also serve as bandstands. At no particular schedule, right in the midst of a pitch, a live *conjunto*, complete with portable conga drums, *trompetas*, wailing trombones, and crooners, will burst from the top of the stand and sashay down toward the aisles. Volunteer cheerleaders rise to put their side's booster section through a collective bump-and-shake. One fiendish *merenguero* does his bit for the Estrellas by waving a massive pennant of San Pedro green. This big banner serves as his baton. Each time the conductor sweeps it over the stands, his orchestra responds with a collective "Wha!" Slowly he gathers speed, until he has the whole park bawling, "Wha! Wha! Wha!" There are twenty thousand babies out there crying for their milk, or a two-out rally.

Decked out in a *campesino*'s straw cap and a T-shirt emblazoned with the Dominican flag, a gray-haired, swivel-hipped old gent known as el Guayaberudo makes the dugout his runway for intricate rhumbas and devil-may-care cha-cha-chas. He works in tandem with Balthazar, a Mongol-browed, grinning, two-ton, all-jelly midget. A loyal fan promoted to official mascot, he gets his own Aguilas uniform plus a full-page entry in the yearbook and takes to his task with the supreme relish of a man who knows he'll never have another moment in the spotlight. Atop the dugout, Balthazar manages to shake in a dozen directions without taking a step. The crowd howls, the señoritas blow kisses, and the ballplayers take turns touching the holy knees of this freakish child of God.

All lines blur: lines between shoeshiner and star, team and *fanáticos*. Unlike their infamous Venezuelan or Mexican counterparts, Dominican rooters are less prone to throw rocks but more likely to wink and caw and send hugs toward their idols. The stands are full of young couples knowledgeably discussing strategy, whiling away another tropical twilight with their arms around each other. Children pass through the stands bearing banners advertising what's playing at the local cine: *Hoy—Dónde está el piloto?* That's Spanish for *Airport*. Or *Hoy—Abajo fuego*. Nicara-

137

gua is "Under Fire" but not this place, not yet. No outfield bleachers here, just empty field beyond the ring of ads for Bermudez rum. The most expensive tickets, still less than a dollar, are almost never sold out. From afar, the cheap, uncovered foul-line grandstands look like packed cattle pens. No one leaves early, not five hours into the game.

Why should they? This is the only game in town—and two games in one. In each cluster of rows, bookies take bets on each pitch, every situation, gesticulating to indicate odds with a frenzy that would make a quote man at the stock exchange proud. Rum is what keeps the bids coming. A rum lady serves out paper buckets of ice and plastic cups to her *regulares*, keeps the booze flowing and the *refrescos* chilled. To stimulate a thirst, there are *papitas*, potato chips, or home-made *empanadilla* turnovers, balls of mashed yucca, thrice-fried greasy chicken parts and even greasier green banana slices called *tostones*, croquettes of *bacalao* instead of Crackerjacks, packaged pork rind *chicarrones* instead of popcorn. Also plying their wares in the stands are tarot readers, fortune tellers, and magicians who go about in tuxedoes with shredded tails but shirtless beneath, coaxing bouquets and doves from their torn pockets.

All the more reason for ballplayers here to put on a "game face" of grim concentration. They want everyone to think they're straining themselves mightily while they sit on their duffs in the splintery dugout, and that trotting to the bullpen and back extracts a far greater toll than it appears. Baseball is the impossible game that anyone can master. All it takes is pluck, a rudimentary knowledge of spitting, and an ability to carry off this mask that hides a shit-eating grin which would reveal to one and all just how cushy a deal you're getting. Not that these local *peloteros* aren't wickedly underpaid—sometimes only three hundred dollars a month—or don't sacrifice family life and suffer the long bus rides. None are immune to the pressure or exempt from the tragedy of a life that loses purpose along with youth. It is just that baseball, once you master a few repetitive tricks of hand-eye coordination, is not terribly taxing. Even in the tropics, only one player truly works up a sweat, has to towel down between innings. The pitcher sits at the far end of the bench, a jacket sleeve draped over his already overengorged arm. To the rest of the team he's contagious. For them, it's enough to slip into sanitaries, feel the itch of woolens, strut tall in one's spikes before cousins, bookies, and *barrio* mates. The "game face" guards this secret, though not too well. Someday these fellows will have to go to work for a living. And so will I.

In the meantime, their cry is, "*Vamos, coño! Coño, coño, coño!*" This article of filthy speech favored throughout the Caribbean is particularly beloved by the ballplayer. *Coño*, depending on the context, means cunt, shit, asshole, fuckface, jerk, pal, brother, cousin, man, lovable son-of-a-cuntlicking fool! In the mouths of these men, it is nearly always affectionate. The more they cuss, the more the team becomes "one big family," says the outsider Chuck Cary. "See, they just can't keep their hands off each other!" The grabbing and mauling and horseplay goes on through the innings, no matter what the score. A tweak of the behind here, a casual fart aimed at a pal, a surprise mussing of the hair, or a mock flirtatious arm leaned on a *compadre's* shoulder while they show off for some *chiquita*. Spent bubble gum is destined for the seat of one another's pants. Chewing tobacco is for dribbling on the knee of one's benchmate or the shoes of all who pass. They can't even keep their juices to themselves.

Army officers, sporting enough medals that their uniforms nearly get up and do the merengue all by themselves, drop by for some hug. A parade of holsters, shiny snub-nosed pieces, pearl-handled Colts often blocks my view of the game, reminding me of Cuba's infamous player-manager Adolfo Luque, who once put a pistol to the head of a reluctant reliever. "I think they've got a contest to see who can go down to Woolworth's and pick out the biggest pop gun," mutters Chuck Cary, the good jaded Yank. These *pistoleros* and carabinieri are not just tolerated in the Dominican dugout, but embraced as living mascots, better luck than the midgets. In this island's intimate genealogy, they're always someone's nephew or cousin, this in-law called the law. *Coños* all.

On this team, as among the rest of the work force, there's terrific underemployment. Eight guys for every one job, probably splitting a decent salary into eighths, too. Six backup catchers, four fungo hitters, innumerable volunteer outfielders tender and willing in their never-mussed uniforms, a couple of team loonies, more equipment managers than equipment. Today's men on the bench are yesterday's shoeshiners who've found more lucrative, if less steady, pickings. It is enough to put on the uniform and be fed and be called a *pelotero*. When asked why he's become a ballplayer, one second-stringer shrugs and says, "*Porque no hay trabajo.*" Because there is no work.

The roster's swollen with batboys who are grown men, walking good-luck charms like Plutarco, a batting practice pitcher disguised as a scarecrow in a numberless hand-me-down jersey. Plutarco's eyes blaze from deep sockets. His gestures are sudden and manic, his bumming of cigarettes ferocious and obsessive. There's an odd hitch in his gait, an exaggerated lameness that extends to his logic. With a malicious glint in his eyes, Plutarco is always mumbling rumors. "See the way that kid throws? Ask him about his parrot. You know the problem he has past the seventh inning? His grandmother worked for the colonel. . . ." It takes me a few days to realize that my Spanish isn't the problem. Between tobacco spits, Plutarco is speaking in tongues. He is the dugout representative of thousands on the street, one of the many who have caved in under a too-frequent dashing of hopes. Plutarco insists he was a prime prospect for the Pirates until he sustained a freak arm injury. This singular misfortune makes up the sum of his life. But Plutarco's convinced that the injury was someone else's fault, part of a plot against him which began with his being born poor and Dominican. He is sure the Pirates still need him. He's planning a comeback. Perhaps some unseen beneficiary's pity allows him this asylum with the Aguilas. Or maybe he just shows up each season bringing along his own increasingly tattered uniform. After a time, I try to evade his vengeful looks and move elsewhere along the bench when he hovers. Yet it's Plutarco who marks my last day with the club by approaching sideways in his usual conspiratorial manner to shove a going-away gift in my guts. It's a bottle of *vino de piña*, pineapple wine, a ghastly sweet local delicacy. In return, he wants me to put in a good word for him with the warden of this sanitarium that supplies all outpatients with mitts and spikes.

Another honorary Eagle for life is Octavio Acosta, a gentle moon-faced soul who now coaches third base after an illustrious career as player, manager, scout. After fifty years in the brown and yellow trim of the Santiago team, he fills out his uniform like a walking beer keg. He's seen all the greats, played with the legends. But Octavio never boasts, rarely reminisces. Maybe's he's reticent because he's seen so much terror as well. About the Trujillo years, he'll say, "The man could make trouble for ballplayers if he didn't like someone in your family. He liked to keep the best ones in the country, to himself." But Octavio, like so many Dominican old-timers, seems a big swollen rudderless fish beached on the shore of the present. The dictatorship is nothing to dwell upon, not unless one wishes to encounter shame. And shame does not seem to be in this nation's repertoire.

Then there's the cool dude everyone knows as Elpidio, who sports an aqua-colored beret and dark shades on a round dark face atop a rounder body. It's hard to believe that this guy's an equipment manager. For one thing, his hands never dirty themselves with equipment. He can always hire a car-watcher or two for that. Elpidio just hangs loose in the dugout, head leaned back, chubby legs crossed like a Buddha. He looks like he could have been a stand-in for Charlie Parker, the second alto on the bandstand. I feel myself honored and duly mascotized when Elpidio's sideman, a bearded and extensively tattooed Anglo trainer, enlists me for a most important errand. Since I'll be in Santo Domingo for the final showdown a day ahead of the team, I'm instructed to make a shopping trip to the one U.S.-style *supermercado* in the country. I've got to scoop up all the Red Man and Copenhagen chaws. The team is counting on me to stuff its jaws. Unfortunately, I find the place out of stock. I return empty-handed, not yet one of the boys.

When it comes to one player, I'm just another fan. The home lockers across the field serve as the lair of the great Manny Mota, guru Mota-ji of the pinch-hit. Down here, Mota is common parlance for reefer, but there's nothing illicit about Manuel. For years now, he's been the manager of Licey Tigers, the team affiliated with the Dodgers. Summers, he coaches for Los Angeles, grooming himself for a big-league manager's job that may never come. While the Aguilas are forced to change in an unlit, airless conduit between the dugout and team bus, the Tigers of Licey disrobe in all the splendor baseball's richest franchise can buy. L.A.'s pocket change means carpeting, soft lighting, a steam room, and a training room, names posted above each locker just like in the *mayores*. I have to talk my way past an equipment manager, who protects the divine Mota's lair. My way is smoothed by the tradition which dictates everyone on the squad wash away the day's raspberries and boos and transgressions, whether or not they're dirty. Wearing only a towel, how can Manny protect himself from a devotee's advances?

"You're my favorite player. I have all your baseball cards." I can't help blurting out my uncreative mantra. But Mota shows none of the Latin graciousness that has eased the awkwardness out of my prior interloping. Only some occult Motaesque signal from his assistant lets me pass into the inner sanctum. One look at my godhead without his clothes shows me this is no other-worldly type. The man is at once dried out and dangerous. If he were a steak, he'd be tough and chewy. He is hardly the blissful one who slashed away a moment after rising from the bench, getting fate over with as quick as he could. Instead, he is utterly humorless from squeezing out every last drop of potential. He doesn't smile, just gnash. His face has muscles. Is it surprising that the most productive pinch hitter of all time should exist in a state of permanent squint? He looks ready to be reactivated for another pennant stretch run—as he was at age forty-four. Even in boxer shorts, he looks calculating.

And what knowledge am I seeking from my private godhead, except perhaps how it feels to shoot a grounder through the right side? Or whether it's true that he holds the dubious record of most fans killed by foul balls, lifetime? Or that all his children are named some variant of Jesús, like Jesusa and Jesusita? How he felt that he was never given enough at-bats to qualify for a batting crown or only played sixteen times in the field during his last five seasons? Instead, I assess my spiritual leader's current state of consciousness by the rows of photos framed and hung in an ascending pyramid on the fake wood paneling behind his desk. At the bottom of this hierarchy are stock publicity shots of Mota's favored contemporaries: the McCoveys, Stargells, Gibsons. All are signed with some variation of "To my good buddy Manny, the toughest out this side of the Pecos." On the next level are the snapshots of Mota's presence in hallowed antechambers: Mota shaking hands with Lyndon Johnson, Mota shaking hands with Dodger owner Peter O'Malley. Everyone is famous to somebody else. On the top echelon are the genuine deities of whom Mota is but a humble disciple. First, Tommy Lasorda, his current boss and the man who bleeds Dodger blue. On the same rung, Ronald Reagan, front-office boss of the empire of baseball, *el líder máximo*. Above this temporal power, at the apex of the pyramid, must reign the deity. It's a greased-back Al Campanis, long-time Dodger Director of Player Personnel.

This is the guy Mota is counting on to promote him someday, the same hale fellow and "good baseball man" who'll get caught telling a national television audience that blacks "lack the necessities" (mental or otherwise) to move into baseball's executive ranks. Leaning back in his swivel chair with a resigned, devil-may-care manner, Mota certainly looks ready to guide even the most lamentable collection of men. He does his best imitation of Walter Alston imitating Miller Huggins imitating John J. McGraw. He repeats the nostrums from everyone he's played under: "If you act like a man, you're gonna get treated like a man." Mota the man, like Mota the hitter, is unswerving. This Manny is the only Manny I'm going to get.

The one they call el Chilote can't keep up the managerial mask. Returning from an emergency conference with some pitcher who's lost his nerve, Winston Llenas can't help batting his frog eyes in my direction. He bursts into a grin that stretches all his freckles and puffy cheeks, as if to ask, "How can we spend our lives getting worked up over something like this?" My answer is a shrug seconding his wise detachment. Then Winston Llenas, former big-league infielder who aspires to manage up North, puts a new chaw in his mouth, plants one spiked foot on the dugout's top step, and becomes another serious fool scanning the field for his destiny.

Before the playoffs' final showdown, Tony Peña knows it's best to think about almost anything but the game. A true leader down to the timing of his distractions, he does not pace like the others, but slumps on the cosy front stoop of dugout steps and opens the morning newspaper. He does not read it, he attacks it. He nearly rips out the pages as he turns. On the back of the tabloid, he spots a photo of an overturned Minnesota school bus. Clumps of snow, that strange stuff, spot the picture. Twenty-two killed. Tony Peña swallows hard on his chaw. His grimace makes every artery in his neck bulge. "Fuck!" he shouts with an accent that gives the word two syllables. "Fuck, man. You see this?" He wants to show Ted Power, show everyone on the team. Those school kids could be his own honey-colored, droopy-eyed Tony Junior, adorable when he follows his dad to the clubhouse, trying to drag a bat. Tony Senior's grief is immediate and unaffected. "Fu-uck!" He's using anything he can find to work himself up into the righteous indignation required for victory. He is the best baseball can produce, a man who's convinced that he'll be young forever. And maybe he will. He's the planetary captain taking all misfortunes upon his shoulders. He feels personally responsible and wishes he could turn that bus up, make everything right. He is the ultimate catcher. He wants the ball. Tony wants the fucking ball. He would like to flash signals for the universe. "Leave it to me, *coño*. I call a good game."

When the team has won the first round of the playoffs, and *cerveza*, not champagne, is pouring all around, it's Tony Peña who rushes to embrace me. The captain makes me feel as though I've contributed a diving catch, a timely pinch hit. Just when I most feel that I'm crashing this party, he assures me that I, too, am an Eagle of the Cibao. Or maybe he's acknowledging that the roster holds a place for a seasoned onlooker, the designated watcher.

At a rare team practice the next morning, I can no longer stand by. I coax a big-league glove from one of the relievers. He doesn't really want to part with his barely broken-in Mizuno, but I've learned to talk player lingo by now. "Come on, man, I won't break your mitt." Now I can take my place in the Estadio Cibao's hallowed, if threadbare, outfield, before the high right field walls plastered with rum billboards, and await balls sprayed out from the batting cage. My euphoria's only slightly dampened by the fact that the usual hordes of barefoot street-kid interlopers act so nonchalant compared to me, so much less eager for the chance to shag flies with the big boys. One has a tennis ball, for between-pitch catches, and flings it toward his newest pal.

Such lazy movements, so monotonous and utterly transfixing! It takes only a toss or two for me to lose my jitters and gain full control over the dirty yellow ball. I snap back into a mode that's been in the making since Manhattan stoopball with a Spalding (hit the parked cars across the street and take your base), New England vacation summers with the Red Sox games blaring on the transistor, in verdant California parks on LSD, with my buddies and my dad and—like this *tigrito*—anyone who would humor me. Simulating pop-ups with high tosses, grounders with squibs, or gyrating in Tiant Perry Palmer Marichal mimes, I muster all variations for my receivers. Neither I nor my tiger cub receiver dare break the good silent peace. This respectful rapport of pitch and catch. There is nothing more that these boys and I could be saying to one another if we spoke, and it doesn't matter when we drop one or two. If they really wanted to further world understanding, the members of the United Nations Security Council should turn off their simultaneous translations, tear off their diplomatic suits, scrap agendas, grab mitts, and reconvene as one circular catch.

Too soon, though I've been preparing for a lifetime, there's a hard projectile veering off the cage around home plate, appearing in my eye-corner radar screen. The real rawhide arcing in an erratic wobble off the bat of Miguel Dilone. He's swung late, though with a considerable professional crack, and the result of that swing is looping toward right field and me. A miscarriage of geometry that I've got to handle. Every shot to the opposite field is like that. The opposite field sounds like some distant cousin of a black hole and I always seem to find myself in it. As I come toward it, it continues to spin away. Moving through the thin sky, the ball turns into a strophe of light. Try and catch a sunbeam! My feet back-pedal at first, then softshoe and finally scurry forward to make amends. They calculate without the need of slide rule or any other awareness of what they're doing. The thrill of all physicality, properly done, is that it is scheming without guilt or premeditation. But I've miscalculated from inexperience and the orb's not in the pocket but up the heel. I must continue to coax it, nurse it, slip as it slips toward grass and gravity, spoiling my nonchalance and turning this routine fly into a shoestringer. I have caught a ball launched by a bona fide big-league hitter. Now, to show I belong with the big boys, I must return the white joy quickly, rear back and heave a nice strike to the cutoff man. In my excitement, I overthrow, sending the relay skittering past second, over the mound, and toward the opposing dugout.

The *tigritos* aren't impressed. The one on my right pounds the tennis ball impatiently into his mitt, then holds it toward me asking permission to resume the important work of our catch. All the miles flown, the cash expended, the gamma globulin shots endured, the stomach balms swallowed, the credit card charges and the hours of brochure-scanning, the culture shock and anxieties, all the debates about journalistic ethics, the doubts and the stiff necks, the grueling shuttle across the island through the heat made these last few days of the playoffs, everything was for this. The ball that I'd craved for a lifetime is gone. Gotten rid of as quickly as it was conceived, like all true pleasures.

Is this all there is to it? Just a matter of cradle and heave? When the players speak, why do they tell me exactly what I expect to hear? In baseball, as in sex, expertise is the end of the adventure. Certain things are better off left at a respectful distance. Never get this close to anything you love.

"You gotta be crazy to play this game!" says Tony P., providing as good an excuse for our passions as any. "You is crazy!" says Cecilio G. "Eat my shorts!" says Ted P. "No comment," says Bárbaro. "It's a super experience," says Marvell. "I gotta get back to my baby," says Hoss. "I coulda be a Pirate, if they give me the chance," says Plutarco. "I know just enough Spanish to shake off a sign and get laid," says Chuck Cary. "It's only a game," winks el Chilote. "I can't go out there and run the bases for them," says Octavio. "I thank God for giving me the talent," says the bullpen catcher. "I been once to Richmond, Veer-hinia," says the third-string e-short e-stop. "Don't tell anyone, but I'm here because my cousin's a colonel," says the batboy. "Because I get good pussy," says the young buck. "Because I gamble away every peso," says the old vet. "Because it's in the family," says Es-stanley. "Because the Big Dodger tells me," says Manny. "Because I'm a deer in the forest," says Omar. "Because I'm still looking for the perfect swing," says Miguel. "Because there is no work," say the others. "Let's keeck some fuckin' ass!" says the unknown benchwarmer. "*Vamos, coño!*" say all the rest.

TROPIC OF BASEBALL

The ballplayers hit the beach like invading Seabees. What else is there to do on a day without a game? "Hello, mister. You *pelotero?*" Before we've crossed the tiny lot under the palms that line this popular cove along the north coast, the *secretarios* see us coming. They don't take dictation, but they'll be our assistants for the day—bearing beer and lotions, machete-carved pineapples on a stick, condoms probably. These barefoot bearers swarm gleefully, as thrilled by this glimpse of the Aguilas as by the prospect of customers: "*Primera base!*" They can identify Hoss Hostetler because he's the tallest creature on the island. "*Primera base! Sí, sí!*"

The one who commands them from the start is a tousle-haired, newly arrived reliever I'll call Clu Rayburn. How come this country boy looks so experienced at playing beach blanket bwana? Is there a touch of manifest destiny bred into his DNA? In bygone days, Trujillo's CIA-trained henchman, Colonel Tony Imbert, hunted sharks from this beach while a military band played to cover the shooting. Now, privileges belong to Clu. Before the rest of us lay out our towels, the *secretarios* are competing for orders and a crack at Clu's Walkman headphones, a turn at wrestling his professional arm. It's a kind of feeding frenzy, except that Clu's doing most of the devouring. The kids have never seen anyone with an appetite this big. The *secretarios* have barely lined up a row of Presidente bottles in the sand when they have to shuttle back to their mammas' ice chests for more cool ones. The jostling hordes get in the

147

way of his sunbathing. But it takes no time for this redneck to become a red back. What a broad unyielding back it is!

Clu's broiling, grinning presence seems to expand without plan. The sheer draw of his money and goofy self-assurance is enough to tip the whole sweep of sand in his direction. The Playa Sosua is one country saloon and this son of the South is ready to buy drinks all around. The *secretarios* pass the word to their pals who sell puka necklaces, amber earrings, carved tortoiseshell doodads. A swarm of barefoot peddlers spreads open their felt-lined cases. The pitcher doesn't bother to bargain, just adjusts his one-way shades and buys one of everything. He even purchases a three-sailed model outrigger made of polished shells as a tabletop memento for his "Daddy." The only frustrated vendors are the ones who bear trays of local oysters shielded from spoilage with folded banana leaves. A perfect case in point of the misunderstandings built into the so-called North-South dialogue, these freshly plucked calcified kisses are probably the finest treat this coastline can yield, but the first no-no of every guidebook's prudent health precautions. So the vendors are left baffled, the tourists deprived. May the world be your oyster, but watch out for hepatitis!

Clu Rayburn has other delicacies in mind. With hormonal radar, he's picked out the first *chica* within an eight-blanket radius. He springs for a cheap embroidered cotton dress and tosses the bribe in the general vicinity of her blanket. His prey is a red-headed, coffee-skinned genetic mix-and-match. She can't be more than sixteen, but she appears to be the oldest of three sisters in white bikinis and matching visors.

"*Cómo se llama*, Mama? How 'bout a brewski?" The *secretarios* bear three bottles as a peace offering. The girl accepts with an air of resignation about all that's bound to follow. Clu Rayburn tries to prove his worthiness of her attention by grabbing a broomhandle away from a young boy in charge of stickball in the dunes. Frisbee has not yet arrived on the Dominican beaches. Only bat and ball, swing and miss—the same poses found in the canefields. The girls don't seem especially impressed, but the pitcher ends his imaginary route around the bases with a slide into their blanket. "Well, looky here! Won't you at least tell me your name?" It's Elizabeta, I hear that much, and the pitcher's soon regaling her with gifts from any salesman she chooses.

Inexorably, the Yankee increases his sphere of influence. An amber necklace breaks her will, and the girl seems to know a walk down the beach is part of the bargain. The encounter is solidified so quickly, and with so little tact, that I can't believe anything will come to pass. *Secretarios* traipse along to verify the conquest. They bring conflicting reports, amplified by obscene hand gestures: Clu and the girl have gone into a shack, no, they're doing it in the breakers. When the pitcher returns by his lonesome—gals always need more time to straighten up— he grins and makes no effort to reconcile the accounts. He does his best to look properly wasted, sunskewered, fucked-out. He's unconvincing only in that he's so indestructible. This gringo isn't monstrous just because he gobbles everything in sight. What makes him monstrous is that nothing leaves him sated or changed.

Clu charges into the water and leads the players out toward the pink reefs offshore, paddling comfortably in bitter currents. Wading alongside me in the shallows, a paunchy man in polka dot trunks begins to chatter. "A charming little beach, no? Nothing compared to the ones back home. You see, I am a Miami Cuban now, but first off, and always, I am a Cuban! I come here because this is the closest I can get. It's something like Cuba twenty years back, no, forty years back. . . . But we must not speak of politics."

I didn't realize we were, but this fellow's enjoinment indicates that he can speak of little else. Few Cubans can.

"The tragedy, my friend, is that we needed a revolution, yes, but we did not need a social revolution. All of us wanted to be done with petty tyrants. Every Cuban favored elections and an end to indiscriminate killing. But our island life was sophisticated, cosmopolitan. To be a Cuban was a joyful thing. Changing everything from top to bottom was too painful a process. It was not required: this separation of families, these public breast-beatings, finger-pointings. This diseased idea that somehow all of us were unworthy!"

The late-afternoon sun is slipping behind a rare cloud, but the old Cuban hardly notices, bounding up and down in the water and splashing himself.

"Perhaps where there is a revolution, it also revolutionizes its victims. Do you understand me? If it could be shown to me that ninety percent of the Cuban people are better off for it, then I would say the pain was worth it. Especially my own pain. In this sense, I'm still hoping to be won over. In truth, I must hope for this revolution as few others do.

149

Because unless it achieves its aim, my sacrifice, my Cuban life, ceases to have sense."

The identity to which this exile clings seems sturdy as a life raft. But neither of us is willing to venture into deeper water. I hadn't planned to attend this colloquy on dialectics convened waist-level in the Caribbean. I only want to go for a swim, *voy a la playa.*

"I went back three years ago. But that was no longer Havana. Not the city of my birth, the vibrant capital. *Mi Habana linda, hermosa, mi ciudad!*" Spanish is the language best suited to remorse. "I went back to the house of my family. I stood in front of it, trembling. I could not bring myself to go in. And you know what happened? Some of the small children of the neighborhood, playing in the street, saw me standing there, a prosperous stranger in expensive clothes, and they started calling in Russian. They could no longer tell that I was one of them. 'Tovarich!' they greeted me in the place where I was born. To me, my countrymen called, 'Tovarich!' "

I dare not speak what seems obvious: The Dominican Republic is Cuba fifty years ago. The same shacks, sugar mills, sauntering army men, inequities. The casinos of Santo Domingo were once the casinos of Havana. I don't mention that one of the first cries when Fidel Castro's guerrillas arrived in Havana was, "On to Santo Domingo!"

I rejoin the team in time to bid the *secretarios* adieu. At sunset, we scale the bluff to Sosua, an enclave that's notable only for having been settled by a colony of German Jews. The Dominican served as their refuge when Trujillo's man in Paris, the international playboy Porfirio Rubirosa, realized a buck could be made selling visas to those fleeing Hitler. Profit overruled ideology for the local brownshirts—a fact confirmed by the signs posted at dirt intersections, bearing Biblical script looking as incongruous here as on a can of kosher Pepsi. The Hebrew writing leads tourists toward a one-room synagogue that looks more like a Quaker meeting hall, painted a pastel yellow devoid of sobriety. In the Caribbean, the temples are jolly—and hardly hurricane-proof. No Star of David distinguishes this tall, slatted shed from the rest of the town. By now, the congregation has died out or moved on to New York. The town which gave them refuge is now dotted with the sort of plumbingless guest houses and hygieneless fruit-shake stands that cluster around every spit of Third World sand. Japanese hippies in rubber thongs stroll between a half-dozen thatch-roofed seafood restaurants, patios draped in fishnets, *grocerías* featuring Coppertone and Cokes, hole-in-the-wall souvenir shops plying fake yet menacing Taino fertility symbols, even a health-food bar featuring carob pudding and chamomile flower soup that some expatriate from Santa Monica has named the Casa Naima in honor of the John Coltrane tune.

The team makes straight for El Albatross, a cramped, wicker-and-bamboo version of Rick's Café Americain, where Sam the piano player has been replaced by piped-in disco and *mulata* hostesses serve an approximation of burgers and potato skins. More members of the Aguilas have beaten us there. From the volume of their guffaws, they've started in early on the beverages. The regulars at El Albatross would be the envy of their nine-to-five countrymen: Yanks and Aussies and Brits living off the fat of exchange rates, an unconflicted, suntanned avant-garde in South Seas shirts who've not so much broken free from mechanized living as they've been banished to paradise.

"Have you sampled that new French place down by the beach?"

"Damn right. I'll try anything new."

"It's French in name only, mind you."

"Just more damn sea bass. *Mero a la parilla, mero criollo, mero* up the wazoo. . . ."

"Have you spied that new Chinese vegetable stand in town? Things are definitely looking up."

"You mean they've actually got more on the shelves than *plátanos*, green or red?"

"They've got cauliflower, man. Real cauliflower."

"Leave it to the chinks! No more of that monkey food for me!"

"Me, neither. But the natives sure go for it. All they need is a sack of dried *frijoles* and then maybe four or five bunches of bananas a day. They never get tired of it. It's cheaper than cat food."

"Monkey food, you mean."

And so on into the night, as the ceiling fans twirl and a magnificent Dominican barmaid flashes her teeth and wiggles a rump encased in blue denim. A couple of surfers who've totally lost their cool are twirling the dial of a table radio, their ears to the speakers, trying to get the latest football scores on Armed Forces Radio. The ballplayers have worked up quite a thirst. With each round, Clu insists on a toast.

"Here's spit in your spitball!"

"*Sí, sí!*" The team barks the open-sesame word out of the sides of their mouths, sarcastic Groucho Marxists.

"Hope the brew keeps flowing, the babes keep growing! And y'all keep it legal, you hear?"

"*Sí*, boss!"

"May you reside forever in the tropic of baseball!"

The gang carries on a rambling analysis of next season's pennant races until midnight. When it's clear that the bar girls are going to close up the joint without inviting any of the team home, we make our way back to the beach parking lot. We stagger under a sky that's more twinkle than background, the Milky Way thick as spoiled cream. This inviting, still night even makes me want to sleep under the stars, or pitch a town right here upon Columbus's "fertile isle which, once seen, is never to be abandoned." But we've all got schedules to meet, games to play.

In two years, Clu Rayburn will be out of baseball—felled by arm trouble after one dazzling September in the bigs. In the meantime he's driving the way he drinks and screws and flings his *número uno* fastball. He doesn't slow for potholes or S curves or the occasional donkey cart. "Totally blind!" he hollers each time the headlights of an oncoming car offer their challenge. Of course we're stopped at one of the frequent roadblocks. In this instance, when the gendarmes would have good reason to haul us into some dungeon or at least extract a bribe, we're waved through as soon as Clu starts shouting, "*Peloteros! Aguilas!*" The cops shout back encouragement for tomorrow's contest.

"Totally loco!" With each retelling of our escape, the delighted Clu jacks up the speed. I can see the headlines flashing before me. "Three players die in Dominican crash." No, there would be no banners, just a wire-service notice at the back of the sports page, next to the "Transactions" column or "Anglers' Corner." I think of Ken Hubbs, plane crash; Danny Frisella, dune buggy mishap; Lyman Bostock, mistakenly hit by a bullet aimed by a jilted lover. Theirs are the most vivid deaths in my bank of obits. "Old players never die, they just quit playing with their balls. . . ." And the young ones get asterisks beside their lifetime records instead of tombstones. The finest of the fine print might mention the promising right-handed rookie scribbler who went down along with them. I suppose writers are expected to die in the line of duty, but there's something spellbinding about the premature end of a ballplayer. After all, I'd never gone 10–6 at Burlington or fashioned a 3.24 ERA at Tetford

Mines. Never mind the reports I'd never file, the destinations left unvisited. What about all those statistics never accrued, the columns of SBs and RBIs untotaled, the hits left in the clubhouse? What about the Baseball Annies left unconsoled?

"The ocean by day and baseball by night!" I hear Clu declare. "*Chicos*, will we ever have it so good?"

THE SHORTSTOP
PLANTATION

Epifanio Guerrero is a hard man to catch. I'm not the only guy on this island who's found the Toronto Blue Jays' master scout one step ahead and one promise gone. He's been called a sneak, a thief, and a spy by competitors who wish they'd landed Jorge Bell, Tony Fernández, Alfredo Griffin, Damaso García, Silvestre Campusano, et al. Over his twenty-year career, Guerrero's been accused of most every ploy: professing lack of interest in a player only to sign him moments ahead of a rival, selecting a player for the Dominican amateur team in order to keep him out of another organization's clutches. Recently, he's become a wanted man in Nicaragua for sneaking a prized player out from under the noses of the Sandinistas. "I carried a camera so I'd look like a tourist," Guerrero admitted. "I said to everybody, *Compañero, compañero.*" But when asked for the secret of his success, Guerrero likes to answer, "It must be my eyes."

Or his slippery moves. I've returned from Puerto Plata to Santo Domingo because Epy promised an interview, but this morning, his wife answers the phone. "Oh, no, Epy just left for Puerto Plata! He help inaugurate the Brewers' training complex." Señora Guerrero offers the excuse with such good cheer, I have the feeling she's been through this dozens of times. She also tells me that her husband had to stop at a small village in the mountains to bail a certain hot prospect out of jail. Such are the scout's myriad duties. "But don't worry, please. The boys will be over to get you."

154

The Shortstop Plantation

I expect the men in the white coats. Instead, a shy teenager in baseball pants ambles into my hotel lobby, doing his mother's bidding under protest. "You the writer?" he mumbles my way. Apparently, he's seen his share of those. He speaks English without an accent, and, except for his wavy black hair, looks no more Latin than Beaver Cleaver. In the front seat of a flashy gun-metal Toyota van, two more laid-back, milk-fed specimens lounge with their spikes on the dash. They are Guerreros all: three of the five sons who form the next generation of this baseball-obsessed clan. Pat, Sandy, and Mike—these are your average American kids next door, pimply and insolent. The van is their clubhouse, crammed with faddish pursuits and hormones. While they're not past commenting on the relative merits of strolling Dominican *mulatas*, the Guerrero boys take great pains to assure me they've netted Americana girlfriends who're pining for them in the States. They've got the latest heavy-metal band blasting from a cassette and laugh smugly after agreeing, "We bet you don't go for this." And I'll bet they don't go for merengue like I do. Age, not nationality, separates us.

I'm in the presence of the very kids that Vic Power and Rubén Gómez and the old-timers complained about. Progress has done its work when it is taken for granted. Aside from their garb, nothing about their dimensions or demeanor suggests potential ballplayers. On their commute to the Blue Jays' camp, the brothers volunteer little about that aspect of their lives. Yes, they're all going to be big leaguers. For sure. No, their father never pushed them. Only Mike, a shortstop in the Brewers' organization, shows a bit of the fire-in-the-belly requisite for the trials ahead. For the brothers, this is just another day at the office. They are going into the family business as though it's dry cleaning.

Forget their old man. What better guides can I have to this up-to-the-minute innovation in the Dominican flesh trade? "Are you surprised yet?" the kids keep asking. The poverty on all sides is merely amusing to them, someone else's picturesque problem. The Toyota rumbles past the suburbs of Santo Domingo, lurching toward the realm of continual potholes. If the Guerrero clan still takes some delight in their *patria*, it's only through perverse back-handed compliments. "Amazing, no?" The road grows ever more pitted through outlying farm settlements and the town of Villa Mella. "Just wait. More surprises!" The Guerrero farm is down the bumpiest road on the island, the worst since my trek to La Isabela, that first New World ghost town. The sign which announces their father's renowned fount of baseball talent is half-covered in jungle growth and rusting away. I can barely make out the words, "Complejo Deportivo E-P-Y."

Nowadays the baseball "training complex" is as recognizable a mark of foreign domination as the sugar mill. At last count, sixteen of the twenty-four major league cities are represented with some sort of facility on the island—with richer clubs like the Dodgers planning Caribbean installations to rival their spring training plants. The stated purpose of these camps is to give promising young players room and board and a chance to concentrate on improving their game. In the mad scramble for talent, it's just as important to have a look at developing players in a setting that's hidden from the prying eyes of rival organizations.

Rules adopted recently by the big leagues state that no player under seventeen years old can be invited to such a camp and that all players must be signed to a contract or released into general circulation within a month. No central authority enforces such rules. Rumors abound concerning players lured out of school by tales of impending big-league glory, kidnapped from their families, taken hostage, hoarded for years. If anything mitigates against such abuses, it's the Dominicans' loose definition of security. On this snug island, no secret can be kept very long. Nor can it take much arm-twisting to enlist most kids. The best that can be said is that this is one Latin country where the suspects dragged from their homes in the dead of the night are usually coveted shortstops.

The clubs justify these combination soup kitchens, boot camps, and holding cells in terms of the welfare of the athlete. As every personnel director will tell you, the Latin athlete will be better prepared for the challenges of el Norte thanks to such innovative facilities. Basic instruction in English supplements advanced seminars in coaches' sleeve-wiping hand signals; the fundamentals of the game are coupled with a crash course in the gringo way of life. These kids from poor families have to learn not only how to handle umpires but a knife and fork. What's required of them is a leap into the realm of "proper work habits," team psychologists, and "self-imaging."

"These camps are all a bunch of baloney," I was told by Howie Haak, the legendary Pirate scout known to generations of Latin players as Señor Howie. According to the crusty octogenarian, "The other clubs are wasting their money. All we do is pay the groundskeeper to trim the grass—and he don't even do that! Teaching English? Hah. The good ones are gonna learn it on their own. They don't fuck around. At least, the kids are given a couple of solid meals a day that they might not get at home." In a Santo Domingo park, I watched Haak run a general tryout by the same methods he's used since 1954. "That's when Branch Rickey told me to drive around Cuba for a month—and I'm still at it. Joe Cambria was the first one to cover the island for Clark Griffith. Of course, there were plenty of Cubans in the big leagues in those days. They had to sign this phony form sayin' they were of white ancestry. But hell, Tommy de la Cruz was as black as they came. Gil Torres, he was one red-headed jig. Then there was Manny Girón, he was the best player from Panama. But after a game, he'd just sit there and cry, he was so homesick. When I went to sign him, I found him at the top of a coconut tree. In the old days, the Dominicans used to sleep eight to a bedroom and live off coconuts. And they'd steal everything that wasn't nailed down. Of course, everything would be nice and quiet during the baseball season. Soon as it ended, everybody would start shootin' up the place." And Señor Howie is still at it, shouting, "*Abajo! Abajo!*" to young outfielders who throw sidearm, begging scrawny pitchers, "*Tiene otra* pitch? *Tiene* curveball?" The scout's fine eye confirmed one player's dream and crushed another. "None of this bunch is worth a damn. *Malo, malo!* Where'd you find them, Hector, gravedigging? Back in '55, in Santiago, I picked out Julián Javier from two hundred and twenty kids. He was my first signee in the Dominican. I got him for four hundred dollars. I could have had Marichal for two-fifty. I signed thirty just like him who never made it. Now we don't get such a big turnout, because of those damned camps."

The Guerrero kids remind me that their father originated the trend. "It was his idea and his money too," Mike claims. Though I learn later that Epy borrowed eighty thousand pesos from the Blue Jays (around $27,000 at today's exchange rate), I can believe it. Epy's breeding ground for ballplayers is a rundown *finca* crawling with chickens and hairless mutts. Three concrete shells with chinks for windows form the main compound. Two are dormitories for the current players-in-residence, but they resemble the dreaded *bateys*—company-built, sewerless hovels provided for Haitian canecutters. The middle building, which serves as an office, is bare except for a permanent exhibit of Guerrero's awards and press clippings. His sons lead me through a small kitchen to a room strewn haphazardly with ballplaying gear—hardly enough to develop major leaguers, and yet, more than I'll see in all of Nicaragua. On a cot are boxes of hardballs that have been hand-stamped "Epy." To save money, says Mike, his father buys them wholesale at the factory in Haiti.

According to one of the posted articles, Guerrero's staff consists of "five baseball instructors, a cook [his wife, Rosario], a religion teacher [his sixty-eight-year-old mother, a Seventh-Day Adventist], and a groundskeeper [Gabriel Pimentel, who served as a chauffeur for Trujillo]. An English teacher visits the camp several times a week, a doctor once a month." I see none of the above in evidence. Mike Guerrero summarizes the instruction provided here by telling me. "They warn us about drugs and fooling around with girls. They tell us everything before it's going to happen." I don't find any chalkboards which might be used for lessons, nor video machines to display the kinesthetics of a proper swing. Of course, the nature of baseball resists the new and the scientific in favor of time-honored methods. But this place seems another perfect illustration of underdevelopment. Seclusion has to be the camp's major asset, if not its purpose. This complex is just a jungle clearing with foul lines.

But there's a beautifully seeded lower forty to this farm. The main diamond looks straight out of a major league spring training camp, surrounded by a grandstand of three rungs resting on cinderblocks, plenty of extra hitting cages and pitching rubbers. The Guerrero boys join a nestful of young Jays in "taking infield." That means fielding whatever comes at you. I can't tell if the lackluster approach of these recruits has to do with the noontime sun or the absence of their *jefe*. Seeking shade, I discover that I'm not the only one who's made the trip out. This awkward, buck-toothed intruder wears a bush jacket better suited for hunting real game. He's so painfully fair-skinned that he could have been airlifted down from the North Pole. He does indeed hail from the Great White North. But this Canadian tax accountant has never been happier to be out of his element.

"These people, they really know how to treat a guest!" The Canadian whips a thick deck of Polaroids out of his jacket's ammo pocket. These blurred snapshots are his reason for being here, his passport to the isle of *el béisbol*. They show the many Dominican prospects he'd befriended the previous summer while they were playing for a Blue Jays' farm club in the Toronto suburb of St. Catharines. "There's me with José and Felix in my backyard. This is my wife and daughter with Luis, the kid out there past second. . . ." He took it upon himself to organize a contingent

158

of local boosters to initiate the Dominicans into the realm of white bread and drive-ins. To astound his pals, he's brought pictures of St. Catharines in winter, complete with snowmen and ice sculptures, to complete the Dominicans' acculturation. "I'm an ambassador of the Canadian way of life, eh?" At the bottom of the pile is his most recent documentation of goodwill among men—photos from the past week's triumphal tour. Each shows the accountant grimacing through severe heat rash before a thatched hut along with at least two dozen representatives of some player's immediate family, plus various neighbors, goats, and mules. The Canadian keeps repeating, "They've done me right, these people. There'll always be a log burning for these boys in St. Catharines. . . ."

This Toronto fan is so gushy over his boys that I hardly register, "There's Tony! What do you make of that?" Then I realize he's speaking about American League All-Star shortstop Tony Fernández. The nonchalant teenagers hadn't tipped me off to the presence of this superstar. His visor reads, "Jesus Is the Solution." Thanks to Epy Guerrero, this Pentecostal Christian has made baseball his solution. As a boy in San Pedro, Fernández would climb the ballpark fence, shine shoes, work with the grounds crew, do anything to get close to the ballplayers and study their moves, often fielding grounders with a glove made from a milk carton. Untreated bone chips in his knee meant the boy could barely run. But Epy Guerrero's eyes had seen enough to ask the eleven-year-old to come with him to Santo Domingo where he could be clothed, fed, and prepared for a major league career. The boy declined because he would not be parted from his family. When Fernández was fifteen, Guerrero paid for an operation to repair his bum knee. The other scouts taunted him for signing a *tullido*—a cripple. They did not suspect that Fernández would take the Toronto job away from Alfredo Griffin, one of the San Pedro idols he used to emulate. He is the classic example of a *tigrito* who grew up into a lion.

Of all the athletes I get to assess, none is so thoroughly in command of his physical tools. Unsmiling and taut-skinned as an uncooked black bean, Tony Fernández is the most sober of magicians. Because his head once looked overlarge for his scrawny body, he's known as Cabeza. And, though there's no scrawniness left, his straining, worried face still seems to dominate, an exaggerated caricature atop one of those souvenir bobbing dolls. Like most of the better Dominican players, he's joining the league for the last two weeks of playoffs. He's come here to work out his winter kinks, but I don't see how Tony could stand much more conditioning. His forearms look like they have been on a Nautilus program since the crib. Yet he spends an hour hitting balls one-handed to sharpen his follow-through. Afterwards, he moves to a semicircle of soft sand that looks like a shot-putter's lair while another player tosses ground balls two at a time, first to one side of the circle, then the other, fast as he can. Fernández dashes back and forth to scoop up every ball. Behind him, the youngest of the Guerrero boys imitates his idol's gestures, trying to keep up the pace. While Cabeza keeps the drill going, the teenager slumps with his hands on his knees, gasping for air.

Fernández is accompanied by his agent, Epy's brother Mario. A second-rate infielder at best, Mario Guerrero bounced around four teams before his release at age thirty. He left the game with a reputation as a griper and a quitter. One Latin play-by-play man told me, "Mario was the only ballplayer I've ever known who used to complain that he was playing *too much*." Since turning agent, he's been surrounded by controversy. The appearance of collusion with his brother can hardly be avoided each time he gets a jump on signing a Blue Jay prospect. With Fernández, for instance, one Guerrero negotiated his contract while the other Guerrero was present on behalf of the club. Maybe Mario's good looks keep people from trusting him no further than he could bunt. His flashing dark eyes and Grecian nose are set off by one of those perpetual three-day beards. My suspicions grow when he insists it was his own choice to cut short his playing career. "I had wanted to be a big-leaguer since I was six. When I got my dream, I had no interest anymore." In other words, you didn't fire me—I quit. Never mind that his batting average never climbed much higher than the dreaded "Mendoza line" of .200, named in honor of all light-hitting infielders. I have the feeling that Mario had to give up hardball because he couldn't get by on charm.

Or maybe this rebel couldn't play along. Outspoken from the start, Mario insists he became an agent because, "I always wanted to defend the players. Especially Latin players. There's no way the ballclubs want to give money to Latin ballplayers. Before, they used to tell the Spanish player, you gonna do this, you gonna make that. But now, the players got free agency, arbitration, they gotta know how to use all these ways to protect themselves." When I ask him about the many reports of Latin players being roped into phony real estate deals or paying exorbitant fees to unscrupulous agents, Guerrero says, "It's true. I could tell you a lot of stories. A lot of Latin players don't know the ropes, they get taken advantage of because of their English. But it's more than just dealing with contracts. The players need someone who speaks their own language to tell them what to do when they hit bad, run bad."

Offering tips to some of the young Blue Jays, Guerrero the Younger looks like he can still run and hit pretty well. He appears to savor this role as an inculcator of a discipline he himself was not fully able to maintain. He tries to correct a hitch in a young player's swing. Over and over, he pulls at the prospect's elbow to keep the hitter from "opening up" too much on his stance. The adjustment is minute, and it's hard to gauge any improvement in so short a time. For a hitter or a concert violinist, technique must become blind habit.

While Guerrero tinkers with these subtle adjustments in mechanics, a Cadillac pulls up alongside the backstop. This corporate brougham and its glow of burgundy newness seem so incongruous in the jerry built camp. I can't see who's riding inside the UFO's tinted windows. A chauffeur jumps out to open the door. Another Dominican, the first I've seen in a pinstriped suit, bows like a Japanese businessman. He's along as assistant and translator to a nondescript, rangy gent who I recognize from closeups of VIP boxes as Bobby Brown, president of the American League. *Doctor* Bobby Brown, the announcers always are quick to point out—as though the medical degree he earned after playing for the Yankees goes to the credit of all organized ball.

The Doctor acts just as I might have expected. He stands there soaking up sun and smelling of money. He looks like he's just come off the tee at Pebble Beach. His white polo shirt has *American League* sewn over the breast instead of the Lacoste alligator. His loafers have tassels. His thinning reddish hair is Brylcreemed down. Brown leaves as abruptly as he arrived, managing a perfunctory chat about the weather with Fernández, one of his league's developing gate attractions. He's the only person in the camp with less to do than me. I can't imagine why he's come here except to justify a beach junket.

"He's checking up on us," Mario Guerrero whispers. But how's the league president going to spot underage aspirants during this quick public relations swing? Perhaps he's serving notice on the brothers Guerrero that somebody upstairs is keeping tabs on their tandem efforts to corner the market on shortstops. But the Guerreros are hardly restraining trade as much as the colluding owners. Besides, it's too hot for anything as strenuous as a reprimand. Like the rest of those who rule on behalf of "the good of the game," Doctor Brown seems ridiculously faded and stiff-jointed, surviving off the vigor of this young man's sport. This is how sugar company chairmen of old must have looked, coming down from Boston or New Orleans to have a quick look at their lucrative plantations. Doctor Bobby is this newer harvest's foreman, straw boss, and massa. Only now it's the actual brown bodies of the young field hands that must be brought to ripeness, processed, and consumed. Of course, this *presidente* probably thinks baseball is doing these kids the favor of their lifetime. Might as well sign them all, since they're cheaper by the dozen. But how many of those he surveys will soon be sent back in disgrace to the cane fields? How quickly will this unforgiving game chew up and spit out all this nimble flesh?

After Fernández has worked up a good lather, I hitch a ride into the capital with the All-Star and his agent. I keep hinting that I'm already late for an afternoon rendezvous with Matty Alou, but Mario Guerrero won't be hurried. The return trip to Santo Domingo takes three times longer than the heavy-metal boys took to come out. And Mario's set of wheels hardly compares to Doctor Bobby's. The bucket seats of his beat-up Datsun look gnawed away by island cattle. Where the radio should fit on the dashboard, there's a Medusa's head of detached wires. Mario drives cautiously, a man preoccupied with contract or perhaps woman troubles, lugging all the way in third gear. The agent plods along partly because of all those damnable potholes, but mainly, I imagine, because he's aware of the potential millions in earnings represented by the arms and legs of his front-seat passenger. We curve around so many squalid little plazas, so many corner lots of smoldering trash heaps, so many bodegas plastered with hand-painted messages on behalf of Coke and Balaguer—everything's on one repeating loop.

Mario and Tony hardly converse, which is unusual in these parts. Even in the car, Cabeza seems to conserve his energies. He's one ballplayer who imparts no air of impending high jinks. He's more like a deacon, with something measured, deliberate, even didactic in the way he sweats. "All I want is a little peace and quiet," he tells me, almost apologetically. But workmen are pounding and mortaring from a scaffold that covers the facade of a two-story house where we will drop him. Through the open front door, I glimpse numerous unidentified relatives gathered around a blaring TV console. Mario Guerrero assures me later that Fernández lives in the most exclusive section of town. But his block's a slanted cul-de-sac of semidetached stucco *rancheros* that would be considered starter units in South Florida. In the Dominican, even affluence is a makeshift affair.

With baseball done for the day, pressures dissipate and there's nothing to do but savor the island's available pleasures. Mario Guerrero seems eager to get the proceedings going, shouting out remarks to peasant girls he fancies. He's more distracted by the many roadside coconut stands. His bumper sticker should read, "I Brake for Coco Frío." We will sample a bit of the tropical bounty, a lunch plucked from the heavens! But Guerrero wants only the best for his honored guest. Before yielding to temptation, he passes as least ten vendors in shorts with stacks of coconuts at their feet and machetes in hand. He leaps from the driver's seat to hover over a vendor. Cocos just aren't what they used to be, his expression tells me. Guerrero's pleasurably vindicated when he discovers this teen-age boy's stock is old. He throws the vendor's first offering to the curb in disgust. Mario makes the boy hack off the tops of four or five coconuts before he finds one where the milk's not too watery, and there's enough firm meat to be scooped deftly with a piece of shell. He passes this one through the open window into the car. Tony Fernández raises the hairy gourd and leans back against his headrest at once, sipping fervently with eyes closed, like a devotee receiving communion. I don't know if I can do the same. The milk looks bluish, smells like the pressings of old socks. "Drink it down," Fernández urges as soon as he's through, ever the evangelist. One look at his All-Star muscles tells me I had better comply. "This fruit is like magic, it's the best medicine for you. This milk purifies the entire system." I lift the coconut to my lips, wondering if it can cleanse this island of the last five hundred years.

THE TURTLE CAN'T DANCE

At Santo Domingo's Centro Olímpico, a decidedly non-Olympic sport holds sway. In the shadow of the concrete oval that surrounds the track, on every inch of available grass, kids too young for tryouts have laid out their own infields. Built for the Pan-American Games, this leaf-strewn jumble of shabby fields and empty parking lots feels like a sleepy, underutilized corner of Central Park. Street vendors who've sprung up in the shade nearest each diamond peddle gooey syrups of guava and *tamarindo*, poured over the shaved ice that is death to gringo intestines. The infields are rutted, the turf overgrown, and the backstops are stencilled, "B-B-1, B-B-2, B-B-3. . . ." A half-dozen big-league teams base their Dominican scouting operations on these ill-kempt patches. A *tigrito* leads me to a diamond where there are more muscle-bound loiterers heckling than playing. "Oakland?" I ask. "Sí," the *tigrito* nods, awaiting his tip. "Los Atléticos."

Is this really my home club's modest place in the sun? One of the five youngsters fielding grounders appears to be wearing socks and sweats that simulate the club's "away" uniform. Very away. Here, the garish team colors that the aggressively gauche owner Charles O. Finley called "Kelly Green, California Gold, and Wedding-Gown White," might be Banana-Grove Green, Conquistadores' Gold, and Formerly Clean. The fellow who is spraying out sharp grounders from home plate wears gold chains that rattle with each whip of his torso. But almost any ten-year-old back in the States could put together a closer approximation of an A's uniform with a cap from Granny Goose Potato Chip Cap Day, T-shirt from Seven-Up T-Shirt Day, and pants from Safeway Pants Day. Though this coach has on knickers with stirrups, the effect is spoiled by a pair of suede penny loafers. The only hint of his allegiance is the surplus sweatshirt from some failed promo campaign that bears the slogan, "I'm A Winner—Oakland A's."

I see no sign of Juan Marichal, the Hall of Famer who's recently signed on as Oakland's man in Santo Domingo. The long-legged instructor looks in better shape than any of the scroungy troops he is urging on with a steady trill of thickly accented Spanish. "*Allí . . . allí . . . allí!*" he cries at almost any example of proper execution, bursting into a smile that sabotages all sternness. He interrupts the drill only to glance over and pull at one of his eyes—encouraging me to take a gander at one prized pupil. The youngest of the group scoops up every squibber sent his way. I concur, "*Un natural!*"

When the workout breaks, he beckons me toward a single bench under a concrete overhang studded with nails from which droop Adidas gym bags. The coach is Ramón Genoa, but goes by a nickname, Papiro—as in papyrus. Funny, he doesn't look Egyptian. He possesses the usual winning Dominican combination of chiseled features and a brown complexion. He is also typically irrepressibly quick-moving and quicker-lipped. Oddly, he was never a *pelotero*. A youthful injury ended his playing time. He's been a dedicated student of baseball technique ever since. Papiro tells me that his salary from the A's is three hundred dollars a month, hardly a living wage from the Levi-Strauss company that owns the Oakland franchise, but not bad for a country where canecutters still average a dollar a day. The instructor doesn't mind the money, but voices a complaint common to subordinates. Marichal, *el gran escucha*, or chief scout, flies off to Miami while he does the work. He is confident that he can find a more promising position in the Big Apple, where he hopes to move soon. "*Nueva York es grande*," I warn him, but Papiro's broad grin tells me he's not the warnable kind. He thinks that another Hispanic hitting instructor is just what the South Bronx needs. When I tell him that I live in California, as far as I can get from Nueva York, he says, "I know. Long way. Two hours on airplane, maybe."

Papiro's naive optimism rubs off on his troops. The baby-faced "natural" showcased earlier introduces himself with a cocky diffidence and a slight courtly bow. He bears the distinguished monicker of Vincente Paul

Javier, though everyone calls him Papucho. "He my son," Papiro tells me. "I am godfather." And what will Papiro get for all his hours of coaching and big-brotherhood if Papucho makes it to the bigs? "He remember about me," says Papiro with a grin. "Or I kill him!" For now, Papiro has more urgent matters on his mind. I can't follow, so Papucho translates. "He wants to know if you like to party! Do you like hear Dominican music this night? Okay! See a true Dominican show? Pick you up aroun' eight? Awright!" The coach has one more question. "Now he wants to know what you think of Dominican ladies!" The response on my face cracks up the squad.

Thanks to my man Papiro, I've finally got my invite to the fiesta. Tonight's the *noche!* After all this time on the island, I'm primed to tango with flowers in my teeth, wind up with a pineapple over my head and lipstick on my collar. So where is my favorite hitting instructor? For once, this tardiness takes me by surprise. The one job people start on time around here is friendship, because it's the one job that can never get done. Ninety minutes have passed since our appointed hour and I begin to resign myself to an evening of Homesickness Box Office. Just before ten, I decide to take my last shot at the hotel casino. On my way across the lobby, I notice a familiarly angular figure leaning against the reception counter, chatting with the night clerk as though they're old pals. In white chinos, Papiro looks even more like some overgrown species of daddy longlegs. His black shirt's dappled with a print of irises and open to the navel. His grin's broad as ever, his thickets of curls glisten with apres-workout Afro Sheen. He indicates neither surprise nor relief at seeing me. He pantomimes the excuse of having left both my last name and room number in the back pocket of his emerald-trimmed Oakland A's pants. From the ease of his lobby-lounging, I get the feeling Papiro would have happily waited for me all night.

I respond by holding up my lurid, satiny bundle: a cheap facsimile of an official A's warm-up jacket. I'm bringing this along not only because it's the flashiest item in my traveling wardrobe but as an indication to Papiro that we're part of the same team. He doesn't seem to notice. He's too busy shaking off the doorman's entreaties on behalf of a line of desperate cabbies. He leads me along the curb of an eerie, near-evacuated boulevard. Papiro knows just which cars are *públicos*, the main hubs in Santo Domingo's unofficial system of transport. At last, I'm riding in one of these springless Chevies that work on an unspoken system of fares and are so crammed that it seems the entire population is on its way to some family outing. The faces in the darkened back seat tell me life's no picnic in Santo Domingo. None of these tired folk react to my English or Papiro's baseballese. Hopping out to catch another car, Papiro offers a pittance to the unprotesting driver, assuring me that I would have had to pay three times more. After each of three quick shuttles, Papiro shakes off my attempt to contribute. Tonight's his big chance to display largesse.

The last car leaves us on another ghostly boulevard. Papiro leads me several blocks down a darkened side steet. This is his *barrio*. It doesn't look zoned for juke joints. I only see stucco houses the size of miniature golf obstacles and front lawns no bigger than cemetery plots. Are we still going dancing, I double-check, and not to Mamma's? Papiro delivers an authentically brisk Dominican reply. "*Más despacio, por favor!*" If he were my hitting coach, I'd never know when to bunt or swing away. Fortunately Papiro knows how to grin in the affirmative. A string of yellow bulbs at the end of the third block signifies our destination. As we approach the club, I try to explain the tourist's difficulties in finding local settings for local music. Papiro looks baffled, as I thank him in advance, for saving me from some casino floorshow's "folkloric" revue.

Street vendors have gathered around the entrance. Their kerosene lamps glow from inside plastic bins whose shelves are lined with thrice-fried chicken parts. The front door looks like a toreador's pants: matte black drizzled with a spiraling trim of metallic sparkle. From a sidewalk desk half the size of his lap, a hefty bouncer enforces a cover charge for *el show*. "*Esta Noche, Super Travestia!*" A couple of Polaroids tacked to the door reveal several odd creatures waddling on stage, lumpy mermaids in gold lamé skins. I don't need Spanish to know that Papiro's brought me to see the neighborhood's favorite female impersonators. I try to look pleased while he reaches for his pesos. There's bound to be a live band.

Except for a few Day-Glo posters of naked ladies pulsating like frogs gulping for air, the club's insides have also been dipped in black. A bar occupies one end, a glassed-in booth for a deejay the other. In between, there's a small square of parquet floor before a couple of ceiling-high mirrors. The ceiling fixture is one of those rotating mirrored globes that leave all beneath it pocked with light. It's past ten on a weeknight, yet we're way too early for the festivities. We have our choice of tables and Papiro insists on giving me the place of honor closest to the dancing. I'm flattered by this front-row treatment until I realize this entire end of the club is wall-to-wall loudspeakers, balanced and wedged together like building blocks. These ramparts of amplification soon begin to vibrate and nearly topple under the attack of a rasping merengue. *"Soy un hombre divertido!"* once again. Papiro's theme song—and everyone else's. I'm hardly seated before the coach carries over several half-pints of rum, Seven-Ups for a mixer, and the usual paper tub of ice.

Before we begin any serious drinking, Papiro takes me around to meet the bartender, the club owner, and various other *barrio* luminaries. He wants them all to take note that he's keeping company with *"un periodista de béisbol famoso."* With the music going, I can't tell if they sound impressed but I doubt it. Everyone here gets the same treatment from the gang, beginning with a sixties-style, full-fisted black-power handshake. In silk shirts, pressed jeans, soft loafers worn without socks, these small-time operators would be at home in New York or Nairobi, a roadhouse in Guadeloupe or Bahia. I can't imagine what they do in the daytime to keep themselves in these threads, but their real job is clearly to stay abreast of the latest music and fashions by which to celebrate the night. Their culture is at once insular and boundless, a culture of the drum that sabotages and eventually overwhelms all other influences. The laughter here reminds me of the cavalcade of laughter with which I've been feted by all the ballplayers. Where knowledge is sounded rather than writ, a man's laugh is his true signature. And where there is laughter and there is music, all listeners are made equal.

But does the music have to be so loud? In ten minutes, my head's throbbing, my inner ear ravaged. I begin to suspect these cats have to keep increasing the decibel levels because they've suffered permanent hearing loss. Or perhaps silence is a sentence to obscurity—and this bodega's wall of sound is simply more of the Latin's love affair with the noise he can make. Just as no color's ever lurid enough, no beat can be too emphatic. They have to keep turning the volume up on life.

As I watch Papiro rocking so contentedly to the music, I can't believe he'll ever uproot himself and move to the States. I'm the one who keeps bringing up America, my America. I shout that this bar reminds me of several dives along San Pablo Avenue, the blighted ghetto strip in Oakland. I expect Papiro to be amazed, or consoled, to hear that the emerald city of Oz, fount of those green-and-gold dollars, is not really so different from here. Or that the city I hail from is mostly poor and black. *"Hay muchos negros en Oakland, muchos Latinos."* I don't possess the vocabulary to get more analytical. I don't know quite how to tell him that the home of the A's is also famous for the Hell's Angels and the Black Panthers, the highest infant mortality rate in the country, and drug kings so resplendent that their funeral processions stretch in high limo style for forty blocks. In Oakland, too, music and liquor are the means to "get over," get by, get through the night.

So I whip out my ballpoint and start a map on my napkin. I dare not look up to see how Papiro's taking this feverish sketching. He probably thinks I've lost my head. I'm aware that I'm not really providing this information for Papiro's edification, but so I can have a turn at showing off my home turf. I delineate San Francisco's ear-shaped bay, complete with coastal ranges and ocean waves, craggy peninsulas and the city limits of its shore encampments. Papiro wants to know the length of the bridge that I've drawn from "S.F." to "Oak." Seven miles, I tell him. He looks impressed. Then I draw a circle around the whole area and write the number 4,000,000. Papiro knows I mean people, not dollars. That's nearly the population of his country! I find myself bullying him with the North's indisputable bigness, though it's a bigness in which I usually find no comfort. A typical gringo, I swathe myself in facts to avoid the moment. Papiro rewards me by shaking his head in disbelief, but only until a favorite song starts up.

Without warning, we're joined by two squat young ladies with huge eyes, pug noses, big crowns of coarse reddish hairdos. Are these the *chicas* Papiro promised when he made his invitation? He introduces one as his fiancée, planting his arm across her tiny shoulders as though to emphasize the other's availability. I try my luck—and my Spanish—on this "cousin." She gives off the air of having been dragged along by her gypsy earrings. I never do figure out if she's been invited for my sake. I don't even succeed in making her smile. All my homesick chatter about Oakland leaves her nonplussed. Like Papiro's, her reaction reemphasizes something I have to keep reminding myself: We're not that far away. These "foreigners" all have relatives in the Big Apple, they watch "Magnum P.I." every night. In the world's no-host party, complete with noisemakers and hats, we Norteamericanos are the braggarts, the blowhards, the sloppy drunks who like to show off our wad of bills. Most people know us much better than we know them. We have no secrets and they have so many. You'd think they'd use this imbalance to their advantage.

169

After more rums all around, Papiro and his girl must get up and move. He dances the same way he coaches, deftly and at full throttle. I keep thinking he'll have to flash signals, rub his shirt like a third-base coach, but his fiancée seems to know each stutter he's going to make. Pressed together at the hip, Papiro and his partner are effortlessly coordinated in their thrusting. Don't the two of us want to join them? Papiro keeps beckoning me, admonishing me. He shows undisguised amazement at how well I'm managing to stay glued to my seat. He can't believe I won't display my own hip-slashing, *merengazo* moves. Here, a man who doesn't dance is no man at all.

"The turtle can't dance . . ." I'm not exactly the unhip creature of the old Dominican children's rhyme. I have hips, but I also know the value of a nice, hard shell—preferably soundproof. My best excuse is that old hillbilly joke, "I never could dance standing up!" Truth is, I'm the kind of American who dances best without a partner. I don't think I can manage a reasonable facsimile of the local, cheek-to-cheek gyrations. And I'm not one to leap up and boogie at the first opportunity. Play, sport, and game. These may be the most frequently used words in my prose—words without synonyms, words for which no other words will do. Sport, game, play. These words seldom apply to my life. In the nick of time, the deejay switches to technopop and I ask the cousin to writhe beside me. Now that the synthesized beat is so devoid of polyrhythms that a centipede could follow along, I display my version of the bump, the pony, the jerk. Papiro slaps me on the back with the same infectious delight that he offers his prized shortstop.

Each time the bass thumps, my ears are pricked with steel-headed Q-tips. By the time we finish our turn on the floor, the rest of the tables are full. So I resort to excuses for taking a breather. Papiro can't hear my cry for fresh air, but he gets the idea. Outside, when Papiro asks if I'm having a good time, his words barely reach me through a mountain of cotton. It's as though there's fuzz on the needle of my stereo and I've no means to brush it off. I don't want to appear ungrateful but I can't help cupping my palms over both ears. Papiro finds this my most hilarious contribution to the evening. Next break, he asks if I'm hungry and I nod eagerly so I can stall for time on the lusciously silent street corner. Apparently the men get to snack while the ladies powder their noses. He treats me to the cart's full menu: greasy chicken breast and a side order of prefried plantain chips which the vendor reheats in case we haven't had our share of rancid oil. Will *el show* start soon? Papiro's answer is the dreaded word, *"Ahorita."* That "little now" often widens to encompass decades.

I have to wait through the unannounced appearance of a local merengue idol. I can't believe a genuine recording artist would bother with such a small club, until it occurs to me that we're in the capital. This may be one of the classiest joints in the whole country. Papiro nudges me. We're in for something special. In a pink polyester jumpsuit, the singer looks slighter and frailer than he does on the album cover he cradles under one arm. Like so many Dominican men, he seems whiskerless; his eyes are moist and doe-like. To Yanqui eyes, they seem sexy eunuchs, half-studs and half-valets. The singer hasn't brought his brass section along, so he lip-synchs his way through several recent hits. In his honor, the volume goes even higher. At the finale, he tosses a half-dozen freebies into the crowd. A good-natured tussle for vinyl ensues, like the one for foul balls at the ballpark. No one protests when Papiro lunges across the next table to spear a prize for his gal.

El show commences around one-thirty. A succession of middle-aged drag queens, a bit thick under the chin to be entirely convincing, sings along to the same quivery, over-emotive Broadway show tunes favored by aspiring fems the world over. "Tomorrow, tomorrow, I love ya, tomorrow!" In sequined gowns and brocades, elbow-length gloves masking rough forearms, they make particularly vulnerable figures in this realm of rigid sexual roles. But the audience of hetero couples hardly looks threatening or threatened. A good-natured competition develops over which Beau Brummel can shove more peso notes down more bogus parts of each queen's anatomy. The tippers who scurry forward get an added bitch-in-heat wriggle as a reward, plus their own moment in the spotlight. By the last number, the girls display so many bills they look like bulls pricked by too many picadors. For my host's sake I try to look properly enthralled.

After Rosita comes Tanya: enough androgynous livestock to last until dawn. Papiro and his date keep giggling and cooing as though they've never seen anything so outrageous. Somehow, I get it through to him that I must be getting my shut-eye. And shut-ear. The disappointed coach shrugs his shoulders toward the ladies—what a party-pooper! He still can't understand why I won't keep up stride for stride, sip for sip, shimmy for shimmy. I can't understand what these insouciant Dominicans have to dance about! The old question, the division of the planet, still comes down to chicken or egg. Are these people so good-natured because they've been oppressed? Or have they been oppressed because they're so good-natured?

And I still don't know what to make of this culture that is not very efficient at anything except song, color, commotion. I'm not sure how to judge these people who do not seem to be very good at anything— except living. If people, including me, keep leaving the "land of the free" in droves to get inspiration from these supposedly unfree places, that's because the freedom found here isn't a guarantee found in some musty archive, an absence of proscribed coercions. Freedom is the step in your walk. Freedom is the way you put your shirt on in the morning.

Grudgingly, Papiro escorts me outside to flag down anything that might pass for a cab at three in the morning. Eventually, a '57 Chevy coasts by, headlights off. Papiro begins a quarter-hour of bargaining with two nasty characters in the front seat. Only when he's satisfied that I'm not going to get taken for another sort of ride does he shove me on my way. However, the driving seat duo begins running a game on me almost as soon as we're out of Papiro's sight. Though I can bearly make out their grumblings through my damaged apparatus, I get the drift of their unconvincing cussing over having to go so far out of their way. I may be deaf, but I'm not that dumb. Suddenly they can't remember the location of my hotel and suggest dropping me in a deserted alley on the opposite side of town. I manage a single, "Okay. 'Stá bien." These gents aren't after an abduction, just twenty pesos more.

On my last day in the Dominican, I wake up legally deaf. A screaming spat between two waiters barely gets through. The clatter of breakfast dishes arouses a response less like hearing than wincing. Does the U.S. embassy have an emergency service for its merengue-numbed nationals? When I stop at the Centro Olímpico diamond on my way to the airport, Papiro exhibits no hangover, aural or otherwise. In the hot sun, he whips his fungo bat with martial briskness, shouts baserunning tips with directorial passion. Frequent siestas must be his secret, or maybe it's plantain omelettes for breakfast. Or maybe he's looking "busy" for the sake of his boss. A white Mercedes is parked beside the soda vendor's rusted cart.

The full complement of future A's has shown up—so many that another assistant has to take roll call from a clipboard while they line up along the foul lines of the shabby diamond. At this unkempt boot camp, not one of the recruits meets inspection in the same uniform. They show the colors of twenty local sugar-mill teams, amateur squads, or stateside logos borrowed for good luck. They answer *"Presente!"* to flowery *apellidos* that sound ridiculously distinguished for a bunch of unemployed teenagers. In the pounding January sun, it's impossible to distinguish the "can't-miss" prospects from those who've been invited to take their chances or from those who've just shown up. By the end of the day, some will be sent home. For now, all of them hope this will be the first step in a journey to a place they know nothing about, can't find on a map, and pronounce "Oky-lann."

They seem hardly aware of the man who holds their fate. Sitting forward on the covered bench, he squints at their efforts from behind designer shades. But Juan Marichal is hardly incognito. Today a bushy mustache adds sobriety to his baby face and he looks a bit chunkier, but he's still the dapper "Dominican Dandy." He wears his coordinated Adidas togs the way some men wear a tuxedo. Around his neck, a golden dog tag glints, stamped with the words *Hall of Fame.* Does he show the label to remind others or himself? Everyone knows this *inmortal* started out as just another *niño de campo*—a child of the fields, measuring out his years by the sugar harvests in the northern village of Laguna Verde. "I lived and worked on a farm as long as I can remember. . . ." he wrote in his autobiography. "There, close to the land, many truths exist." Maybe that's why he, too, has come home to the friendly embrace of his native culture. "Only in the Dominican Republic," Marichal waxed, "can you pump a pig with wine and rum and take it to the bakery to cook in giant ovens. Only in the Dominican Republic do they make the white cheese where the juices run liquid. Or the holiday dish of meat and *plátanos*, wrapped in banana leaves, part with hot spices, part 'cold' spices, so no one's taste is offended."

"El Millonario" samples the same guava drinks, speaks the same street vernacular as the greenest rookies. When a new first baseman arrives who's unusually oversized and red-headed, and he shouts at the squad, "Who invited the gringo?" a dozen quips fly back, too colloquial for translation. Here, where everyone's a *pelotero* or wants to be, there's a charming equality among aspirants. The Dominican talent boom is bred by the ongoing presence of yesterday's legends, touchable and very real and all too willing to pass on the tradition.

"When you want to play, you got that inside," Juan Marichal tells me. "I pitched down here one year for one peso. The team was having problems, money-wise. They couldn't pay American players and the owner was the godfather of my daughter, so I agreed to draw some people in the stands. He offered me anything, but I said, 'No, *compadre*, I want to pitch but I don't want to get paid.' So to make the contract legal, he gave me one peso. I think the team still owes me that. I'm the type of person who's gonna try in every way to be your friend. And if you don't like me, that's your problem. What else can I do?"

Nada más. When it's time to catch my flight, I'm not allowed to leave without the formalities that cement friendship. The workout is suspended so everyone can wish me godspeed. Even the soda vendor makes a last futile attempt at a sale, shouting, "Oak-lann A's! Oak-lann A's Man!" Tomorrow's Atléticos make me jot down their addresses in my steno notebook, just in case they aren't instantly promoted to the mainland. With my adiós, I express the hope that all of them make it to the diamond of their dreams. Behind a backstop in a shady park on a balmy afternoon, it doesn't seem that any of them have that far to travel. But Papiro follows me to my car, an uncharacteristic hesitancy slowing his loafers, his smile put on temporary hold by chagrin. Here's the payback for the night on the town, for all the free rum! When I don't catch his Spanish, Papiro starts playing charades, modeling then removing some invisible garment. It turns out he covets the satinized Athletics' warm-up jacket I thought he'd failed to notice. It's Columbus and the Indians all over again. In return for their loyalty to the big club, Papiro and his brothers could ask for so much more.

LEFT FIELD
JARDÍN IZQUIERDA
Nicaragua

"There's no stealing here anymore, not even in baseball."

—Fidel Castro

SPORTING GOODS
AND DOING GOOD

Sis-boom-bah! Another squadron of Yankees is disembarking, but this time, the Nicaraguans are striking up the band. Two portly gents are blowing as hard as they can on a trumpet and clarinet while three protégés in short pants crash cymbals and pound snare drums. These village greeters remind me of the bandaged fife-and-drum corps that roused the troops of another revolutionary war. Their frenzied tooting may not sound like much—off-key Dixieland, bar mitzvah music with a hint of bolero—but it's about all the cacophony that the town of Boaco can muster. And it's amazing what effect a little brass has on the human psyche. I wish I got this much pomp and timpani every time I stepped off a bus.

This attempt at VIP treatment is due me because of baseball—which I've signed on to play in the name of goodwill. My tour group, called Baseball for Peace, has come here to face a literal farm team, as well as deliver badly needed baseball equipment donated by American citizens and even a few major league clubs. For months, this provincial supply hub in the hills north of Managua has lobbied to be the first host of our curious delegation. Proud elders form a receiving line on a slope of mud before the first row of whitewashed hovels that stagger over a half-dozen hills. Peasant women nursing babes emerge from dim cinder-block shanties. A few ranchers glare down from horseback. Oblivious to flies or formality, dozens of children with ruler-even bangs crowd around. Hardly overawed, they rush to show their prowess with the only toy

177

they've got: two wooden balls on a string that, through deft wrist-twisting, knock one another until these colliding yo-yos clack like applause. No one seems to mind that my cohorts and I emerge from our mobile locker room wearing a grubby assortment of play clothes, knee-high tube socks over our sweat pants to give us the look of a genuine ball team.

Too bad the marching music summons our opponents, heading up the steep path from town. Their spiked shoes scrape on the cobblestones as they climb, but otherwise this motley selection of regional all-stars looks almost as amateur as we do. Each player models a different hand-sewn uniform, crookedly lettered across the chest "Nica" or "Los Criollos" or "Roberto Clemente." But the patches on their knees and the extra lengths of string wrapped around their shoes to hold on the cleats don't comfort me. These athletes have a lean and hungry look—what's worse, an athletic look. The deep-set black eyes give these boys a determined expression even without their "game faces." Just as they reach us, grins break out and the captains unfurl a Day-Glo pink banner across the width of the main street. At each end is a passable imitation of our tour logo: three baseball bats crossed to form the inverted "Y" of the international peace sign. Across this banner is stenciled "BIENVENIDOS, BÉISBOL POR LA PAZ!" The home team has even added the English words "peace" and "love."

"Can you handle love twenty-four hours a day?" Someone had called this up and down the aisles soon after our flight left San Francisco. "Cause you're gonna get smothered in love down there. You're gonna get it gift-wrapped, ready or not!"

Somehow I had expected more skepticism from Paul, a middle-aged hipster with a cocky swagger who laid down his raps in the emphatic delivery of his native Bronx. I saw at once that Paul was going to be our clubhouse sparkplug, ready to exhort us on to greater deeds whether we've asked him to or not. But this former community organizer with thinning hair, sunken chest, and empathetic eyes is a successful fuss-budget coffee importer who's as wedded to the gourmet revolution as any other. "The sweetest beans on the planet, right in the midst of the frigging war zone!"

Politics makes for strange bedfellows, and even stranger roommates. And what about politics plus baseball? To avoid such fellow travelers, I'd long resisted the siren call of Nicaragua. In fact, it was my perverse ambition to be the last man in town to make the pilgrimage. In a place

178

where recycling newspapers entitled people to call themselves progressive, more people traveled the Berkeley-to-Managua shuttle than the BART trains across the Bay. Of course, these support groupies returned periodically to knit up their intestines and sip cappuccinos, sort out their Sandino pins and posters, give slide shows and hold fund-raisers while serenaded by Chilean exiles in ponchos.

Despite mounting outrage over the effluvia of distortions fed us by the American media, I kept telling myself that Vietnam had been my colonialist war to oppose. I'd lost my taste for being an uncritical camp follower about the time that the ho-ho-ho went out of Uncle Ho. And my anticolonialist revolution had already come and gone in Cuba. How could anyone top a government whose first act had been to make admission to baseball games free for the masses? Or solidified their hold on power by barnstorming the nation as a bearded nine called *los Barbudos*? Nobody in Nicaragua compared with Che or Fidel—their speeches weren't as exhaustingly eloquent, their humor as irreverent, their cigars as long. I preferred the Cubans' hedonism and impulsiveness to what I perceived as the Nicaraguans' long-suffering Catholic stoicism. Give me the rhumba over the catechism any day! In the age of electronic snapshots, Central America just didn't seem as photogenic as the Caribbean. Of course, I kept hearing that Nicaragua looked better in person. But I continued to exercise that dubious right to pick and choose my spots to get compassionate. Such are the pitfalls of the consumerist society, offering its buyer's guide to regimes based on solidarity inspired per dollar spent. Besides, I'd acquired enough problems of my own that I didn't need to participate vicariously in a distant land's tortures or triumphs. Ten days of teamwork couldn't make up for ten years as a free agent.

On a previous jaunt to Cuba, I'd learned that the combination of group travel and left-wing causes could be poison. Both have a penchant for false promises, both tend to take their rank and file for granted—and for a ride. My "Cubamobile" claimed a focus on "Sports, Recreation, and Culture." Yet the main sport on display turned out to be swimming in hotel pools, recreation meant guzzling *mojitos* and daiquiris, and the biggest sample of Cuban culture was provided by dining hall musicians, rescued from the streets by a planned economy, who crooned a new verse of "Guantanamera" at every meal. August turned out to be the worst month to have scheduled a seminar on Cuban athletics. Most wisely, the

179

nation's impressive "sports cities" were in recess. One of the numerous cigar-chomping officials told us, "At this time of year, the only Cubans you'll see running are running for a bus."

So why was I taking that bait again? The answer had to be those two squat syllables: *béis-bol*. My interest in Nicaragua wasn't piqued as much by tales of land reform or the poems of Rubén Darío as by rumors that Minnesota Twins' pitcher Al Williams spent his off-seasons back up in the hills of his homeland fighting with the Sandinistas. Watching *Under Fire*, the Hollywood version of the Nicaraguan uprising, I'd noticed that the filmmakers established authenticity with a shot of a young boy trying to throw a hand grenade with the motion of his hometown idol, the Orioles' Dennis Martínez. The father-and-son team who ran San Francisco's Turnica, Nicaragua's state-sponsored travel agency, went ape at my mention of baseball. Why, one of their best friends was manager of the Matagalpa team, a cousin was the batting coach, an uncle a legendary player! Baseball's extended family is always small, and in a tiny realm like Nicaragua, incestuous.

Along the equally intimate grapevine of *béisbol* came the first crude translation of "The Centerfielder," a story written by Nicaragua's current vice president, Sergio Ramírez. Positing baseball as the poor's only solace, the story describes a former player's loving memories of great catches as he is about to be tortured by Somoza's National Guard. This seemed a new high point in the connection between baseball and politics. "That last inning of the game against Aruba, zero to zero, two outs, and the white ball was floating gently home to my hands as I waited, arms outstretched; we were about to meet forever when the ball clipped the back of my hand, I tried to scoop it up, but it bounced to the ground— far off I could see the batter sliding home, and all was lost. Ma, I needed warm water on my wounds, like you always knew, I was always brave out on the field, even ready to die."

Later, I heard that Ramírez's epic novel of the revolution, *To Bury Our Fathers*, had been structured in nine chapters to mirror nine innings. What other metaphor could best frame a country whose motto for its male offspring is "*Nació con un guante y una bola en la mano*"? Born with a glove and ball in hand—and God bless the child that's got his own! This was starting to sound like my kind of country. In Colonel Oliver North's infamous slide show for conservative donors to the *contras*, he even included an air reconnaissance photo showing baseball dia-

180

monds—and revealed stupendous ignorance by offering them as indisputable proof of Cuban influence. Following their amateur team's early elimination from the Los Angeles Olympics at the hands of Japan, all Nicaragua had been plunged into mourning. "That night," the popular saying went, "even the *contras* cried."

The straw that broke the back of my obstructionism was a mimeographed handbill announcing the second annual hardball tour of "Baseball for Peace." A sometime sportswriter and Mendocino folk musician named Jay Feldman had concocted this most whimsical among the many initiatives of direct aid for Nicaragua. Despite my cynicism over the therapeutic benefits these gestures offered the donors, there was no denying that a surprisingly large and growing sector of the North American populace had virtually seceded from the authority of the State Department and annexed Nicaragua, turned it into a kind of fifty-first state. This expansionist movement, pointedly unlike those of Yankee generations past, seemed bent on conducting its own foreign policy. If Ping-Pong could promote an opening to China, then surely a more mutually beloved sport was worth trying here. Where governments had failed, baseball might succeed. Bats Not Bombs!

During the thaw of the Carter years, Cuba opened negotiations to bring the New York Yankees to Havana for exhibition games. One attempt came close until commissioner Bowie Kuhn put his foot down. "You notice they always ask to play the Yankees?" manager Billy Martin quipped. "I guess they've already got enough Reds down there." Our own group's goodwill games would be far more than symbolic, thanks largely to an unlikely sponsorship by the *Unión Nacional de Agricultores y Ganaderos*, a militant union of cattlemen and small farmers. But UNAG also sponsors its own first-division squad, *los Productores*, whose cap insignia is a direct knockoff from the Philadelphia Phillies. As part of the union's commitment to enriching all aspects of rural life, they are in charge of maintaining some seven hundred so-called *campesino* leagues. "The country people have been the ones most affected by the war and I consider what we're bringing to be a form of war reparations," I was told when I called Feldman, who'd first learned to play stickball in Brooklyn. "You'll see what it means, if you come with us. Short of making love, there's no way to get closer to the Nicaraguans."

I'm not concerned about making love, but making outs. Some people go to Nicaragua dreading a landmine, but I'm afraid of a live fastball. In the Nicaraguan countryside, I'll be making my virgin attempt at genuine country hardball, and I just hope I get through without being maimed or disgraced. "Dusty Baker of the A's may come along," Jay had assured me as part of his sell. "He's paying the fare for my son, who's a decent high school shortstop. And Bill Lee"—the irreverent Spaceman of the Boston Red Sox—"may join us if he isn't making another comeback in New-foundland. . . ." Without them, our squad of internationalist couch potatoes may set back relations twenty years. What gesture can be more absurd than trying to get in our at-bats behind enemy lines? What political act could be more doggedly naive than distributing catcher's masks and batting helmets to people in need of the bullet-proof kind?

On arrival in this world beacon of hope—having flown via Aeronica, pronounced distressingly close to "Air Ironic," with a stopover in San Salvador for extensive metal detection—we found the corridors of the Managua airport blacked out. Either the authorities were saving electric-ity or some people's janitor had hit the wrong switch. But while the Nicaraguans groped through a customs inspection in semidarkness, our precious cargo of aluminum bats and red batting helmets sailed through. And we were rushed to a lounge complete with plush sofas, coffee tables, the finest Nicaraguan folk art. Across the carpeted Kremlinlike expanse was a mahogany-framed portrait of General Augusto César Sandino, that mighty pipsqueak in ten-gallon hat and riding puttees who once made the U.S. Marines turn tail. "Hopalong Cassidy," muttered Captain Jay. Furnished with Coca-Colas or demitasse shots, along with typed itiner-aries soon amended, scrambled, and ignored, we're ushered over to an abandoned airport cocktail lounge to face the glare of television lights. Baseball for Peace merited a full-scale press conference, complete with reporters from Radio Sandino and the party newspaper, *Barricada*. How could I have doubted that anything having to do with baseball would not be treated with the utmost seriousness?

The revolutionary greeting was a good deal different than my 1980 arrival in Cuba. Our antique DC-3's load of sportsmen for the cause had been made to wait nine hours before entering customs. But we'd been treated to a uniquely Cuban event nonetheless. We'd barely entered the minute transit lounge at José Martí Airport before three hijackings unloaded, one after the other. My first sight in Latin America was a bunch of North Americans in a state of shock. "Welcome to Havana! Have a nice day!" The waylaid tourists were soon consoling themselves by buying out the entire gift shop's bargains in Upmann cigars and Russian vodka. In one corner, Russian pilots in Elvis pompadours and blue leisure suits paced nervously, suddenly outnumbered, conspicuously on the wrong continent. In another, a contingent of wizened *campesinos* in their best black suits awaited a flight that would take them to two years' volunteer labor in Angola. All the currents of twentieth-century history seemed to crash together that day; the cramped airport lobby was transformed into history's waiting room. Only the hijackers, and our tour group, would pay for the crime of being between countries, between ideologies.

Yet Boaco is rolling out its threadbare red carpet. The regional all-stars drop their banner to slap our backs and offer jock-style *abrazos*, jersey to sweaty jersey. Then we all head down the hill toward town, holding the lurid pink sash of slogans aloft. Party officials, kids, clarinetists fall in behind for a euphoric, anarchic parade. The two squads wind their way over several hillocks crowded with claptrap barrios, picking up more marchers, more barefoot children who want to climb on our broad backs or clamor to try on our mitts. We rumble past the stark, defoliated plaza, town cathedral, cantina, feed supply, receiving waves or bemused nods of approval from those villagers reluctant to risk getting trampled.

The only touches of decoration on the rotting wooden doors and peeling walls are daubed slashes of red and black that make the town look like one giant Mark Rothko canvas. These colors, smeared like lamb's blood to make a plague pass, are a testament to each household's allegiance with *El Frente Sandinista*. The only thing in Nicaragua that does not appear in short supply is paint—and slogans to use it up. So far as I can see, this revolution's main achievement is in the field of graffiti. Nicaragua has to be a grave disappointment to dedicated Marxists. Unlike Cuba, with its clinics and schools, the future here is still in blueprint form. The term *progreso* can't be fairly applied to a country like this. "You start to rejoice when a tree's planted," one long-time Nicaragua watcher tells me. "You notice when a single pile of trash gets removed."

The marching band continues the tinny razz-matazz, that sounds more like belly-dancing music than John Philip Sousa. Suddenly, a loudspeaker mounted on an old Toyota pickup at the rear of the procession blares out its own concert. All local efforts are drowned out by a scratchy recording of "Off We Go, into the Wild Blue Yonder." Don't they realize this is the theme song of squadrons poised to bombard them from Honduras? Or that our bunch might feel more roused by "The Internationale"? Can they believe this music actually makes us feel at home, or are they playing it to somehow orient themselves? Nicaragua, one quickly notices, isn't recognizable as Nicaragua without signs of the U.S. of A.

Our parade tumbles down a last slope and dead-ends in the mud. Sinking six inches into black goo is a crude circle of corrugated tin sheeting, just high enough to keep out the snoozing, spotted pigs. Porkers grow so big here and wander so freely that our team comes to refer to them as "Nicaraguan dogs." Vintage leatherneck humor. Against the entrance to home plate, this contented livestock roots, roots, roots for the home team. I stoop to follow my teammates through an entrance that's merely one peeled-up flap of tin. Boaco's only ballfield is a cleared area of black dirt clods with basepaths added. What little grass grows in the outfield is trimmed by grazing cattle. The field of play is demarcated by a ditch that leads down into the underbrush beside a swampy arroyo. Anything hit there is definitely a home run and fair game for the village kids. Far removed on either side of approximate foul lines are three rungs of crumbling concrete steps that may once have been fully covered. The stadium, if it can be called that, has been stripped to build shanties for war refugees.

Still, it's standing-room only at the old ballyard. Farmhands eager for a little diversion pass round home-brewed cane liquor in hide-covered flasks. There isn't much else to do in these parts on a Sunday afternoon. But you can't do anything in Nicaragua without a ceremony, often an interminable one. Town officials insist on lining up both teams on either side of home plate, World Series–style. The one piece of technology they've got in this town is a bullhorn, which materializes out of nowhere so we can hear a fifteen-minute oration from some burly rancher, a lyricist in cowboy hat. The local accent's almost as thick as the flow of rhetoric, but I do catch a reference to peace as "our faraway star."

Spanish and sedition are both long-winded affairs. Is this ability to make with the high-blown chatter merely the usual Latin flair for the dramatic, or a long-cultivated means of making much ado about so very little? In the land of Rubén Darío and Ernesto Cardenal, a flood of public daydreaming may be the only way to unite an underdeveloped reality with overdeveloped imaginations. On the pillar of a hacienda's back porch, a calendar-shot of a Nicaraguan beach is accompanied by

184

the usual waxings: "Quiero Ser . . . Tu Sol, Tu Mar, Tu Tierra, Quiero Ser Tu Razón de Ser." "I want to be your sun, your sea, your earth, I want to be your reason for being!" In Nicaragua, even the kitsch is Byronic. I soon learn why from the woman in charge of Boaco's recently opened *casa de cultura*. Wonderfully shy, yet radiating a contentment that cannot help but encourage flirtation, she strikes me instantly as one of those durable women who make up Latin America's greatest resource. She's also a typical small-town wife with an unabashed appetite for knowledge of the world beyond. I quiz her on the American writers available in her library. Mark Twain and Jack London are about as contemporary as she gets. So I trot out the obligatory inquiry, "Why are there so many poets in Nicaragua?" Without skipping an iambic beat, she beams up at me with a mouthful of gold teeth, announcing, "Nicaragua *is* a poem!"

Before we get to show our stuff on the field, we too must produce some fine words. In scrupulously democratic fashion, Captain Jay wants each of us to take a turn as official spokesman. The bullhorn goes up and down the line like a hot potato, ending up in my hands. Perhaps I'm emboldened by the fact that I know I won't be understood. Or that nothing I say can be news to these rhetoric-benumbed peasants. I clutch the bullhorn, knowing this is the chance of a lifetime to play Fidel on the pitcher's mound. As I step forward into the circle of Sandinistas, Jay nips any grandiose ideas in the bud by cautioning, "Keep it nonsectarian, *chico*. And be sure to apologize for the size of our gift." So I start out, "We know that these few bats and balls cannot meet all your needs, but we hope you accept them as a token of our desire to see sportsmanship replace war." The pause for translation gives me more time to think. "Baseball is the game for all the Americas. May this expression of our two peoples' love for baseball serve to strengthen our two peoples' love for peace." A few more captive audiences and I just might get the hang of this.

Jay grabs the bullhorn and gets down to business: "Among the gifts that we bring to you today are contributions from the San Francisco Giants, the Baltimore Orioles, the Seattle Mariners." Though these clubs have only chipped in with some leftovers from unsuccessful promotional giveaways, Boaco doesn't have to know that. And the public utterance of these mythic entities, enlongated into "los Marineros de Seattle" and los Gigantes," sets off a palpable wave of belonging. Never mind if fifty team portraits of the last-place Mariners will hardly advance agrarian reform. The assurance that some big-league teams may care about the fate of Boaco may be more immediate help to local morale. Later, I'll be entrusted to hand-deliver thank-you notes in which Nicaraguan officials greet baseball's owners as "Hermanos Norteamericanos" and apprise them of the progress of the revolution. Just what the Orioles' millionaire owner Edward Bennett Williams and the Giants' real estate tycoon Bob Lurie want to hear.

Our hosts stress that baseball in these rural areas could not continue without our meagre donations. When the first of the sporting care packages is lugged from our van onto the pitcher's mound, the audience crowds closer. Before the overflow of people can be cleared from the field, the first boxloads of helmets and chest protectors, already coming apart at the seams, are nearly ripped apart. A phalanx of brawny ranchers has to guard their new treasures. Already, I see why people who won't be caught dead "giving at the office" to the United Way do so here on behalf of the united front. Nicaragua serves as an abundant source of ideological inspiration and a basket case, so pathetic that one can stoop to give and give and never fear that one might be seen as stooping too low or giving too much.

A swarm of kids hovers over the duffels full of balls and mitts reserved for our use. Quickly we do-gooders have to turn guard, fending off the constant tugs and pleadings. A few older brothers volunteer to patrol the sidelines, warning us against thieves with the universal gesture of a finger opening an eye. Once they've done their duty, they, too, demand payment in gear. Though the Sandinistas have launched campaigns to eradicate the mentality of dependency, they've made few inroads here. Whatever sense of self-pride grows in these villagers is still outstripped by need. As the game progresses, the insistence grows to hysteria. Though the alms these children seek may be in the form of rubber and cowhide, the begging in Boaco's as bad as in Calcutta. A single used tennis ball tossed casually from our bus sets off a near riot. Throughout the country, the kids call out, "Dáme un lápiz!" They've come to expect a pencil from every foreigner. Now we've changed their tune to, "Dáme una bola!"

The town elders, it turns out, are begging too. Later, we'll be whisked away to the bare office of a regional "corporation for sports development" founded in our honor. Pinned to the unfinished concrete walls are architectural drawings of a new ballyard for Boaco. The architect himself, a local boy made good in Managua, is there to answer all questions concerning his five-thousand-seat, pillarless, obstructionless marvel. To build this state-of-the-art stadium, of course, Boaco will need plenty of greenbacks—and that's where we come in. These grandiose plans seem to embody the new society's predicament. These villagers seem too patient, too used to procrastination. As they once blamed their slow progress on the dictatorship, now they can blame everything on the war. Transfixed by stirring drawings of a stadium that can never be built, these people do not seem to be stirring themselves to maintain the one they already have. A day's volunteer work could smooth the infield, get rid of the cow pies. Instead, they spin visions of Astroturf and play in the shit.

So must we. At the end of the presentation, Captain Jay is careful to caution that we're not professional *peloteros*. Changed out of jeans and plaid flannel shirts, our starting lineup looks a bit less like the local Hegelian study group. The sight of our first baseman Tim taking his position actually causes a stir among the local folk. Little do they know that this hefty six-footer and former Chicago Cub prospect is now a reporter for the Communist Party's West Coast organ, *People's World*. Though an injury prematurely ended his career, he still possesses the supple, confident hands, the fluid uppercut swing that bespeak an easy Yankee mastery. Balding and way over his original playing weight, he at least knows how to carry himself like a ballplayer.

Captain Jay's taken short, and in center, he's stuck his strapping, tousled-haired teenage son, Blue Jay. Our tour is quite a family affair—for Jay's also enlisted *his* father, the Manhattan jeweler Ben, giving us three generations of feisty, tough wisecrackers who perfectly illustrate the stages of Jewish-American assimilation. On top of the three Feldmans, we have two Fieldmans. Their family resemblance is less traceable, the motives for participation less straightforward. Son Jeff is the best ballplayer we've got, a blue-eyed, flat-topped, gum-chewing, Walkman-toting high school catcher who could be a Marine paratrooper. Father Arnold's rightfully proud of his all-American progeny. He has already told everyone who'll listen that he's a proud Reagan Republican who's come along to watch his son whip "the enemy." Whenever he gets the chance, Arnold tries to whip them in debate. From the start, there's widespread suspicion about Arnold's conservatism. The trouble is that he appears to be having too good a time.

Prowling the foul lines with a video camera, our designated redbaiter is just another emergency substitute along with me and Terry, a translator of Chilean poets, and Warren, a Sacramento refrigerator salesman. Another extra named Bill never even heard of Nicaraguan baseball until his general-interest tour of the country was cancelled a few days ago. On the ride here, he whipped out a driver's license which showed him in a cleric's collar. He's had himself ordained in the service of his one-man crusade against federal income taxes. This professional crank spends his days dashing off irate letters-to-the-editor and press releases in the name of organizations of which he's the only member.

Finally, we've got a cheerleading squad of one—a gangling, cheery woman in old-fashioned, flowery print skirts who happens to be the oldest person I've ever seen wearing braces. This appreciative creature flashes them at almost every remark. Back in San Francisco, Barbara serves on a commission recommending sites for a new ballpark. Down here, her frustrated fandom and maternalism has been channeled into a concern for oppressed peoples in general and brawny, brown-skinned ballplayers in particular. Barbara lugs around looseleaf snapshot albums full of the Nicaraguan national amateur team she entertained during a series of exhibition games in California. She lovingly displays every Julio and Arturo in Kodachrome to anyone who'll look. She even knows their batting averages.

Yet even in utopia, the first inning's a bitch. The two teams seem to operate at different speeds. Despite a pitcher and shortstop on loan from the locals, our regulars can't stoop for grounders until they've passed or judge the hops on this rutted surface. A fly ball sails over the head of our left fielder while he's chatting with a gaggle of kids. Our third baseman fields a bunt and zips a throw to first only to find that no one's covering the bag. After the nine-run debacle, Paul calls us into a huddle for a unique pep talk. "These people deserve better. So let's pay them back with a little class." A few ignominious innings later, the love man is exhorting us to "kick some Nicaraguan tail!"

I'm relieved that I haven't been asked to step into the fray. Trying to disassociate myself from the carnage, I wander over to watch an inning or two from the stands. With no training regimen to break, I gladly share a swig from the flasks passed my way by the farmhands. My Spanish isn't good enough to make excuses for the club. If we'd lured along a single minor leaguer, a prospective batting-practice pitcher, these humble folk would have gone wild! But their disappointment contains no fury. The villagers shrug their shoulders at the world, and I shrug back as I'm finally called to take a turn in left field. I can't do any worse than my predecessor. My only fielding chance is a home run that takes but a single bounce to roll toward the wet warning track at the banks of the creek. I let a horde of kids chase after the stray. They will go on searching through the entire game. They don't seem to realize that, thanks to us, this town can afford to lose its share of balls. But there is no joy in Mudville, a more apt name for this burg than Boaco. Final score: Locals fourteen, Peaceniks zip. Blame it on the treacherous field, spattered with cow patties. Call it a shellacking for peace.

FOUL BALLS
FROM THE GODS

"**B**aseball is very problematic," admits Carlos Cuadra, the Sandinistas' man in charge, "because it did not come to us in a very sporting manner." With anything this crucial, there are differing theories concerning origin. Call them imperialist creation myths. Which divine hand was the first to reach out and lay a rulebook in the open palm of some dark-skinned *chico*? What uniform was worn by the manager of the first team? Did a platoon of coaches in combat boots barnstorm the land, distributing ground rules along with Wrigley's gum? As often happens in Nicaragua, there's a pointed lack of coordination among those who ought to know. Come back next year, I'm told, and the archives will be in order. We are creating a Nicaraguan Hall of Fame. But in Nicaragua, order has been synonymous with repression and next year is only a hypothesis.

Jamil Zuniga, head of the Sandinistas' Institute of Sport, insists that the game was brought to Nicaragua around the turn of the century by the sons of the land-owning autocracy. At Harvard and Yale, they acquired a gentlemanly pursuit requiring knickers and mitts and four soft bases. Soon enough they were teaching the game to their field hands, whose physical development quickly allowed them to surpass their masters. And if these Nicaraguan collegians exported the still embryonic game as long ago as the 1880s, then what makes the National Pastime any more ours than theirs? A favorite Cuban boast is that their own professional leagues were founded before either our National or Ameri-

190

can leagues. The rivalry between Havana and Almandares predates that between the Giants and the Dodgers. Most likely, the Cubans served as missionaries through the Caribbean—just as today they are attempting to teach the sport to their Russian allies.

But why, in the midst of soccer-mad Central America, should baseball have retained its sway over Nicaraguans? On closer inspection, the ongoing loyalty to baseball found both here and in renegade Cuba makes perfect sense. The two anti-American nations treasure all aspects of American culture, including Hollywood movies and fashions and jazz. The ability to appreciate and nurture baseball suggests a level of cosmopolitanism and development in mass communications, even a taste for the absurd, which would also encourage nationalism and political sophistication. And in the family of nations, the sons who most resemble the father are the most likely to challenge the father's authority.

An argument could be made that a national zeal for baseball exists in exact proportion to the number of times that nation was invaded by the Marines. Yet Haiti was invaded and occupied longer than either Nicaragua or the Dominican Republic—and not a lick of ball has ever been played there. So there must be something about the culture here, and not just the weather, that offers a predisposition, a bias, a proclivity. U.S. occupations may have been responsible for introducing the game, yet wherever I go, local aficionados are quick to correct my assumptions about the link between the bat and Teddy Roosevelt's big stick. In the Caribbean, baseball wasn't shoved down anyone's throat; the candy was seized even before it was dangled.

"Baseball is in the heart of all Latin people. They feel in baseball, they think in baseball," said Pancho Coimbre, the Puerto Rican and Negro League great. "Don't say the Marines bring the baseball," scolded Ruben Gomez. "Oh no, this game, it's in our blood!" As proof, he and other of his countrymen offer the so-called "ceremonial playing ground" of the Caguana Indians, preserved as a tourist attraction at Utuado. Though the shape and form of this site more closely resembles a crude soccer pitch, Gomez claimed this as "the first baseball field. Oh yes, the Indians played baseball in Puerto Rico. And you know the Spanish people, they hadn't arrived here yet. Sure, it was better known when the Navy came because they had the press." A typical ballplayer's view: history as the concoction of press agents.

Anthropologists in Cuba have also tried to justify their country's ongoing passion for the game through evidence of pre-Columbian ball. Call what the Indians played lacrosse or basketball with skulls, but calling it baseball just isn't cricket. Others look to the Spanish side of the cultural ledger to explain the zeal for baseball, pointing to fourteenth-century court drawings which depict games of pitch and catch. Others point to the Basque form of handball known as *la pelota*, that's come to America as jai alai. But cricket is still the apparent model for baseball, evolved first into the street games of "stoopball" and "one-cat" in the urban centers of the British colonies.

My favorite tale of genesis is advanced by Cuadra, a bearded militant who looks more like a graduate student than a baseball commissioner. His parable, both plausible and poetic, is an admission of dependency and a confession of expropriation. Citing an eyewitness now in his nineties, Cuadra claims that around 1902, the U.S. Navy included a ballfield in the construction of a base near Puerto Cabezas. After landing along the Atlantic Coast to quell some local uprising, the invaders first put their characteristic mark on the land, hacking a diamond shape out of the jungle. But the Seabees had no intention of sharing their game. Out of racism or arrogance or habit, they disdained playing catch with a bunch of dusky natives. After all, a half-century would pass before the integration of the game back home. So the curious locals had to watch from the other side of the fence. Denied admission, they became the archetypal knothole gang. The Nicaraguans mimicked the sport's numerous gestures and rituals. They studied the white men's curious ways and waited their turn.

Their patience was rewarded, as this slow-moving game always rewards its fans. Plenty of line drives gone astray to chase down and collect, a slew of equipment donated by foul tips and mis-swings, pop-ups gone into orbit. Baseball's construction, after all, is purposely open-ended. The grassy terrain fans out far beyond home plate. The pesky white orb flies even farther, as uncontained as the consequences of the history which these invaders had set in motion. Just as the U.S. had burst from its confines, the game leapt from its boundaries. The confirmation of this tale can be found in the barefoot Nicaraguan children still poised today, ready to claim every foul ball from the gods.

No wonder both countries attach such importance to making sure they're not playing with Uncle Sam's balls. Cuba's vaunted sports factory has the feel of an old-time movie studio, good only for churning out one-reel westerns. From the half-dozen production sheds of Havana's vaunted sports factory flow all the toys required by a nation of players. "Here in this factory," director Guillermo de la Cuesta told me eight years ago, "we make everything required for our nation's pursuit of fitness—623 items." Like many of the sports officials I met, he was defiantly corpulent and puffed on his cigar the way a high school football coach blows on his practice whistle. Like a good socialist bureaucrat, he started out properly humble. "I only represent the fine things you will see here. I have not made any of them."

He explained that the same workers our group watched sewing hides or stitching up volleyballs had also helped design the plant and much of its machinery. "This labor began less than fifteen years ago, after the United States imposed its criminal blockade of our country. And it was not an easy proposition, nothing like nationalizing a sugar mill. It was not a matter of spare parts. Before the revolution, we were entirely at the mercy of the United States for manufactured goods. Cubans had never fabricated a single piece of sporting equipment. So we had to start at the beginning. We had to invent everything."

The director paused before a doorway leading into a dirt hut where medieval blacksmiths might have felt at home. "As youthful revolutionaries, we were not prepared to run our industries. It has taken time. We continue to receive technical assistance from Bulgaria and Czechoslovakia. We process raw materials from both these nations, from Hungary, the U.S.S.R., Japan, Germany, Italy, and England. . . . But most of what you will see here is our own technololgy, our very simple technology. That is why we must ask you to refrain from taking photographs."

Cuban paranoia over Yankee imperialism was going too far. What expertise could be swiped out of these badly ventilated stables? What was so secret about an old man shaping bats from Cuban ash shipped from the Isle of Pines? There didn't seem to be anything unusual about the seamstresses with kerchiefs wrapping their hair who sat under fluorescent lights, putting the final stitching in a number of soccer balls. Chess pieces were popped from plastic molds, basketball covers peeled from circular furnaces, badminton shuttlecocks were assembled like Swiss watches. Guillermo de la Cuesta explained that "the baseball presented particular problems. None of the other socialist countries practice this sport. So what you are about to see is a Cuban patent." This looked like an ordinary twining machine to me, wrapping string around a silver ball-bearing with spastic efficiency. "This is why our Batos brand is the only non-American baseball that meets the standards of international organizations, the only one allowed in tournaments."

Posters slapped on the corrugated walls urged workers on to their monotonous tasks: "Revolution Is to Build!" "Advance on the Glorious Road of Socialism!" And a portrait of Fidel toting his rifle in the Sierra Maestra: "Commander-in-Chief, Give the Orders!" Back in his trailer, de la Cuesta gave us his best Fidel imitation. First, the director stressed that the Cubans enjoy unrestricted access to every piece of equipment, even the hand-shaved racing shells. "Eighty percent of our production goes to schools and other institutions. They are used freely—as a lending library." Next, he pulled out a prototype of an oversized, rigid trucker's cap, copied straight from the Peterbilt, "good buddy" variety worn by Tennessee teamsters. "What do you think, eh? Pass it around. Try it on. The people have been sent caps from their relatives in Miami. So we must match it. We are always trying to improve ourselves."

Pride in self-improvement brimmed from de la Cuesta, who spent his prerevolutionary days as a roulette dealer and numbers runner for the Mafia. "Many companies come here to learn from us, too. American companies. I can't give you their names. If only it wasn't for your government's criminal blockade, we could visit their plants also. We would love to spend time with our 'dear neighbors.' It is only natural that we should be trading partners. As it is now, we must take a flight to Eastern Europe for technical advice. It's a long trip, and very expensive. We can only afford to send one man once a year. But if we could go to the United States, well, I could leave in the morning, carry on my business, and be back in Havana that evening to share a bottle of rum with you."

Guillermo de la Cuesta banged on his blotter. Behind him was a collection of objects that could be found together only in Cuba: a wide-bodied Soviet television console, various sizes of Batos baseballs, a portrait of a grimacing Che Guevara. An assistant brought in a tray of fresh-squeezed guava juice, but that didn't slow down this eloquent equipment manager. "Commerce and human relations have to be set aside from political creeds! Let me believe what I want to believe. Don't tell me I have to think as you do so that I can buy from you. We don't ask the people who place orders with us if they're Communists. That's the best policy. My parents were Catholics. They believed in God. I

194

believe in science and material things. Yet I respect them, and they respected me. When my mother was buried, she wore a cross and a rosary. I did not ask that they be removed. I am a Communist, but I wouldn't violate her ideas. Just don't put a cross on me. What I am saying is that you can do what you want in your country, just don't tell me what to do in mine. It's that simple. When a neighbor in your apartment house tells you that you must sleep in long pajamas, and you want to sleep naked, then you tell him to go to hell. That's human rights!"

In Cuba, where sports and politics are inextricably linked, it is never really possible to roam very far from one or the other. In Nicaragua, too, our group's first sightseeing stop is the sporting goods factory established with Cuban assistance. This form of cottage industry housed in Quonset huts is considered so critical that it is supervised by uniformed Sandinista army officers—with a briskness and efficiency hardly evident anywhere else in Managua. More miniature and hand-wrought than its Cuban counterpart, this place is the socialist equivalent of Santa's Workshop. Only here, the elves aren't spurred on by rosy-cheeked images of Saint Nick but by the scalding countenance of Che and the ubiquitous likeness of Carlos Fonseca, a murdered founder of the *frente*, whose four-eyed stare reminds me of a Leninist Wally Cox. The nation's attempt to produce its own balls and gloves saves hard currency and works a statement of self-sufficiency out of rawhide.

Exactly two dilapidated lathes are set aside for the entire production of "Managua Sluggers." A couple of sixteen-year-olds in black bandanas and torn T-shirts are responsible for sculpting the square blocks of lumber into functional bats. Yet these days, both machines are rarely in simultaneous use. Suitable native hardwoods are found only in the remote forests of the battle zone. The supply line has been severely disrupted. The Sandinistas claim that the U.S.-backed *contras*—well aware of baseball's role in maintaining the regime's morale—often target and ambush truckloads meant to be turned into baseball bats. Though Nicaragua is a cattle-breeding nation, leather needed for the gloves has also become scarce. Boots for the army receive first priority.

On a single rickety American-made machine, the rubber cores of balls-to-be bob up and down like the Adam's apples of nervous suitors. The stages required to create a hardball—the accumulation of twine, the stamping out of figure-eight covers, the hand sewing, the final pounding down of the stitches with mallets, the careful weighing of each orb in the cradles of postal scales—drives home this sport's anachronistic nature. Its wealth of specialized paraphernalia bespeaks baseball's nineteenth-century origins. From masks to chest protectors to weighted fungo bats, the various accoutrements needed to maintain teams and leagues add up to quite a burden. In comparison to soccer or basketball or even tennis, baseball is an expensive sport for a poor country.

No machine can duplicate the efforts of the patient women who could be grinding corn meal instead of pounding out first baseman's mitts. Their sewing piecework isn't sweatshop dresses but the preassembled balls that rest like prized circuitry chips in customized stirrups. Beside them, half a dozen women cut boomerang-shaped pieces of suede that are somehow formed to the human hand, with fielding fingers and *cajonés profundos*—deep pockets. This is a sport that could only have been concocted in an era of cheap human labor—which is why the baseball, that most American of objects, is no longer made in the U.S.A. The manufacturers of capitalist balls have moved their plants to low-wage Haiti. The Rawlings Company refused me permission to inspect their Port-au-Prince operations, citing the protection of trade secrets. In contrast, the Sandinistas are eager to show off how they manage to produce 9,000 balls monthly.

At the end of our tour, the army officers stage a test for us. Notches indicating height have been drawn against a back wall, like a growth chart for some precious child. From the top of a circular staircase, the sergeant drops his factory's Danto brand to measure its bounce against Japanese, Cuban, and U.S. competition. "Weel-son, *número dos!* Spaldeen, *número tres!*" The Sandinista tester beams even though the local model proves suspiciously springy.

Back in the visitor's room, each one of us is given plastic-wrapped samples which set off a round of frantic souvenir buying. The army men have to call in secretarial reinforcements to keep track of our group order. "That's forty-seven righty outfielder's gloves, sixty-two hardballs. . . ." We'll take any piece of equipment stamped with the magic words *Hecho en Nicaragua*. The blue suede children's mitts are as functional and flashy as any back home, and a bargain at less than five bucks. Paul the coffee roaster must have a left-handed version for his six-year-old, even if

196

it means retooling the factory. Never mind that the shelves of the Nicaraguan sporting goods stores are empty. Baseball for Peace snaps up nearly as many items as we've brought south to donate. In half an hour, our precious dollars exhaust the stock-on-hand of factory and nation.

VIVA
SANDINO KOUFAX!

At six in the morning, they're pounding down the door to our Managua motel bungalow. Tim sits up in the nearest cot, throws off his flimsy sheets and greets the caller, buck naked. It's not the secret police. A grizzled farmer clutches his straw hat to his chest and his young son to his knees. The two of them have driven down to the capital just to see our first baseman. Our tour will get used to this peculiarly Nicaraguan habit of well-wishers turning up unannounced in one town or another, in spite of gas rationing and frequent transportation snafus, as though the country were one hacienda kitchen. All night long, says the farmer, his son stayed awake talking about the big *primera basista*. Now this frail boy in his best gingham shirt presents his idol with a letter. The boy doesn't seem to register that Tim's in the buff. Father and son encourage Tim to read the letter aloud. In formal Spanish, the first baseman is requested to give greetings from the children of Nicaragua to his children back home—they can't imagine that Tim has none. And to please ask his president, personally, to stop the war. The letter also inquires humbly whether Tim might think to send this boy a Wilson-brand first baseman's glove so that he might follow in the path of his hero. Half alseep, Tim reaches in his backpack for a spare ball. Father and son back out the door, bowing. "There I was with my hand on my dick!" Tim mutters before trying to get some more shut-eye. "Then I'm handing out my autograph! Man, this has got to be baseball heaven!"

198

Viva Sandino Koufax!

The former Cub farmhand and current red bear has found his nirvana: a place where his sweet swing can be hitched to his politics, or vice versa—and where each cursed Yankee dollar buys a wad of continually devalued cordobas. Tim will remain here after our tour to serve as a batting instructor for the first-division team in Matagalpa. In the meantime, "Baseball Heaven" becomes the title of our group's epic poem, our stanza of Nicaraguan free verse. In what other firmament could we find sworn revolutionaries who interrupt their dialectics to remind us that their favorite player is Ernie Banks? Where else would our chief guide, a mischievous mustachioed union leader and nerveless street-fighting veteran named Emigdio Siqueiros, spend most of his time glued to game broadcasts on his transistor? Or could we, simply by showing up, get the finest players in the land to stay up in darkened hotel dining rooms patiently offering their trade secrets on which scams to grip for the slider, the scroogie, the forkball? And where else could our ragtag squad get ogled like superstars, asked to scrawl our worthless autographs on dozens of souvenir balls? I sign mine "Sandino Koufax."

It's all too *perfecto*—the word used all the time in a country where a simple yes is never good enough. In Nicaragua, where everyone's presumed to be a poet, we're presumed to be ballplayers until proven otherwise. Hitting the back roads like a bunch of old-time barnstormers, we experience the grinding bus rides that are the staple of life in the minors. In this instructional league, we work out the kinks by spreading mirth and equipment to hitherto neglected locales. Each stop begins with the announcement of our names and positions from speakers propped against cattle posts, and ends with brew, barbecue, and kind words at the nearest tavern or hacienda. When everybody's drunk enough, the Nicaraguans rip off their hand-sewn, sweat-stained uniforms and give us the shirts off their backs. In return, we leave 'em with a rousing, off-key rendition of "Take Me Out to the Ballgame." This is the leftist equivalent of a baseball fantasy camp—the sort of place where oral surgeons pay thousands to play an inning or two with their boyhood idols. The Natural meets Walter Mitty meets Fidel.

In Matagalpa, as close to the war as we ever get, we're told that "whenever the troops have a moment away from the front, the first thing they do is pick up a ball and a glove." At a welcoming breakfast, a Paris-educated lawyer named Marco Gonzales speaks on behalf of the region's coffee growers. "We would no longer be Nicaraguans if we stopped

199

playing baseball. What was once the opiate of the masses has become the balm for our wounds." Gonzales claims that Nicaraguans remain "mentally very healthy people," despite losing thirty-five thousand lives in five years. And baseball, this legacy of prior wars, is "our way of coming away from war, of making certain that our people never yield to a war mentality."

It is just beyond the next hill that one never crosses: *la guerra,* invisible yet omnipresent. Somewhere nearby, a game adds up its score in casualties inflicted and families uprooted. For us, the threat takes a slapstick form. A softball designed for the blind, emitting a steady beep, sends the Nicaraguans scattering in fear of a time-bomb. On the way back from an exhibition in the hinterlands, our van often gets mired in puddles that have stretched to small ponds across the single, unmaintained lane of brown dirt. In the mountains, three hours from nowhere with darkness closing fast on the jungle, none of us dare speak our fears. If our UNAG driver Silvio doesn't get us through these washouts, we'll be easy picking for the *contras.* The whole team has to evacuate the Toyota and watch the moves of our most valuable player. Mission accomplished, he winks and flashes his gold-filled front teeth. In designer jeans and polo shirt, Silvio always looks dapper. Each morning, he rises an hour before the group to hose all the mud off his treasured vehicle. Near the end of the trip, I hear he first learned to handle a set of wheels as an ambulance driver. Life in Nicaragua is one controlled skid and Silvio, a wizard in a Red Sox cap, knows just when to spin his wheels.

Riding beside him is compañera Lisa Rosenthal. Like so many North Americans settled here, even those who have gained positions of trust, her presence in Nicaragua is almost entirely accidental. An aspiring modern dancer from L.A., Lisa came down on a summer tutoring program before the Sandinista uprising and has never been able to bring herself to leave. She has survived the siege of León and *contra* ambushes and come through looking like an advertisement for Jane Fonda's workout. Though she's not good at translating ground rules, she never falters in her account of Sandino's flight from the Marines. But this honorary Nicaraguan has also absorbed the Nicaraguan style—which dictates that militancy never get in the way of diversion. A nattering swirl of flirtation surounds the *gringita.*

The UNAG officials who accompany us are hardly the image of toughened cadres, either. The easiest way to spot what might be called a

Nicaraguan elite—that is, those who come from families that did not work with their hands—is to look for penny loafers and a chemise Lacoste. The architects of this new society seem to be frustrated preppies. Though they show a predilection for the front of the bus, they're easy about allowing the back to be filled with ever-changing passengers. Everyone in the country wants to hop a lift with a bunch of ballplayers. Coffee growers in Stetson hats pay their fare in sacks of fresh Matagalpa grind, one pound to a player. Out of nowhere, a painfully thin adolescent squeezes into the half-seat beside the back door, holding an official Little League scorebook so dog-eared it may have been passed down for generations. I never figure out if he's asked permission to act as our official scorer and play-by-play man. His mop-haired younger brother totes a briefcase filled with coils of thick wiring and an antiquated microphone, probably the first public address system invented. The gizmo must weigh a ton. The two kids get their biggest thrill when Blue Jay or Jeff pass along their Walkman headphones so they can hear something "really radical." Our Apollonian surfers look twice the size of the teenaged Nicaraguans. The brothers admire our American swagger and gadgetry the way we would like to admire ourselves.

We've recruited two ringers to make our team respectable: a pitcher and a shortstop, of course. On a moment's notice, they left their families and gas station jobs in Boaco and grabbed their mitts. They get free chow and two days, one frigid night at La Selva Negra (the Black Forest), a mountain resort known to honeymooners throughout the country. At a rum-swilling party in one of the rustic cabins, we even teach them how to play charades. "First word . . . a Broadway musical . . . on the nose!" Did somebody say there's a war going on? Only toward the end of the tour do our two new teammates let down their guard. "Everything's fine if you belong to the party," one whispers after too many beers. "If we could, we would follow you home. Don't you need a pitcher for your team in California?"

Our most useful recruit is an Arizona agronomist named Circles. I never learn if this is his real name or one of those visionary monikers with which people anointed themselves in the sixties. Circles doesn't look old enough to have seen the sixties, but he perfectly embodies their spirit. This Harvard-style hayseed in tortoiseshell glasses and neatly pressed coveralls reminds me of the first volunteers for the Freedom Rides through the South. Now he rides with us, tackling inequality on a global scale. Circles fills our heads with more than we'd like to know about the redistribution of arable land to the lower and middle peasants. At last he settles down to the task of reeducating the pugnaciously reactionary Arnold. As our van rolls through disputed territory, this odd couple goes toe-to-toe over the free market system, Che Guevara's true intentions in Bolivia, whether there's really any more difference between Democrats and Republicans than between Trotskyists and anarcho-syndicalists. Both seem delighted to have finally met their match. Arnold hasn't traveled this distance solely to revel in his son's strong throwing arm. By inclination and training, he's a devil's advocate. And he's come to Nicaragua because he can't get into a scrap like this in the suburbs of Virginia—though he'll probably use Circles's very arguments to shock and outrage his colleagues. Each day, the rest of us grow more convinced that the Republican lawyer is undergoing a change of party affiliation—and equally convinced that we'll be the last to hear of his conversion.

Arnold gets more "brainwashing," as he calls it, at interminable meetings in airless rooms. The life of a ballplayer can't be all fun and games and we've got to suffer question-and-answer sessions that lead to hours of ponderous oratory. Commissioner Carlos Cuadra, the Sandinista placed in charge of baseball, demurs at first when asked for a summary of his background, then traces his activist lineage back three generations in an hour-long digression. Cuadra reports dryly how his grandfather was murdered by the first Somoza, his father was driven to Costa Rica by the second Somoza. As a child of exiles, Cuadra's thoughts were "with Nicaragua twenty-four hours a day. I loved it though I didn't know it." Expelled himself after becoming a student militant, Cuadra says he was able to sneak back into the country only during the chaos of the '72 earthquake. A hundred hair-raising escapes so he could become the Commissar of Hardball! Like so much else in Nicaragua, Cuadra's tale would seem slanted to provoke sympathy if it weren't true.

After a few such sessions, our squad begins to mutiny. The great ideological schism within Baseball for Peace occurs one breakfast over the question of whether or not to show up for a scheduled audience with Vida Luz Menenses, a prominent poet who's Vice Minister of Culture under poet-priest Ernesto Cardenal. The popular position, championed by the two teenage boys, is that a team practice would be more useful than a discussion of poetics. Some argue that we mustn't insult our hosts by failing to attend planned activities. The majority counters that we insult them more by failing to give them a good game. Besides, asks this action faction, what does baseball have to do with culture? I'm one of the few who goes to seek an answer from the vice minister. She's a severe woman in her forties, who lectures from under the protection of dramatic, gray-streaked bangs. She raises the only laugh by trotting out the standard joke about the Ministry of Culture's headquarters: "This used to be one of the Somozas' mansions, and it has twelve bathrooms. We like to say that this is because the Somozas spent a great deal of time washing their hands." When she outlines the new government's efforts to revive and preserve native expression, I'm amazed to find that she counts baseball among them. "Like North American music, baseball is a cultural influence that will always be with us," the vice minister declares. "All we wish is for people to become educated so they can make their own choices."

There seems little choice at all in Matiguas, an archetypal mountain village of loose donkeys and gully-washed streets. After wandering across the block from the town ballfield, I share a doorsill with a bubbly old coot in a cowboy hat covered with mock leopard-skin. This farmer hasn't shaved in a week and looks like he's been on a bender for longer than that. As a conversation starter, he points to his crotch and wants to know how to make reference to the anatomical part *en inglés*. Before long, we're teaching each other introductory scatology. You say *"pendejo,"* I say "piece o' crap." A few buddies join us, acting all too merry in their involuntary indolence. The leopard man explains that they've all been smoking marijuana. He even says that there's *cocaína* for sale in these parts, a claim denied by Sandinista officials. This voice of Nicaraguan irreverence rubs his twinkling red eyes and asks the question I've been dreading all week. "Why do you bring us baseballs when we need spare parts for our Italian tractors?" For emphasis, he points toward a stalled rig in the middle of the street. "Do you know we haven't been able to lay irrigation ditches in a year? What good are bats and balls to people who are starving?"

The other men on the stoop nod. I can't tell if they're ranchers or winos. Maybe they're both. "We are slowly starving to death. There is nothing to be done about it." And they all have a good chuckle. "Tell your people back home that we are not Communists. The worst thing for farmers is Communism." But when I ask my stoopmate what he thinks of Somoza, he uses his thumb and forefinger to form the sign of the rifle. Like everyone you meet, he, too, claims to have fought with the *frente*. After our squad manages its first triumph—whipping a makeshift collection of farmhands who haven't laid their hands on gloves or bats since last year's harvest—my stoned friend joins most of the other town luminaries for a chicken-and-beans luncheon in the town's single dank corner tavern. He, too, raises the long-necked bottles of Victoria beer high when the town's Sandinista mayor, who would look quite at home along the Pecos with his pointy boots and checked cowboy shirt, offers another round of barroom histrionics. "When the *frente* began, we were only a few. And look now! We have become everyone! Your presence here today proves it. Once we were few, now we are the whole world!"

But how will the dirt streets bear the traffic? Half of Matiguas wears an imported T-shirt that reads, "My Job Is So Secret—Even I Don't Know What It Is." A perfect explanation for the town's condition. But the locals want more Americana to bear on their chests, and we soon begin our ritualized swapping, our cross-cultural transvestism. Though the wind from a sudden rainstorm whips through the open pillars of the dirty bodega, I strip off my shirt reading, "Billy Ball—Oakland A's" for the chance at a coarse Spandex jersey hand-lettered, "los Criollos." A former pitcher for the Dantos gives me the top he wore at the World Amateur Championships in return for a cheap nylon windbreaker that he's been eyeing enviously. We leave with the names of a dozen Nicaraguan towns on our chests, while those who wave us off have become adopted citizens of every major league city. But the relative positions of privileged and underprivileged can't be traded as readily as our uniforms. We're still the good Yankee traders, getting the best of the deal.

Yet our group's obstinate loyalty to childhood pursuits dovetails perfectly with the Nicaraguans' own Catholic trust in the power of innocence. No, call it an embrace of the naive. This upheaval supervised by priests and would-be saints had been one of the least vindictive in human history—with fewer than forty of Somoza's hatchet men executed or murdered in acts of retribution. "The only way we know we're on the right path is that we bear no bitterness," says Daniel Núñez, the head of UNAG, whose brother had just been killed by the *contras*. "And that is what makes us so certain that, in the end, you will be on the same path with us." The Nicaraguan idea is that we should all be as children—until the corruption and power-lust that whirls and plots on all sides has exhausted itself. Until the other side takes its fancy gear and its fragmentation bombs home because nobody will play with them.

Baseball for Peace does not become a real team until our first day off in the schedule. Like a bunch of veritable jocks, we vote to skip the Museum of the Revolution and head for the beach. Poneloya is a half-hour drive from León on the Pacific coast. From the size of type on our map, I expect a mammoth resort. In Nicaragua, as I should know by now, one abandoned hotel at the highway's dead end, all veranda and filigree work painted pink, constitutes a mammoth resort. Once the proprietor is found and awakened, he offers beer and, in an hour or two, lunch. Lisa's request for the local variety of sea bass elicits a long story about a group of village fishermen who've wandered too far out into international waters. They've been missing three days now. From the owner's deadpan tone, it's hard to tell if he thinks the fishermen have fallen prey to the sea or the *contras*. The war is just another excuse for being out of fish.

Not a promising start to our outing. Neither is the immense placard across the entrance to the beach, reading "Zona Peligrosa." There's more stencilled red print fading out underneath, but we get the idea. Cool yourself, gringo, at your own risk. Being gringos, we're willing victims of our own arrogance. Everyone plunges into the surf, a Marine amphibious assault going the wrong way. The breakers crest a good fifty feet out, offering a long ride in through coursing foam. Our group divides up between those beyond and those in front of the undertow. After ten minutes, one bobbing head seems a little far out into that inviting sea. Blue Jay has pushed his all-American indestructibility a stroke too far. The riptide will not let him return to Nicaragua's safe haven.

"A boat! *Una barca!*" Silvio's impish smile indicates that, unlike us, he is not prone to hysteria. Sure enough, within a few minutes, the boy finds a current that takes him to where he can swim in with the undertow, not against it. Blue Jay's father and grandfather sprint along the sand, leading the rest of us, until they can huddle once more with their young. They hug and cry in the shallows, three pale but tough terrier bodies cast from the same genetic mold, clad in boxer shorts and baseball caps gone soggy.

When lunch arrives at last, the team hoists its Victoria beers with greater purpose than ever. The waves become larger with each telling, the tide stronger. Despite the alcohol and the heat, everyone has spare adrenaline. Our captain goes to the bus for his pants, his mitt, and his spikes. He corners one of the barefoot Poneloyans. "Is there a field in this hellhole? *Dónde está el diamante?*"

Before we know it, we're being led through a scraggly papaya orchard toward a clearing of baked mud. Nicaraguan oxen, placid as Asian water buffaloes, graze in left field. The right field line is your basic malarial swamp. Behind home plate, our distant backstop is the bluish, cold-eyed cone of the volcano Momotombo. The infield is rutted, the bases wherever we imagine. Here the team stages its only true practice of the trip. And everyone responds by making the plays with a crazed sense of affirmation. After each miraculous backhand stab, we whip the ball round the horn, hit the right bases and the cutoff men, back each other up the way it says in the how-to manual none of us have ever read. Sweating and half-delirious from the heat, our khakis covered with splattered mud up to our knees, we revel in the crisp heaves and crazy hops. We stoop and pluck and toss how we've been taught by the dads here and the dads we carry with us. Captain Jay dubs this scabbed-over clearing of hardened chocolate pudding our "home field."

To be alive and pursuing the snaky twists of a hardball is consummate joy. A crowd of scrawny day laborers wanders over to watch the crazy foreigners. How can anyone play in the noonday sun? But this is not India and the natives are as mad as the mad dogs for the colonial game. Tiny, undernourished eight-year-olds dismount from tired ponies to take a turn with bats twice their size. Before long, we invite the Nicaraguans to take the field. Most of them outshine us. Though they've probably never played with such new balls or soft gloves, they're accustomed to the erratic bounces created by this ravaged, bursting piece of ground. "*Buenos manos,*" we shout, the universal baseball compliment. Having managed our own close escape, we're now more attuned to how the Nicaraguans live. In the midst of all this hostile lushness, the sight that pleases us most is our own survival. Having set our feet down at last in this looted land, the only landscape worth beholding is the human being.

Back on the bus, Captain Jay whips out his harmonica. He wants to teach us the turn-of-the-century tune sung by North American prospectors in Mexico which supposedly gave rise to the word *gringo*. As our van sloshes off into the sunset, we try a new version of "Green grow the lilacs all covered with dew." Our improvised lyrics begin, "We are the gringos who'll play ball with you. . . ."

THE FAMILY OF FAN

Who cares if the Crackerjacks have been replaced by cookies sprinkled with chili peppers? If the only hot dogs are the mangy kind who scrounge in the aisles? Or that pig-tailed señoritas hawk fried plantains, barefoot vendors move through the aisles balancing trays of iced cakes and enchiladas on their heads? This is the sort of evening for which this somnambulant game was invented, as hot and sultry as July on the prairie, even though it's January in the tropics. No matter that we're on the road to Chichigalpa instead of Flatbush Avenue. Or that this isn't Wrigley Field, but an anti-Yankee stadium named after the "Heroes and Martyrs of September." The only heroes that count here are the ones anointed by the previous inning. The punishment for martyrs will be our booing. Except for the herds of goats grazing near the bleachers, this could be a Norman Rockwell vision of the American heartland—so much in the heart that it's called Central America.

It takes a nation in its birth throes to show how our national pastime might have looked in the days before computerized scoreboards or press releases, Astroturf or covert operations. But could baseball or America have ever been this innocent? Are there proper terms left in our language for these bits of Iowa airdropped into the jungle? Call them glorified corrals, roofed cow pens, lost bullrings, petrified circus tents, lean-tos with turnstiles, creaky wooden horseshoes, park benches with lights (when there's electricity), bandshells that double as stables, lemonade stands with scoreboards, platforms that elevate the common man above the mud, but just barely, ungrand reviewing stands for lush mountains, way stations for farm boys to lounge in in their fatigues, prosceniums with the back wall removed, grounded canoes, slivers of shade, havens of indolence, temples to insouciance, monuments to impermanence. Nothing in Nicaragua qualifies as a superdome, a super-anything.

Yet an hour before game time, there's already a line before the one rusty gate to the grandstand. Mobs press against the face-sized square cutout in the clapboard facade that serves as a ticket booth. A seat in the grandstand costs 250 cordobas, about fifteen cents at the black market rate. This guarantees only a spot to stand through the game. Some of the more limber and resourceful rooters climb the netting behind homeplate. The single banked tier of wooden benches sags with the weight of too many *fanáticos*—a word which, even in this most politicized country, is reserved for this most apolitical and enduring of allegiances.

They've come early to crane their necks at the seemingly anarchic swirl of pregame warm-up rituals, no more easily observed than any form of magic. Before how many innings in how many parks have these same patterns swirled, these same autonomic routines of pepper and fungo gyrated? A flattering p.a. system broadcasts pregame interviews—but they have less to do with the starter's tender elbow than the condition of *"nuestro pueblo heroico"* and the *muchachos* at the front. Billboards cover the outfield fencing—these are nothing like the Ebbets Field trademark, "Hit This Sign and Win a Suit from Abe Feldman!" Beer ads alternate with exhortations to produce more for the sake of the *frente*, a Pepsi logo adjoins the anti-*contra* rallying cry, *"No Pasarán!"* Fewer than a hundred miles from the war front, baseball passes freely through enemy lines.

Our tour has come to León, first capital of Nicaragua and a seething university town that's always been the breeding ground of insurrections. "The hair on your head is hot, your thoughts are hot—believe me, Holy Week in León is hot!" Sandinista leader Omar Cabezas wrote in *Fire from the Mountains*, "All through Holy Week, the whores didn't fuck; the bars didn't open; the Chinese restaurants were shut. . . . León is hot. I'm not making this up." This heat-blanched, bullet-pocked, slanted tabletop of a town is renowned for two things: its militants and its crazed *béisbolistas*. No wonder León has one of the few municipal parks blessed with night lights. Or that León is where our delegation has been brought to witness our first Nicaraguan league game.

The Family of Fan

The phrase "Béisbol por la Paz" wafts over the loudspeakers—and wins applause from the few who can hear above the hubbub. Allowed onto the field, Barbara sprints on high-heeled espadrilles toward a brawny León pitcher. He sweeps her up and whirls her considerable womanhood in circles. I can't imagine what the León fans make of this indiscreet scene of international friendship. I try my Spanish on a batboy whose first language is English, of the sing-song Caribbean variety. He's from Bluefields, main town in the long-isolated Atlantic Coast region. The revolution has brought organized ball there for the first time. "Every day's a challenge in this job, brudda. But can you book me passage?" His ambitions are as impenetrable as his dialect. "Are the scouts coming, brudda? At least, this way, I eat every day." Whether he's daft or retarded, I'm never sure. Once the game gets going, I realize this team mascot doubles as a court jester. Each time a hitter's lumber is tossed aside along the first-base line, this oversized bat fetcher races from the dugout with a high-stepping urgency that sets off the crowd's delighted jeers.

Our Nicaraguan guides think they're doing us a favor by seating the group in a fenced-off pen beside a broadcast booth. But I'm determined to sneak down and take my place among the *mestizo* peanut gallery. Oddly, the avowedly antipopulist Arnold is the only one to join my escape. Though his motives may be different, he, too, bridles at our hosts' stage managing. With his fearsome blue eyes and a giant schnozz beak that make him look like a big, bad bald eagle, Arnold draws the attention of Nicaraguans wherever he goes. Once he's loosed his power necktie, changed into a floppy madras shirt and straw planter's hat, Arnold is a different man. It must be a relief to let down all that status. None among us banters so easily or has his common touch. He helps me squeeze into a row behind home plate that looks like it can handle two more customers.

The local boys are thrilled to have us in their midst. In outlying Jinotega, most of the bleacher bums wear tasselled Stetsons or olive-drab camouflage suits. This largely male, mostly beer-bellied bunch looks much like their rooting counterparts in the Northern Hemisphere, modeling a standard uniform of blue jeans and jogging shoes and caps bearing the anointed initials of far-off cities—St.L., S.D., S.F. . . . . I notice my T-shirt reads, "No Lights in Wrigley Field!" I'm ready to air out my lungs with boos and catcalls just like these brethren in denim. The level of *entusiasmo*, they assure me, is nothing compared to the old

209

days. The backstop netting functions as protection from foul balls—not, as in other Latin countries, to shield the players from projectiles hurled by the disgruntled rabble. Alcohol is no longer sold in the ballpark. There's far less drunkenness and less open gambling than elsewhere on the Caribbean circuit. Since the revolution, the demeanor of the crowds has become markedly more fraternal. From Emigdio Siqueiros we've already learned that first-division players must take exams on decorum and sportsmanship. "We're all brothers in the struggle," he says. "It's considered impolite to be abusive to the umpires." Tonight's pregame procession of black-swathed, black-hearted judges brings only a swell of mutterings, a pale imitation of the red-blooded fan's antiauthoritarian response. This "socialist ball" also entails far more extensive collective conferring on the mound. In critical situations, even the outfielders trot in from their posts to partake fully in the nonsectarian strategizing, perhaps a round of self-criticism.

The main reason for the fans' new-found decorum may not be ideological, but a dearth of action to get rabid over. We're watching the two best teams in the first division, yet the play is ragged and often downright inept. The forced transformation of the Nicaraguan league from professional to amateur footing has lowered the quality several notches. While salaried teams here were once stocked with Cubans, Dominicans, and North Americans, the talent is now homegrown and poorly coached. These players can't get any better without the goad of imported competition. Even the best among them must hold down part-time jobs to maintain their nonprofessional status. "And," Commissioner Cuadra has reminded us, "just think of the *compañeros* who might have big-league ability but must now put a gun in their hands instead of a bat!"

Over the past three seasons, teams run by UNAG have lost a hundred and seventy players from their rosters. In a country where everyone who can get his hands on a ball is likely to use it, regional championships have been postponed or cancelled for lack of playing talent. The commissioner overseeing thirty regional leagues was killed by the *contras*. The ranks of the nation's first-division clubs have been likewise depleted. The rationing of electricity has recently forced the cancellation of many night games. Maintaining any semblance of organized ball is an ongoing battle, a kind of second front. "One day, all soups become cold," runs a Nicaraguan proverb the fans like to repeat. "And when this war's over, we'll field the greatest ball team in Central America." How better to envision the benefits of peace?

Given much to groan about and little to gloat over, these men in Expos and Brewers caps have no choice but do what fans do best: reminisce. Our presence among them stimulates a nostalgic round of tall tales. Each fellow in turns wants to show off his knowledge of *las ligas grandes*. The names spill out, nearly transformed but always translatable: Pete Ros-ey, Y-ohnny Bench, Reggie Yack-son. I dare not break it to my rooting compatriots that most of the superstars they name have long since retired. One old-timer recalls seeing Mickey Mantle and Roger Maris, and another tops him by claiming to have witnessed the swat of "Baby" Ruth. And every man in my row says he was there when Marv Throneberry, that buffoon with the fledgling New York Mets, hit the longest home run ever in Managua Stadium. "Marvelous Marv!" the Nicaraguans croon.

The story is repeated of how the National Guard was put on full alert when three North American players (including future A's manager Steve Boros) were reported missing after a fishing trip to Lake Nicaragua. These idols of the day ended up swimming to safety—unaware that this was the world's only fresh-water lake infested with killer sharks. There is still talk about the exhibition played here by the Baltimore Orioles in 1982, the most recent visit of major leaguers. Others harken back to the halcyon year of '72, when the country last hosted the World Amateur Championships. Staging this baseball extravaganza was quite a coup for the Somoza regime, so much so that the brief period of political grace between the end of the games and the massive Managua earthquake was jokingly dubbed, "the five days of Somocismo."

While this game between León and the Dantos unravels, my newfound experts rattle off a roll call of the Nicaraguan *inmortales*: Stanley Cayasso, the local "Iron Horse," and Manolo Cueto, called "el Hombre Diablo," and everyone's favorite play by play man, Sucre Frech. León, they say, was known for its Cuban players and rival Granada for its Americanos. The León fans used to scare the gringos by tossing iguanas with firecrackers tied to their tails onto the field. I hear, too, about the ongoing grudge rivalry between the two Managua teams. Boer, Nicaragua's oldest continuous franchise, named by its North American founders after the South African settlers who were seen as heroes in the fight against the British, was the people's choice and perennial underdog.

211

Their enemy, the Cinco Estrellas, or Five Stars, was owned and stocked by the Somoza family. Now the Sandinista army's Dantos entry has taken over the role of perennial government powerhouse. The standing of their sponsored ball team is no less a sign of the gods' blessing for those who rule Nicaragua than floods and earthquakes were for the dynasties of China.

"The fact that baseball is being played in the middle of a war against us by the U.S. is another triumph for the Nicaraguan people," President Daniel Ortega has said. He knows first-hand the ideological uses of baseball from the days when he'd root for the Boer against Somoza's Five Stars. Each season mounted, every game broadcast, is an advertisement for the stability of his regime and an important tool in upholding morale. Yet in baseball, as in foreign relations, Nicaragua has had to accept ostracism. If countries were grouped in leagues, then this one went from Double-A back to the instructional level. And the *aficionados* know this. Rather than applaud the efforts of their restructured sports industry, they complain about everything from errant throws and missed signs to the inconsistency of the Nicaraguan-made balls. For the true *fanático*, this revolution has been a mixed blessing.

The León boosters express their baseball politics through an unusual variant of ballyard gossip. Snickerings reach me that a pallid-looking second-string catcher is the illegitimate offspring of a local Baseball Annie and some famous *pelotero* from the North. Gleefully, they repeat the rumor that León's freckled left fielder has major league DNA in his chromosomes. Whispers attest to a blue-eyed shortstop's genetic predisposition for crisp singles. If the stories are to be believed, then the rosters of Nicaragua are sprinkled with the unwanted products of touring ballplayers' local flings. There is the uncontestable example of Brant Alyea, Jr., fathered by the "player-to-be-renamed later," spirited out of the country by Dominican scout Epy Guerrero to fulfill his ballplaying destiny. Baseball's conquerors, like any other kind, have left behind bastard children in their own image.

What my fellow boosters want from me, though they're too polite to ask, are Topps and Fleer baseball cards. When I whip out these pocket-sized gifts, the boisterous men beside me grow wide-eyed and admire my handouts like packets of fairy dust. They thank me on behalf of their young sons, the *muchachos* of León, though they are the ones who'll most value these new shreds of sporting evidence. To remind everyone

212

how far Nicaraguan baseball has strayed from the major-league variety, tonight's contest ends when a pitcher fails to back up a throw to home plate. This transgression of the fundamentals would have been inexcusable in the old days. Have the Sandinistas made these fans their latest "heroes and martyrs"? And will we follow suit by trying to take possession of these pitching mounds and bullpens, dropping bombs on a nation of ballfields? Is it possible that these gents in their caps may yet find themselves fighting *mano a mano* against another uniformed team from up North? If the bleacher bums of León are the enemy, then it's only more proof that the enemy is ourselves.

RUNNING BACKWARDS

"**T**he revolution begins in prison,"
Emigdio reminds us from his seat on the hump beside the driver. On a
hazy, hot morning, we're heading north of Managua to the country's
main penitentiary for the second annual interns' baseball championships.
The place is set on a flat brown moonscape. Nothing grows for miles
around. Beyond the discouragement of this landscape, there are few
obstacles to escape. The guardhouse, painted in diagonal candy stripes,
might be the keeper's house of a quaint rural drawbridge.

I find it hard to believe that Somoza staged interrogations here. Yet in
"The Centerfielder," the moral tale by Nicaraguan Vice President
Ramírez, a ballgame between prisoners is used to cover the torture and
execution of a former star on the national team: "He was a baseball
player, so make up anything you like. Say he was playing with the other
prisoners, that he was in center field and chased a hit down to the wall,
then climbed up an almond tree and jumped over the wall. Put down
that we shot him as he was escaping across the slaughterhouse yard."
Today, the sandstone retaining barriers are hung with drooping pennants,
some stenciled with the crude silhouette of a ballplayer clutching a bat.
They look lower and easier to leap over than Wrigley Field's ivy-covered
confines.

Locks and chains are simply antithetical to *el estilo nicaragüense*. Head
counts are surely not their strong suit. There is also something incongruous about jails in a tropical climate. In these balmy regions where shelter

214

from the elements seems a largely irrelevant exercise, this ultimate form of sequestration stands exposed in all its absurdity. The concrete flanks of holding cells, visible for miles across the parched plateau, look like giant radiators. The gray lookout towers seem better suited to the angry, wintry skies of Illinois. But this isn't Joliet, it's Tipitapa. And the convicts aren't out breaking rocks, they're playing ball.

"Sport—A Factor in Mental Rehabilitation," was the slogan I'd seen painted at the entrance to Havana's Psychiatric Hospital. A showplace of Cuban progress, this site among rolling, suburban hills had been transformed into a veritable country club for the chronically disturbed—mostly by patients who cut lawns and trimmed hedges with obsessive fervor. Though psychotherapy and calming drugs are applied, the major therapy in a country once noted for its joblessness is work. But play is not forgotten. Along the far turn of an excellent quarter-mile cinder track, I saw patients taking up positions in the starting blocks, pantomiming their own starter's guns, then repeating frenzied twenty-yard dashes, arms flailing. On the grass in the oval, an elderly man with a shaved head was working hard to improve his distance with a javelin. In the hospital's main parking lot, a dozen or so inmates were being put through calisthenics by attendants in white coats. The jumping jacks were poorly coordinated, but the patients were holding short wands with multicolored pom-poms on the end. This hospital possessed athletic facilities that would be the envy of small American colleges and also provided its own cheerleaders.

And the baseball complex turned out to be bigger than the administration building. Yes, a stadium, complete with refreshment stands, an electric scoreboard, a fully enclosed grandstand, three hundred thirty feet down the lines, capacity approximately fifteen thousand. When it came to treating schizophrenia, was this diamond part of the solution or part of the problem? The well-clipped field was empty, but I tried to imagine the games where the positions were filled by true *fanáticos*. Maybe the hospital boasted its own Jimmy Piersall, running the bases backwards. That same evening of our tour, I saw the hospital staff play a game in the Estadio Latinoamericano, the biggest park in Cuba. The shrinks in this country played hardball. Final score: *Siquiatras* 9, Sane Opponents 0.

The Sandinistas, too, are unequivocal: Their new society can be judged by how well its marginal elements get into the lineup. "We challenge you to visit a prison in Texas," says a polo-shirter who may be

215

the warden, "and see if the Chicanos are allowed to come out and have a game." Despite the sweltering heat, it's standing room only along the foul lines of the two ragged diamonds drawn in a vast table of crumbling red chalk. Teams of convicts from six regions are in the midst of final playoffs. Their fans behave as though the outcome's a matter of life and death. Maybe it is. *Los internos* scream and howl at each bungled grounder and screeching line drive. Runners who cross the plate fall straight into the arms of delirious supporters who hoist their heroes high as a way to make plain the score. These boosters are decked out in blue cotton pajamas, stamped on the back with the white roman numeral of their district jail. Only their headgear is individualized. The most popular caps advertise Chevron and Levi-Strauss. Men and women, blacks and whites, prisoners and guards mingle. Some snooze in the shade of the prison walls, including a few officers with pistols in their holsters.

No ballgame in talkative Latin America is complete without a continuous play-by-play. This time, an intent inmate with pointed goatee takes up the task. *"Dos es-strikes, todos esperan. . . ."* Two strikes, everyone waits—on this field where everyone's waiting for release, the game's built-in pauses become deliciously palpable. Through a single raspy loudspeaker, the announcer bathes each name in the captive lineup with unchallenged adulation. *"Un doble tremendo para Francisco Ramírez Godoy, el gran bateo excepcional!"* He competes with an impromptu band squatting along the first base line. The group plays "Pallo de Mayo," a Calypso-style beat originated on the Atlantic coast by descendants of runaway West Indian slaves. To guitar and bongoes, the inmates dance in jerky and familiarly African thrusts. Whether male with female or male with male, their movements are frankly sexual, an open parody of mating that turns to coitus interruptus when foul balls whisk past. Hoping for a song to take home with me, I push my way into the mass of clapping revelers that surround the musicians sitting cross-legged near the on-deck circles, jamming in the dust. The first lyrics I hear are "Day-o! Day-ay-ay-o!" Moldy Belafonte oldies in Nicaragua Libre. The prisoners go wild to "Matilda, she took the money and run Venezuela. . . ."

Under a thatched stand, a bucket of beers waits on ice for the dignitaries. We're free to wander where we choose. Behind the backstops bedecked with banners declaring this glorious *campeonato*, I chat with prisoners who say they're well-fed and well-treated. As part of a gradual program of release, many are granted monthly home furlough. No torture, they tell me—and they get to practice baseball three times a week! Plenty of time to work on the fundamentals, and to polish their alibis. One fellow tells me he was forced to change dollars on the black market because he could not live on his schoolteacher's salary. When some of his bills were found to be counterfeit, he got three years. But most of the men in blue mutter a single word to explain their presence here: *Guardia*. Somoza's National Guard. One is so delicate and frail, I can hardly believe this Cantinflas caricature once served as a ruthless enforcer of the dictatorship. Then I notice a half-moon indentation in his skull held together with miscolored strands of skin grafts. He mutters ominously through gritted teeth, "We have a saying that in the mountains, everything can change. . . ."

Undoubtedly, a few will run to those mountains when released and sign on with the *contras*. Yet the Sandinista officials keep stressing their commitment to a penal system based on "human considerations." They have even saved a few of our donations for the prisoners' use. The last of our helmets and balls are spread out like a banquet atop the hood of a jeep. Another ceremony is required, and a designated spokesman for the prisoners steps forward, accepting our equipment with the same dignity and grace shown by prior recipients. "Your act is an encouragement for all of us," he says. Before we've had time to think about what we might be encouraging, another band strikes up, this one officially sanctioned. The prison resounds with trumpets and a decidedly Latin beat. The music is the only thing that distracts the men from the games. The inmates take turns leaping into a circle of dancers to show off their quickest, hottest stutter steps. But the person they want to coax into the spotlight is Lisa, our translator. They don't know that she was once a devotee of Martha Graham, just that she's the only woman in tight blue jeans within a fifty-mile radius. Lisa hesitates at first—less out of modesty than a highly rasied consciousness about exactly which sector of Nicaraguan society should get to see her shake her booty. Eventually she takes a turn to give the boys a thrill. The rest of us follow the conga line as best we can.

The prison officials look on approvingly at this finale. "Just remember," the Tipitapa warden reminds us, "those who were dancing, all former National Guard. Today you danced with the *Guardia*. . . ." From a few dark slits in the main holding tank, faces strain to watch. Among them may be Eugene Hasenfus, the pilot of a CIA-sponsored arms-running operation, whose capture set in motion the revelations of the Contragate scandal. Everywhere we go, the Nicaraguans assure us that Hasenfus will soon be set free. They see no purpose in taking out their anger on such a hired lackey. But when we ask whether he'll be among today's rooters, the warden winks and answers, "Who can say? We don't know whether or not he likes baseball."

SUNDAY IN THE PARK
WITH HUMBERTO

If more confirmation is needed that baseball and Nicaraguan history are irrevocably intertwined, we get it at Managua's National Stadium. Originally named after Somoza Number One, the current government pointedly rechristened their inherited showplace the Estadio Rigoberto López Pérez, in honor of the same Somoza's assassin. An equestrian statue glorifying Somoza Number Two that once stood at the home plate entrance was toppled in one of the first acts celebrating the dictatorship's demise. All that remains today is the pedestal.

Closed for over a decade due to earthquake damage, the park reopened to national jubilation. The Sandinistas haven't been able to contribute much beyond structural reinforcement. This is about as much ballpark as a boycotted, war-stricken ex–banana republic can buy. There are real press boxes, plenty of ads for Radio Sandino, the nation's snazziest electric scoreboard, outfield grass lush as the distant hills. The field doubles as the country's main track-and-field facility and the ring of cinder lanes around the playing area makes the foul area huge, the spectators far removed. The stands are a single sweep of concrete tier: This is a land without a second deck, without elevators. The front gates are busted, the stadium rampways urine-saturated; a crooked, hand-printed sign reading "Home Plate" marks the entrance to the box seats.

Four erector-set stanchions punctuate the enclosure. But these are Constructivist sculptures, mere homages to industry reaching toward the

219

socialist sky. There are no banks of lights mounted on the towers. When we ask Commissioner Cuadra about the delay in completion, he explains that the country has only one crane capable of hoisting stadium lights. "One hundred and fifty feet is an enormity to us." The critical piece of machinery has been allocated for electrical installations in the country-side during the past year. The *comandantes* may be fans, but they do have their priorities. The crane has now been brought out in our honor, but it is not at work.

Neither is Managua. This airless Sunday seems best suited for sitting through a doubleheader, yet we find the stadium half-empty. One explanation is an outdoor Eucharist mass that Mother Teresa is conducting the same afternoon. But I doubt that one would draw fans away from the other. A baseball man has room in his life for only one faith. I prefer the rationale that the visiting San Fernando club is one of the weaker in the league, and not a traditional rival of Managua. Scheduled to go seven innings, both games turn out to be scorchers decided in the bottom of the "extra" ninth. The action even features the first brouhaha we've seen under revolutionary auspices. It all begins with a beef over a bad strike call. The Dantos' manager gets the heave-ho after wiping the plate clean so the man in blue can see it more clearly. Afterwards, to the delight of the home crowd, the burly manager scurries from the dugout to offer the ump a pair of spectacles.

Directly behind home, separated from the rabble by a waist-high barrier, a government party occupies box seats. In this section, the vendors have been replaced by plainclothes bodyguards. Captain Jay whispers that we're sharing our section with Minister of Defense Humberto Ortega, brother of President Daniel Ortega. I don't feel remiss for my ignorance, since he is one of the least photographed of a leadership whose attitudes toward photo opportunities is what one might expect from people who've spent much of the formative years of their lives in hiding. Actually, Humberto Ortega is to Daniel almost exactly what younger brother Raúl Castro is to Fidel. Darker, squatter, less outgoing, but, one has the feeling, more steeled, more comfortable in the trappings of power. Humberto, like Raúl, represents the single-minded side of the political personality which the older sibling softens with charm. But Humberto resembles his presidential brother in his enthusiasm for baseball. After pitching an army team to a win over a squad of Nicaraguan sportswriters, the minister of defense was asked if he regretted not

220

having become a ballplayer. He is quoted as answering, "I *am* a ball-player. Didn't you just see me pitch nine innings?"

Of course, Cuba's hard-thrower has always been more of a baseball extremist, interrupting Cuban league games to take a turn on the mound. In the article "I Batted against Fidel Castro," Cincinnati infielder Don Hoak describes a winter-league encounter with *el presidente's* fastball. Rumors persist that the young law student was pursued by scouts from the New York Giants. Others claim that Fidel wrote Washington Senators' owner Clark Griffith requesting a tryout. Was Latin American history changed for want of a better off-speed pitch? We forget that the Havana Sugar Kings were a franchise of our International League—Cuba was what made it international—until 1960. The club was expelled on the pretext that the ballpark had become too dangerous, after a Rochester player was grazed by a bullet from gunfire in the stands celebrating the revolution's first anniversary. Before the island raised its own heroes, some of Cuba's greatest idols had been ballplayers like George Sisler and Joe DiMaggio. "I would like to take the great DiMaggio fishing," Hemingway's old man of the sea muses. "They say his father was a fisherman. Maybe he was as poor as we are, and would understand."

In the rows behind the younger Ortega are his children and the children of the president. They look well-groomed and well-behaved, a bunch of private-school kids on a field trip, nibbling peanuts intently. Everyone seems ballpark relaxed, though their outing is enveloped in security forces. When I leave our group to photograph the stadium's crude mortar patchwork exterior, I discover that the VIP entrance is patrolled by two ticket-takers cradling AK-47's. The phrase Béisbol por la Paz is pure gibberish to these Praetorian ushers. And I have no stub to show. A soldier asks me firmly, but with an apologetic smile, to vacate the area. My pacing, while I try to figure out what to do with the rest of my Sunday, provokes the suspicion of troops stationed before army jeeps in the parking lot. Again, I try in vain to explain about my delegation. But I don't try too hard. In fact, once I realize I've been banished from the ballpark, I feel liberated. I've been granted an afternoon free of guides or games.

But where else is there to go in Managua? This is a city in appearance only, a mock capital with a downtown gutted by earthquake. The few oases of tourist luxury are set amidst slopes of unreclaimed rubble; the cathedral sits roofless; the former Bank of America headquarters, tallest skyscraper in the country, remains unsafe for occupancy; the accumulated wealth in the markets adds up to no more than that of a medium-sized K-Mart. The rum bottles decorating our hotel bar proved empty, the hotel pool "closed for chemical treatment"—for years! Even gigantic Lake Managua was left so polluted by Somoza that it is now useless except as scenic backdrop. This seat of world subversion is a daily threat to itself.

The only other show in town is Mother Teresa, appearing live. Years ago, I'd made the pilgrimage to her Calcutta Home for the Dying Destitute—a modest corner office divided into two tiled rooms where beggars lounged on low cots waiting for the final handout. Today, as in India, I have to ask a cabbie to locate this saint of the starved. He takes me across Managua to a relatively suburban neighborhood, then points me in the general direction of the open lot where mass will be celebrated to mark the end of a week-long Eucharist convocation. For blocks around, the streets are occupied by a slow-advancing, eerily quiet phalanx of believers. It's standing-room only in the field. My Nikon and notebook get me one of the best seats in the house. The edge of the dignitaries' platform offers an upper-deck view of the processionals of bishops and cardinals, white-clad nuns marching in formation. On the podium, the clerics in their finest vestments are gathered before long tables laden with goblets. All in black, with peaked black hats reaching into the suddenly threatening sky, they're a brood of vampires. The Mother comes in like the headline act: by the back way, with more nuns of her blue-striped order as roadies. Once she takes her seat, I grab my camera and make like one of the paparazzi. They're clicking their motor-drives. Mother Teresa fiddles with her rosaries. She's alone with her God. She has the face of a tortoise trying to decide whether or not it's safe to cross the road.

I'm in the presence of another Nicaragua, one that's slightly better dressed and more female. Dangling crucifixes and big purses, mother-daughter teams strain to catch a glimpse of their prelates with a more disciplined fervor than their menfolk display while following a double in the corner. The woman wear kerchiefs on their heads for piety's sake, but what sticks up to punctuate the rolling waves of heads are hundreds and hundreds of North American baseball caps. About half are Yankees, half Reds. The crowd may number five thousand, a moderate show of strength for the Catholic opposition. This urban, tradition-bound Nicaragua does not disquiet me as much as I'd expected. These people do not look so privileged that they'd defend the old way at all costs. It's not blind habit that grips these people, it's the notion that their private crucifixions must not be in vain. Black clouds close in on the ceremonies, but this sort of faith does not take a rain-check

In the meantime, our tour has its climactic audience. In a country where politicians don't just throw out the first pitch but stay until the last pop fly, Defense Minister Ortega's party and our contingent file out together. On tape, I hear the *comandante* say that this was certainly "a lucky meeting." Through a translator, Ortega speechifies, softly but with labored formality, "In spite of the current difficulties between our two countries, we believe our people have the right to enjoy themselves." *El derecho de divertirse.* "And we love baseball like you do. It is our preferred sport." So what else is new? "This stadium suffered damages in the earthquake, but with the efforts of the revolution, we have made it earthquake-proof. We're trying to put up lights, because it's not so hot at night." Tell them that in Chicago. "We thank you for your work. Sports should unite us. The only way we want to compete with the United States is through baseball. If the U.S. presence has left us something beautiful, it's baseball." And isn't baseball the best that the U.S. has given the members of Baseball for Peace? I see heads nodding all around when the minister of defense says, "We'll have no problems in the future, if only they'll leave us beautiful things like this. . . ."

WE REJECT SADNESS

Baseball for Peace plays its last game on the field of our dreams. The diamond at San Dionisio awaits us denuded of all previous connotation, torn out of all cultural context. It's a muddy cow pasture four hours down a dirt road into Wonderland, it's Magritte's pipe captioned, *"Ce n'est pas une pipe."* Nicaragua may be a poem, but after ten days, it's one delirious stream-of-consciousness in which we no longer know where America ends, where our own skin begins. The grandstand that encircles us is made of hills covered with a mossy green so lush they pulsate. Hemming in yet another disputed valley, these stubby volcanic peaks are obscured by a steamy mist, white as slabs of dry ice. These bleached clouds ring our field like curious spectators, a dewy knothole gang that can't afford to get any closer to the soil's warm, dirty action. Forget the Elysian Fields of Hoboken, where the Knickerbocker Club tried out the first nine innings of "New York rules." This has got to be the most beautiful place where anyone's ever attempted baseball.

Our locker room is the van, pulled over into a ditch. Our opponents are a squad of weekend jocks not unlike ourselves. Out of nowhere, *campesinos* in knee-high rubber boots, coveralls, and John Deere caps crowd the foul lines. They don't cheer, just squint at the spectacle in wary silence. Toothless old men hold hands with young boys. Little girls in black braids materialize, handmaidens of the mist. These miniature misplaced *infantas* with flowers behind their ears have to touch us to see

224

if we're real. Giggling in amazement, they politely cover their mouths with both hands. When we ask them their names, they die of embarrassment.

The contest turns into a sloppy, mucky brawl. After three innings, all the players' patchwork uniforms are blackened to mid-thigh. Trying to make wide turns in the mud, both teams waddle their way toward solid ground, gasp for breath, spin out. Milling about behind first base with the rest of the substitutes, I want to do more than trade winks with local cuties or guard our equipment bags from antisocial elements. By this last game, I cannot squelch a desire to throw myself into the fray. A trip to Nicaragua, after all, is all about getting off your spectatorial buns and into the playoffs of history. For North Americans, the whole country is one big singathon of leftist ditties—where "Which Side Are You On?" is more than a question about whether you hit right or left. Audience participation is the rule at this concert. Everybody join hands and clap along, build that school, dig that irrigation ditch. Maybe this trip isn't going to change the world or my life as much as I would like, but it does force this one tangible act. Nicaragua gets everyone into the game.

When Captain Jay calls for pinch hitters, I am the first volunteer. Later, in his infinite one-liner wisdom, Ben Feldman terms my act "bravery beyond the limits of intelligence." But how can I call myself an expert unless I've experienced firsthand the sting left in one's grip by a slider that bores inside and "chops the bat off"? How dare I scoff at some second-stringer for "putting his foot in the bucket" when a curveball comes breaking toward his head unless I'm convinced I wouldn't do the same? Being a fan, of course, means having every right to insist, with indignation, that others achieve regularly what we could never execute once. But I'm too intoxicated by this pickup game in heaven. Besides, the score's actually close.

"Okay, Juanito, let's get up there!" I'm wrenched out of one dream into another. I'm entertaining visions of unlocking the two-two tie with one mighty blow when Jay barks out as gruffly as John J. McGraw, "Let's put a little lumber on the ball!" Everyone's waiting for the next hitter. The burly *campesino* on the mound has his hands on his hips to indicate disgust at the delay. The farm boys along the foul lines have already begun to titter. I scurry back and forth like one of their roosters, trying to find a bat that feels less than leaden in my grip. Jay reminds me to put on a batting helmet, but I'm so flustered I can't remember whether or not it goes over my felt Oakland A's cap. When the peanut gallery begins clucking and whistling, I can tell I've made the wrong decision. This helmet wobbling and tottering atop the bill of my cap certainly does feel peculiar. I'm still thinking about amending my error in haberdashery while I try to take a comfortable stance in the mud.

Suddenly, the volcanic backdrop blurs away. I am at one end of a tunnel with a third-string *lanzador* at the other, toeing the rubber. After thirty years of analysis from behind the backstop screens and batting cages, it's time to step out front and face the full fury of the game I profess to love. I take my stance against the back edge of the batter's box and decide to keep my aluminum bat on my shoulders—my lethal weapon in its scabbard—until I've gauged the relative speed of the pitcher. I wish I had a Juggs gun reading. I hardly see the ball, just hear it strike the catcher's mitt. The crouched *receptor* has set an outside target, just beyond the arc of my futile swipes. I find myself thinking, "That's cheating, isn't it?" Yet I'm powerless to answer the strategy. Wonder of wonders, the ball comes just a tad further inside and up. I take a giant whack that seems to unfold in slow motion. Fans call this the rusty gate—a swing ascribed to aging veterans who've lost the reflexes to get around on a fastball. How can I lose what I never had? Somehow, I get a piece of the ball to barely graze the end of the bat-handle. A murmur of approval rises behind me. Or is it just the scattering of livestock?

I don't have time to check. The pitcher rocks back, then toward me. It seems to me that I recoil just slightly as the next pitch tails inside, though witnesses later assure me that my reflexes did not appear to have been the least bit activated. The ball hits me squarely above my left elbow. I do not react. I'm still thinking about how sissified I must look in my double-decker headgear. I'm also waiting for the umpire's unnecessary confirmation of the thud made by ball against bone. More laughter from the peasants—even if it's out of solidarity, people laugh when you slip on a banana peel. Captain Jay shrieks from the on-deck circle, "Go to first, man! Take your base!" I'm so stunned that I've forgotten the rules.

All at once, I recall my very first time playing with the "big kids" in the Sunday morning softball game. Grounding out to end the game, I had run out my weak effort by running far past first base, running all the way off the field and home without ever looking back. It's not the *contras* who've caught up with me. I've fallen prey not to some back-roads ambush, but to a beaning in broad daylight. How many times over the years has Don Baylor or Ron Hunt been hit in worse places by pitches twice as fast? "Sacrificing your body," it's called. Compared to theirs, mine isn't much to sacrifice. What heights of masochism pro athletes regularly scale! Fear of the ball is something every successful player must overcome. I've written so on several occasions. The intimidation factor, the threat of reprisal with the close pitches, known as "chin music" in baseball lingo, is at the core of each game's unseen strategy. Now I know of what I have spoken. While I try to act nonchalant on the base paths, take my lead, and listen for the barking encouragement of our first base coach, I've got pins-and-needles from my shoulder down. I don't want the *macho* crowd to catch me rubbing myself or whining, but when I run a few discreet tests, I find that I can't move my fingers or raise the arm more than a few inches. Mercifully, the inning ends with the next batter. I tell Jay that I can't lift my glove high enough to take the field. "Okay, kid, you're on the disabled list."

Though my travels aren't quite through, my hardball career is over after a single at-bat. At least my lifetime record will show that I got on base. Grandpa Ben, now the team trainer as well as mascot, begins to knead the bruise vigorously, viciously it seems, to keep the swelling down. The skin above the elbow is one raised, pink grapefruit. Bench-warmer Bill runs back to our bus for some Ben-Gay, but I pass on his offer of Percodan. "What you really need is some ice," the bench-jockeys suggest. *Buena suerte!* Good luck, kid! We're at least fifty miles from the nearest refrigeration.

I can hardly get my shirt off the rest of the trip. Taking a shower—especially a cold one—is no fun at all. But I dare not bring down team morale. And how can I whine to the Nicaraguans, who've suffered wounds more grievous and permanent? Still, each time our two Nicaraguan ringers see me, they rub their own elbows sympathetically. Our group's only veteran hardballers could easily downplay or dismiss my injury. Instead, they're the ones who choose to acknowledge pain. They know all about the sting of the ball. They do not turn away from their fellows, or from the frailties held in common. In Nicaragua, in all Latin America, sooner or later everyone's on the disabled list.

Our farewell dinner is held at an outdoor nightclub that must once have been a swank Somocista hangout, complete with live calypso band and thatched cabanas overlooking a lagoon. Beat and cranky, I find myself seated beside the one member of our entourage to whom I've never been introduced, a baggage-carrier with a rutted *indio* face. He speaks not a word of *inglés*. An evening of forced smiles and nonverbal awkwardness looms. But it turns out this Chico Pintura, as he's nicknamed, is a self-taught artist who does all the sign-painting for UNAG. In place of sign-language, he draws caricatures of the group on his napkin. Each one is more hilarious than the next. His favorite subject is Arnold, and I see why. Chico Pintura draws the outlines of the lawyer's dome in rear view, like Mt. Baldy risen between two shoulders and adds pointy undersized leprechaun ears. With sand beneath, the shape is captioned, in Spanish, "Arnold at the Beach." With waves beneath, "Arnold in the Water." *Perfecto!* At our corner of the dais, we're laughing so hard that we forget to eat. On the last napkin of the evening, Chico Pintura, still chuckling, sketches the item he wants most in life: an ordinary, art-supply-store airbrush.

"In 1522," wrote the monk Las Casas, "the foresaid Governour went to subdue the Province of Nicaragua. There is no man that can sufficiently express the fertility of this Island, the temperateness of the air, or the multitude of people that did inhabit it. . . . And therefore they endured the far greater misery and persecution and underwent a more unsufferable slavery, being the less able to bear it, by how much they were of a mild and gentle nature. . . ." Though the conquerors have changed, the people haven't. Through centuries of subjugation, the Nicaraguans have had much practice at savoring life's smaller pleasures. Small, but never petty. Ignorance, greed, class violence—those are the small-making things, the demons to be laughed off.

"We're a little country with a big heart," is the way Commissioner Carlos Cuadra puts it. To the very last moment of the farewell, he clutches our arms and will not let go—a Marxist ideologue unafraid to act like a little boy losing his favorite playmates. "Please think of our country as a reservoir of humanity for the whole world to draw upon!" Despite the skepticism I brought with me, I can hardly do otherwise. I've been won over.

Maybe that's why I feel strangely resigned when genuine disaster threatens us. Though our tour group has been assured from the beginning that we'll never be out on the roads at night, we've run late on our last road trip. On the main highway back to Managua, a huge fireball explodes in the dark several hundred yards ahead. At that moment, a

We Reject Sadness

teammate and I are sprawled in the back row, relaxed as two campers coming home from the summer, arguing over the cause of Red Sox Bill Buckner's fatal World Series bobble. "Did you hear why Bill Buckner was late for spring training? He was going to catch the train, but it went through his legs. . . ." In mind and spirit, I could not be further from the country I'm traveling in.

Suddenly, the bus swerves to the side of the road along with the rest of the traffic. No one knows the cause of the bonfire that now blocks the nation's main highway. In the flames ahead are the skeletal remains of a trailer and cab. This is no *contra* attack, just a gasoline truck that's jackknifed and overturned. Unflappable Silvio decides to be the first driver to make his way around the wreck. As we swing past, the whole side of the van heats up with astonishing speed. I'm amazed at how little reaction I have. What's this fire after a fastball? Is the bravery which seems so commonplace in these people merely the detachment that comes with knowing that the worst has already occurred?

"You may think us queer people," the coffee rancher Marco Gonzales told us, "because you will see those of us who have lost husbands and brothers dancing and joking with you the next day. That is because we Nicaraguans reject sadness. And we hope you can learn to do the same when you return to your country. We reject sadness fundamentally as a strategy for living." This rejection of sadness—in which *el béisbol* plays its part—is the greatest tangible result of this revolution, the one surefire source of inspiration for the many who make the pilgrimage here. I'm not surprised that the UNAG officials who've been our unofficial mascots and trainers—those winking, joshing dudes, preoccupied with women and game scores—are the first to rush onto the road, pistols drawn, prepared to defend to the death our right to play ball.

teammate and I are sprawled in the back row, relaxed as two campers coming home from the summer, arguing over the cause of Red Sox Bill Buckner's fatal World Series bobble. "Did you hear why Bill Buckner was late for spring training? He was going to catch the train, but it went through his legs. . . ." In mind and spirit, I could not be further from the country I'm traveling in.

Suddenly, the bus swerves to the side of the road along with the rest of the traffic. No one knows the cause of the bonfire that now blocks the nation's main highway. In the flames ahead are the skeletal remains of a trailer and cab. This is no *contra* attack, just a gasoline truck that's jackknifed and overturned. Unflappable Silvio decides to be the first driver to make his way around the wreck. As we swing past, the whole side of the van heats up with astonishing speed. I'm amazed at how little reaction I have. What's this fire after a fastball? Is the bravery which seems so commonplace in these people merely the detachment that comes with knowing that the worst has already occurred?

"You may think us queer people," the coffee rancher Marco Gonzales told us, "because you will see those of us who have lost husbands and brothers dancing and joking with you the next day. That is because we Nicaraguans reject sadness. And we hope you can learn to do the same when you return to your country. We reject sadness fundamentally as a strategy for living." This rejection of sadness—in which *el béisbol* plays its part—is the greatest tangible result of this revolution, the one surefire source of inspiration for the many who make the pilgrimage here. I'm not surprised that the UNAG officials who've been our unofficial mascots and trainers—those winking, joshing dudes, preoccupied with women and game scores—are the first to rush onto the road, pistols drawn, prepared to defend to the death our right to play ball.

SHORTSTOP
CORTO CAMPO
Venezuela

"Now, more than ever, it is necessary to be inflexible."

—Gen. Augusto Pinochet

UNRULY PROVINCE

Someplace out there, there's no more baseball. No hits except on the radio, no runs except the gastrointestinal kind, no errors but the sort that can turn you into a *desaparecido*. No wonder my nighttime arrival in a cosmopolitan city of four million feels like a leap into the unknown—and across centuries.

Having left the plantations that grow shortstops, I feel like a landless peasant migrating to the big city. I ride the green asphalt highways like they are my flume over the huge folds of the Avila range. I'm overwhelmed by the scale of this jungle encampment, growing up the sides of the first hospitable valley away from the Caribbean. In either direction, a vast net of lights undulates with the topography, a weak and flickering web sloped and tilted on waves of a black sea. The approach to Caracas is pure Hollywood. But those aren't the homes of the movie moguls climbing the canyons. With a population that's doubled in fewer than twenty years, this capital has slums to rival Rio or Mexico. If I were really one of the dispossessed, I'd be headed for those mazes of shanty *ranchitos*. For the moment, I'm willing to admire the show. Never has poverty been made more spectacular.

The hotel where I'm dropped is called Aventura, not a promise of things to come but an acronym for the Venezuelan Tourist Board. This Swiss-clean, heavily secured pillar, set in a sedate neighborhood of hospitals and research centers, caters mostly to out-of-town docs. Still, a sign on the sliding doors to my twelfth-floor balcony reads, "Closed for

Security Reasons." Can they really believe the squatters in a construction site below would be able to shinny their way up this concrete maypole? The hotel personnel act under siege. The androgynous night clerk admonishes me always to wait for a taxi, never to stray from the entrance. When I ask him where I can find some nightlife, he responds with a litany of areas where I'm sure to encounter dangerous elements.

Within a day or two, I begin to measure each Caraqueño's affection for me in terms of how dire his or her warnings become. The more people try to scare me, the more I feel welcomed into the fold. There are boulevards that should never be walked down, there are gangs that rape tourists in broad daylight and steal cars from under the noses of the police. The cops, too, are known to machine-gun a suspect if the bribe isn't juicy enough. The common topics of social discourse are burglary and battery. It's like talking about the weather. In place of "Have a nice day," strangers offer, "Don't walk down that street!" They all sing the refrain, "This used to be such a charming country. . . ."

The view out of my window tops anything in Houston or Miami. The newer the skyscraper, the better—and most of these are the result of Venezuela's oil-crisis earnings. Where the exuberant Latin sense of public space has been given the full funding, there are polyhedron arenas, Aztec banking pyramids, fifty-story upside-down shuttlecocks. Set in huge concrete beds, watered with overlit fountains, the office towers seem to have risen overnight from the jungle like monstrous white calla lilies, appropriately oversized Amazonian shoots. Caracas is a sun-belt city with more sun, more city, more belt. A town like this challenges the paternalism latent in all North Americans of whatever political stripe. My own mixture of awe and discomfort suggests this holds for radical and conservative alike. Whether we're building schools in the name of solidarity or representing Chase Manhattan, our underlying attitude is that these poor, sleepy nations to the south can't get along without us. When it comes to miracles like Caracas, we'd rather not admit that anyone but us can pull them off. We want there to be only one American success story.

Perhaps that's why Yankees carry less stereotypical baggage about Venezuela than any other South-of-the-Border haunt. Yes, there are plenty of Indians here but somehow they're not the tribes whose shaman-istic ways Claude Levi-Strauss catalogued; there are descendants of black slaves galore, but again, their African beat goes by no catchy label; there are plenty of righteously oppressed *campesinos* and ornery, inscrutable cowpokes, yet they cannot be called to mind as readily as Zapatistas in sombreros or gauchos with their herd; terrorists are at work here, too, along with drug-runners and the obligatory *generales*, yet few make it into our headlines or crime shows.

When I risk a jaunt to the civic promenade known as La Sabana Grande, I can't see why the hotel staff had me so worried. Dwarfed by massive corporate headquarters watered by fantasias of spraying fountains, this mall of less than a dozen blocks remains the spiritual heart of Caracas. With its outdoor cafes and magazine kiosks, sidewalk booksellers and open-air chess tournaments, La Sabana Grande is a less hectic version of Barcelona's Las Ramblas. Sidestreets echo with the amplified strumming of harpists, whose voices scratch out the lonely plaint of the *llaneros*, Venezuela's cowboys. The only other clues that this is the New World are the Indian features mixed into the faces and a J.C. Penney store.

Turtlenecked professors and bohemian students of life mingle and gab under umbrellas. The signs may still be in Spanish, but now at least I can read the people. After sorting through the baffling homogeneity bred by poverty out on the islands, these harried crowds easily decode into distinct, global types. The bent and ilk of these Sabana Grande strollers is as easily identifiable as their equivalents in North Beach or on the Left Bank: this one the priggish Marxist grad student, that one the garret intellectual, that one the craven poet, there the rebellious teens puffing on their first cigarettes, the schoolmarms and the hedonists, the pedants and pederasts. There are even genuine hippies squatting on sidewalk blankets to sell Indian trinkets. And there are books—Sartre and Marx and Philip Roth, not just the century-old platitudes of some crazed local patriot preserved on *papel higiénico!*

I plunk myself down at the last free table in the Gran Café, a venerable institution that offers a place to see and be seen along with a variety of fare from ice cream to buttery Venezuelan steaks borne by veteran waiters who wear white linen on their arms and a grudge in their hearts. At this *café du monde*, I am free of the burden of that attention which often could not be distinguished from obsequiousness. No one harasses me, importunes, notices. No more kowtowing! No getting addressed as *caballero*—the equivalent of *boss*—just because I'm white. What a relief after all that tropical happy-go-luckiness in the face of absurdly long odds! The waiters are positively Parisian in their fishy-eyed disdain—sneering at me for my cautious, jet-lagged order, dropping their blue-plate specials down with a hostile chunk. These waiters don't mind letting you know that they'd really rather not be waiters. Waiters who are painters, thespian understudies, waiters who dream of being emperors! This is the terrain I know, the one where nobody is as he appears. Here, at my café table, I can savor any great city's gift: the freedom to cultivate in peace one's own peculiar brand of desperation. I no longer have to justify my long face or my tendency toward complaint. I never thought I'd find it so enjoyable to be treated with such disrespect.

Ay, those Venezolanos! Baseball's loudmouthed advance scouts had warned me. As their nation stretches the geographic limits of the Caribbean, so Venezuelans stretch the usually elastic Caribbean patience. With cleft chins, two-day stubbles, eyes that bat impassively at each sign of turbulence, the men strutting past strike me as defiant descendants of those folks who, arriving in "the Kingdom of Venecuela, being more large and long than Spain," according to our monk-on-the-scene, Las Casas, "showed themselves more fierce and greedy than Tigers, Wolves, or Lyons" and "bestirred themselves with greater fury and covetousness in the heaping up of Gold and Silver." Female counterparts with long dark locks, Roman noses, and oversized bone structures parade down the promenade. This bounty of brooding young women makes Venezuela a perennial contender for Miss World, Miss Universe, Miss Inter-Galactic. They're one national resource all the tourist pamphlets like to emphasize. And most every town holds a pageant of virginal flesh as an adjunct to its saint's day fiesta. As a result, the whole country's populated by not-so-congenial Miss Congenialities, runners-up clutching their consolation bouquets. The hard faces remind me that charm isn't what laid waste to a continent, bub.

Yet this blast of haughtiness leaves me refreshed. After so much time in our miniaturized colonies, I've been beached in a bona fide country with its own history, identity, even, God forbid, a functioning economy. Colonized man, after all, is a comparative man. No matter how loud he sings, how well he plays, he's judged against the bigness and loudness of the boss in whose shadow he labors. Here I no longer have to tiptoe guiltily in the wide swath cut by invading Marines. Instead, I dodge the horseclods left by the nationalist cavalries of Simón Bolívar.

This is the site of the first republic on South American soil, which endured less than a year. Here's where *el Liberador* organized the bloody campaigns that failed to achieve pan-American unity but nonetheless freed half a continent from colonial rule. Oil deposits in the swampy region along the western Caribbean coast—where Indians' villages on stilts reminded the Spanish explorers of a "little Venice"—have made this the wealthiest nation below our borders. The major non-Muslim force in the OPEC cartel, a leader in the Contadora group, Venezuela is also one of the more progressive-minded lands—the only South American country which has successfully brought its leftist guerrilla movement back into the electoral process. It is also the only country on earth that boasts a minister of intelligence—intelligence as in brains, not spy secrets.

If Venezuelans are different, that's because Venezuela is different. In the reach of baseball's hegemony, this is the outlying, anomalous, unruly province. Over my first whipped *merengada* of papaya and milk, I find myself wondering how the sport fits in. Venezuela has produced dozens of big leaguers and its fans have a reputation as the most single-minded and vicious. Wasn't it here that Baltimore catcher Rick Dempsey was rescued by Venezuelan Bo Díaz from being ripped to shreds by an indignant mob? But how well can the game be doing here if the depreciation in local support matches that of neighboring countries? How can an American relic go head-to-head with soccer and bullfights? How firm a foothold can this transplant possibly maintain on the mainland of a boundless continent?

I soon have my answer. Turning a corner in search of an after-dinner harp serenade, I find the sky illuminated by a source that's either *Nuestro Señor*—Lord God—or a stadium. I can't imagine why the lights are still in full halogen glare well past midnight. I've stumbled onto the country's main ballpark, a modern stadium leased from Caracas University by two home teams, the Leones (Lions) and the Tiburones (Sharks). As I head closer, the crowds thicken, hurtling toward a subway stop. The last inning must have finished just now. Four hours at minimum—now that's a ballgame, Latin-style.

Skirting the first wave of *fanáticos* dashing home, I follow a main thoroughfare as it rises toward an overpass. In a moment, I'm transported from second-hand Barcelona to deepest Beantown. The Caracas stadium is positioned much like Boston's Fenway Park, with the brick rump of its outfield wall flush against an eight-lane freeway. The souvenir hawkers and sausage grillers who line the park's single convex link to downtown could be Massachusetts Irish or Italian. In their bellows, I almost hear, "Hey, there, pilgrim, getcha Sox caps! Getcha Yaz buttons here! Getcha hamburgs!"

But no crowd in our most ferocious of baseball cities has ever left a game the way this one does. Clutching radios that blare post-game interviews close to their ears, plastic yellow cushions, tooters and horns and timpani, hyperactive kids on their shoulders, these fans show no sign of the sport's usual side effects. Baseball's relaxed pace hasn't lulled or enervated these fans, but left them wired much like the native coffee that's dosed out in dixie-cup shots. The hordes move in an urgent, un-Latin gallop, hurrying home on the brink of hysteria, still pounding at mitts, swiping at the air, arguing calls, doing cartwheels. Baseball, you do leap continents in a single bound! Why should I be so astonished when Coca-Cola and blue jeans do the same trick? Maybe it's because every time I find the game well and alive, it feels like my heart has been wrenched from me and set down to pump away in some hairily unfamiliar chest.

SIMÓN SAYS

"**T**odos Iguales!" scream headlines across the kiosks of Caracas. All even, crieth the four-color tabloids devoted entirely to baseball. The type is so large they might be declaring the dawn of a new social order rather than the current status of playoffs between La Guaira and Lara. As though this were the first time in written history a best-of-seven championship series was knotted at one victory apiece!

In the heat and haze, I grope my way toward what remains of the original colonial center. A walk through Caracas is a negotiation of levels. No matter how crammed with twenty-story *edificios*, each boulevard eventually becomes a rampway, one floor of a vast garage. Once this was known as "the city of red roofs," more recently "the Paris of Latin America." In terms of roads, it is Los Angeles; judged by pace, glitz, and common etiquette, it is closer to a second New York. Caracas no longer shimmies like maracas, but bleats with the cry of stalled taxis. All quaintness still extant has been quarantined to the neighborhood misnamed el Silencio. Around the Plaza Bolívar is a burst of white: white plaza tiles set off by tropical arbors, white stucco churches of the padres, white Greco-Roman halls of administration, set with wooden doors too huge for the colonized to pry open. The old Spanish hub spins in the smog like a wicker aviary.

Everywhere, plaques are chiseled with the stirring rhetoric of the great Bolívar. Talk about a cult of personality! The whole country is a giant

239

game of Simón Says. But what does Simón say to the millions who've become, posthumously, his countrymen? That the job of unifying the Americas is only half finished? Or that the glory days are long gone? Lenin has nothing on the rabid militarist whose memorable declaration is etched on a twenty-foot bas-relief of a battle scene: "If Nature is against us, we shall fight Nature and make it obey." A perfect motto for this megalopolis on the edge of the wilds. I can't imagine what reaction his hometown would now stir in the man who confessed, "For Caracas, I served Peru; for Caracas, I served Venezuela; for Caracas, I served Colombia; for Caracas, I served Bolivia; for Caracas, I served the New World and liberty."

The series of austere rooms hung with formal portraits which form Bolívar's *casa natal* offer few hints of such passion. In a central atrium that offers refuge from the honking cabs, I try to recall what, if anything, I was taught about the man beyond the phrase, "the Latin George Washington." Of course, Georgy Porgy with his wooden teeth had little in common with this high-minded maniac obsessed by a call to greatness. One father of his country left evidence of having "slept here." The question with Bolívar was *who* he'd slept *with*. There was no hint of puritan tidiness in this plutocrat's life of fury and flight, revenge and remorse. For him, leadership was ever a tragic burden, a torment, a useless attempt to intervene in the irrationality of history. None of our constitutionalists could have declared, "My friend, in our veins flows no blood, but evil mingled with terror and fear." Nor would any Virginian have dared anoint himself "the liberator" before he'd won his first battle— nor managed to lose so many along the way. Descended from an assistant to one of the first governors of Santo Domingo, Bolívar viewed himself as the representative of a doomed class. He knew that by seeking freedom from Spain, he was unleashing forces on the new continent that the old elite could never control. Try as he might, he would be the first in a line of generals to hold sway by force over emergent peoples. "There were no Negroes in the Passion," went a popular song which plagued this follower of the French revolution. "Indians there were unknown, Mulattoes there were none. It was an affair for white men!"

Through a languid courtyard set with dribbling fountains à la Alhambra is the National Library. Dare I slip past an honor guard in white breeches and tricorner hats to seek the catalogue listings under *béisbol*? I blow my cover as a distinguished visiting scholar as soon as I turn in my request slips. In the Dominican Republic, I was able to find crude *"álbumes deportivos"* of coarse-screened newspaper clippings and a single paperback, "Juan Marichal: Historia de Su Vida." Thanks to Venezuela's relative economic development, the stacks contain quite a few pamphlets, even full-scale biographies. One is *The Chico Carrasquel Story*. As told to Bob Considine. I didn't realize the beloved Chico was the first Latin named to a big-league All-Star team, Luis Aparicio the first shortstop named to the Hall of Fame. Or that it's a good bet any major leaguer named "Luis" will prove to be Venezuelan. I've forgotten this country produced César Tovar, Dave Concepción, the brothers Davalillo, Pompeyo and Vic—a mere pinch hitter up North, but the all-time hit leader here, idolized as "Victico." In baseball as in geopolitics, Venezuela is the neighbor we've failed to credit.

Here, baseball's origins have been more carefully pinpointed than in the States. No murky mythology about an old leather ball found in the trunk which once belonged to the pipsqueak Abner Doubleday. These historians state categorically that Venezuelan ball was first attempted in a Caracas park known as the Stand del Este. Several books concur that the word *base-ball* first appeared in the Venezuelan press on August 5, 1895. In 1902, another paper described some strange procedure *"que se pronuncia Béis-Bol."* The researchers insist that baseball evolved here independent of U.S. influence, and in a parallel manner. They claim the British introduced the early versions of the sport when they arrived to construct the Venezuelan railway in the 1890s. *Caraqueños*, like kids in Chicago or Paducah, played the street game of rounders—*en español, la rondada*—around the turn of the century. But it wasn't long before wealthy Venezuelans who attended college in the United States brought back the rules and equipment required for the American variation.

By 1903, when the U.S. Navy was summoned to break a German blockade of the country, local teams were skilled enough to play a much-publicized doubleheader with the visiting Seabees. Box scores indicate the locals came back from a first-game pasting to gain sweet revenge in the nightcap. A series of early, barnstorming Cuban clubs—the Caribbean equivalents of the Harlem Globetrotters—helped increase the sport's popularity. Puerto Rico's Borinquen Stars toured to sell-outs in 1918. By the twenties, soccer was the sport identified with foreign elites, while baseball had been established as "native." Venezuela's dictator, the infamous Andean bully General Gómez, practiced his own brand of

241

domination over the game. As part of a ban on "public congregating," he cancelled the entire 1928 season. The current, six-team professional winter league was formed only in the late forties.

Nothing in these exhaustive texts helps me locate my "end of baseball." Before my journey began, I'd assumed that baseball remained largely a Caribbean phenomenon, found only along the coastal cities—as in neighboring Colombia, where the quality of play in Cartagena and Baranquilla has been declining in inverse proportion to the cocaine trade. From what I've learned, the traditional hotbed of Venzuelan baseball activity is also along the coast, in the swampy Zulia region around Maracaibo. Now I know that the franchises of the Venezuelan league reach inland to the industrial centers of Maracay and Valencia. And I've heard scouts talk of prospects scattered through the cowtowns of the country's underpopulated midsection. But the sports historians don't seem to realize that the exact territorial limit of the American game may be more historically significant than the Mason-Dixon or Maginot lines, more useful in terms of cultural anthropology than that perspiring abstraction called the equator. Few Venezuelans seem able to conceive of their boundless nation ever being the end of anything.

Luckily, Ramón Becerra Mijares, a daily columnist and author of one chronology I'd perused in the National Library, invites me up to his newspaper office. This Caracas tower looks impressive enough from afar, but can only be entered by climbing up and over the bulldozed rungs of its incomplete foundation. Mijares strikes me as the archetypal sports scribe. This skeletal figure is probably no more than forty-five, but looks like he's got one gray foot in the grave from days spent chain-smoking in his underlit cubbyhole, while he peers over box scores and wire service reports from the big leagues. This professional trivia retriever would make a fine bookie or pari-mutuel teller. He must have come from the womb wearing a green visor. He reminds me of Emilio ("Cuqui") Cordova, a more debonair Dominican baseball writer who, when asked about the history of the Dominican leagues, had grabbed a pointer and taken me on a guided tour of his office walls, covered to the ceiling with publicity shots of Cuqui with Hank Aaron, Cuqui with Leo Durocher, Cuqui *con* Cuqui. Presented with a North American colleague, Mijares can't tear himself away from culling back issues of *The Sporting News*. Instead of an interview, he hands me his book and offers me a spare desk. I don't have the heart to tell him I've already skimmed his life's work.

Simón Says

After some desultory page-flipping, I ask Mijares for an assessment of the Venezuelan league. He complains about the same downward spiral I'd noted in the other ballplaying countries. Thanks to a recent devaluation of currency caused by the drop in world oil prices, top North American players are increasingly difficult to hire. Despite the continued enthusiastic participation of upcoming native stars like Ozzie Guillén and Andrés Galarraga, the quality of play is declining and attendance is off. Still, Mijares stresses, grass roots interest is as keen as ever. Then I at last get around to popping the question. Does he know where I can find the continent's southernmost outpost of the sport, *"el fin del béisbol"*? The scribe absorbs my concept without the slightest double-take. In fact, his quick reaction makes me wonder if this clubhouse Charon has already sent a stream of budding sports symbologists in the direction of the River Styx.

Mijares informs me that little leagues are spreading throughout South America. I'd heard rumors to that effect, though I still can't quite picture Inca ball in the bleak highlands of Ecuador and Peru and Chile, samba ball in soccer-mad Brazil, or, egads, penguin ball in Patagonia! Still, I should have known that the sun never sets on our *paz americana* or its game, not with night lights and satellite link-ups at the ready. Even on Antarctica, there are bound to be a few M.I.T. geophysicists with thawed mitts. Perhaps the ultimate diamond is etched in moon dust. My budget requires that I settle for an approximate point where our pastime relinquishes its monopolistic hold on sporting hearts and minds, or at least ceases to be the mania of first choice. Señor Mijares leads me toward a conference room mounted with a gigantic wall map of the country. Using a pointer, he plots out my options like a general reviewing a battle plan. My search is going to be more of a haul than I bargained for. This Venezuela is one mother of a country.

I'd better catch one last game, in case I encounter jaguars or cannibals along the way. Just before sunset and long before game time, the stampede begins, this time in the direction of the Caracas U. stadium. I pause in the fray to purchase a cushion, a T-shirt commemorating Davalillo's fifteen-hundredth hit (no doubt a bloop single to left), my Leones yearbook, a blue-and-white Caracas cap (fifty cents), plus one wax paper–wrapped *arepa*, the national Venezuelan nosh: a soft, grilled cornmeal cake stuffed with your choice of cheese, chilis, chicken, or anything that crawls. Outfitted like Joe Fan, I stand in a long line for *preferencia* tickets, but soon learn they're not as preferential as the *sencillas* behind homeplate. Those seats have been long sold out for this third game of the semifinal playoff series between La Guaira and Lara (whose "Cardenales" uniforms are direct knock-offs of the St. Louis breed). My battle cry of *"Periodista!"* gets me into the packed sections. I'm soon sorry I've passed this sliding gate of no return. A half-dozen ambulances sit at the ready near these prime seats. Stationed beside them are an equal number of paddy wagons, full of tactical squad drones in blue jumpsuits, clutching riot batons. Their uniforms read, "Brigada Especial." There are more cops on alert before a ballgame in Caracas than there were in Berkeley after Nixon invaded Cambodia.

Before the first pitch, the fans have formed one standing, chanting, rocking, surging mass. But they've gone upscale since the violent ol' days. Too urbane for pelting the field with rocks and bottles, the crowd has brought along whistles, tambourines, and conga drums that pound in a constant invocation of the baseball gods. This is Rio during carnival. And nobody's even appeared on the well-manicured turf. Maybe that's why the dugouts here have been built flush into the base of the grandstand, like high-security corporate bunkers. An electronic scoreboard as sophisticated as any back home pulsates with commands to cheer—only here, the fans don't need to be cued. In response to the prerecorded trumpet blasts first played at Dodger Stadium, everyone raises both arms in fascist rally unison. I don't see why management wants to stir them up further.

A top step near the more decorous press box offers some relief from the chants. Behind me, an apparition in a homemade moonwalker's suit strolls up the aisle with a sign pinned to his chest. "FANÁTICO!" reads his appeal. "CON TU CONTRIBUCIÓN IRÉ A LA SERIE DEL CARIBE. TE SENTIRAS ORGULLOSO DE COLABORAR COMMIGO. GRACIAS." Toting a used fire extinguisher for a piggybank, he solicits charitable donations so he can attend this year's Caribbean Series in Mexico—in return for which the fans can be proud to have sent him on his way. Is there a Spanish word for *chutzpah*? If there were, it would soon be overused. Here, nerve is a stronger selling point than trustworthiness. Everyone joyfully pitches a coin into the can. An odd little man in a shiny, oversized leisure suit joins me where I squat. But this fellow isn't merely taking refuge. Brushing his sweep of black hair nervously from his forehead, he looks like a mad scientist. Instead, he's the mad fan. He swings a big attaché case onto his knees, then unclicks the locks. Inside is a clunky, reel-to-reel recorder. He unwraps the cord of a portable mike and jabbers a full play-by-play of the game, complete with humorous asides, dramatic build-ups, and pauses for imaginary commercials. Maybe he hopes to send this sample tape to some local station. Like all the Latin announcers I've heard, he keeps up a nonstop barrage of hyperbole. Catching phrases over the mob's static, I savor once more the transformation the game undergoes in this tongue that turns every moment of life into high drama: three balls and two strikes becomes *"la conte de verdad,"* the count, or moment, of truth; the playoffs *"la lucha por semi-final"*; a double play is turned *"seis-cinco-tres, oooouuuutttt!"*

The *fanáticos* in linen suits and Panama hats get a laugh at the expense of this curious character. They shrug their shoulders toward me as an invitation to join in the derision. Yet I feel kinship with the self-employed announcer who carries on as if he's the only man in the park. For him, the pleasure of baseball is in the grimly methodical, almost monastic pursuit of the game's endless rotating "moments of truth." And truth flees from hoopla. For me and my new pal, baseball provides a mental architecture that must be strolled through as leisurely as one wishes. The charm of the "waiting game" is rarely what happens, but what might happen. I don't see how baseball's slow dance can possibly satisfy this soccer mob's demand for instant gratification. Clearly, Venezuelan fans do not take well to disappointment—and yet, baseball's a contest where a team's a champion if it wins eleven times out of twenty, a batter's an all-time stud if he makes contact four times out of ten. One prevails through patience and keeps on swinging. While this sport and its ramifications have occupied more of my lifetime's mental activity than I'd care to admit, I don't dare expect so much from it as does this nation-on-the-move. Though the old ballgame has driven me thousands of miles on this curious odyssey, it just doesn't seem worth getting this worked up over.

ORINOCO OUTFIELDS

I'm off to mine diamonds, however symbolic, so I'd better find myself an all-purpose bearer and guide—or at least someone to call me *bwana*. A contact at the U.S. embassy recommends a local señorita who charges a hundred dollars a day for simultaneous translation in her brand-new Mercedes. When she realizes this isn't the style of travel I require, she passes on the number of a friend who might do the job. "Actually," the lady giggles, "Irene is likely to do anything!" This Irene speaks English with a flirtatious rolling of *r*'s and urges me to pop right over to her "es-studio." The address, in the swankest shopping area of Caracas, leads me to a freshly poured arcade still looking to lease half its storefronts. At the very back is a young woman in splotched coveralls who introduces herself as the very one I'm seeking. I perform the same double-take that I'll see her countrymen do over and again. Irene may sound like Charo, but she looks like Sonja Henie. One out of six Venezuelans is foreign-born, and Irene's father was a German engineer. "I know, it's a big surprise for everybody!" In pink plastic earrings and wraparound shades, blond hair bobbed to look intergalactic, she could be the twenty-two-year-old next door.

"Well, mister, what do you think?" she says. Venezuelan girls are awfully forward. Then I realize she wants my assessment of various experiments strewn across the studio floor: ungainly, glazed, abstract pin-cushions stuck with feathers and tiers of bugged-out Picasso eyes. "Irene gave herself one year to become an artist." She refers to herself in the

246

third person—her own best creation. "If Irene doesn't get gallery, I go back to the States and make some real money!" After graduation from a women's college outside Washington, she's returned home to a family whose fortunes have waned. "I don't know what I'm doing in this damn country! The traffic, the crime, the inflation, is too much! I come back only for my mother. And the discos!" Irene has even been to a few ballgames. "The fans, they throw the beer everywhere. The trick is to wear the raincoat!" But her main qualification for the job is her desire for distraction. Irene is half society girl and half hired hand. She takes on assignments for petty cash because she really can't be bothered with anything so petty. What other sort of girl would be willing to head off for a weekend to help a strange man find the end of baseball?

Who's to say that going from ballpark to ballpark is an any less edifying form of tourism than traipsing from battlefield to battlefield, cathedral to cathedral? If Irene thinks I'm "too much," she doesn't let on. She'll get enough in devalued bolívars to pay for plenty of disco admissions. "Irene goes anywhere in Venezuela. Everywhere is beauty! And danger!" She seems eager to show off her native country's abundance of both. Yet she offers little opinion on the route we should take. No dotted line on auto club maps delineates the territorial range of Louisville Slugger salesmen or their final stop. According to Señor Mijares and others, baseball has managed to climb the first *cordillera* of the Andes—though it's hardly baseball weather up there all the time and soccer is popular, too. Evidence of the game may be found all the way up to Rubio, a mountain settlement on the southern border with Colombia some twelve hundred kilometers distant. To the east at about the same latitude, nine hundred kilometers across the flat alluvial grasslands known as the *llanos*, the game has a venue at historic Ciudad Bolívar, on the banks of the Orinoco River. Somewhere in the vicinity, the Amazonian highlands begin and baseball withers. Beyond, said Mijares, it's *"puro indio."*

"Are there really Indians outside Cleveland?" I kid Irene. "Lots of Indians in Venezuela," she answers, and that encourages me to opt for the bush instead of the mountains. I can't see myself, or baseball, making it over bleak passes; I want to play anthropologist, not Alpinist. Besides, telling people I've been to the Orinoco has a glamorous ring. "You know what the Venezuelans say?" asks Irene, primed to go in any direction. "There's Caracas, and then there's the jungle!"

This seems sheer urban snobbery, until we leave the city limits next morning in a rented Chevette. Almost instantly, the broad freeways turn to winding two-laners shrouded in banana groves, the towers of housing projects worthy of Moscow or the Bronx become rows of pink-washed and yellow-washed lean-tos. Only the massive scale of the truck stops and their dozen pumps of Venezuelan crude remind me that this is a petrol, not a banana, republic. At our first pit stop, a humpbacked attendant fills the Chevette tank. On the way to the ladies', Irene shouts, "Be sure and count your *cambio*, mister. You never know with these Venezuelans!" Irene's attitude toward her countrymen is that they'll get away with whatever you'll let them. She's hardly bitter; rather, she relishes playing the game. What other way to have a little fun? Though she couldn't have been around for much of the good old days, Irene, too, offers a variation on this-used-to-be-such-a-lovely-country. If only she could see the countries I've been in! With their combination garages, hardware stores, and *fuentes de soda*, these rest stops are better stocked than whole provinces of Nicaragua. Across chest-high, open-air counters, I can order chicken-on-the spit, paperback romances, a complete set of wrenches.

And Irene is the perfect traveling companion. She shows as little aptitude for analysis as tendency toward complaint, leaving both to me! Up on the latest New York fashion and art trends, Irene seems thoroughly Latin in her giddy pursuit of people, food, sensations of the moment. Yet the longer I ride beside her, the more she seems like North Americans of the post-sixties generation. At once spoiled and pragmatic, irreverent yet accepting of the social cards she's been dealt, she rates her nation only in terms of its sluggish job market. And the crime, of course. "My car was es-stolen from right in front of a police es-station! Is too much!" More entertaining than the car radio, she prattles on about the various cuts of Venezuelan steak but can't recall the name of her own president, Jaime Lusinchi. She's a fan of the punk rockers called the Dead Kennedys, but when I express my admiration for Che Guevara, Irene asks, "Does he have any albums?"

The road emerges from the brush to skirt the Caribbean and we could be anywhere on the coast of Mexico. The hills and passes are bleached dry, good only for throngs of floppy-eared cacti. On a ridge above a silty ocean cove is a turnoff for Puerto Piritu, the hometown of Antonio Rafael Armas Machado, no *generalissimo* he, just the outfielder known around the American League as Tony Armas. No wonder scout Howie

Haak told me he first encountered the slugger sleeping in a hammock! A few miles farther on, we turn south from the sea and end up in Wyoming. "Are these the *llanos*?" I ask. Irene corrects my pronunciation, for the word meaning "plains" begins not with a *y* but a *j*. She admits, "Irene has never seen them." All I see ahead are hours of scrub brush, dead branches, black boulders, chalky soil. I'd expected Serengeti-style views of the *llaneros* driving their herds of the horned water buffalo called Zebu. These cousins to the gaucho, first of South America's vaunted he-men, battle the *llanos'* extremes by rescuing parched livestock on horse-back during droughts, in boats during flood. From this highway, there's no sign of those fiercely individualist cowpokes whose motto is *Sobre mi caballo yo, y sobre yo mi sombrero*—"Above my horse am I, and above me my hat!" Supposedly descended from tribes who practiced cannibal-ism, these fearsome fighters turned the tide in favor of Venezuelan independence. The recruits were so impressed with Bolívar's stamina in the saddle that they called him *culo de hierro*, iron asshole. Looks like that's what I'll need.

So much for my National Geographic special! I always did have a knack for avoiding scenic routes—if there's a New Jersey Turnpike in Fiji, I'm bound to ride it—and we're doomed to spend the rest of the day on this hypnotically undeviating course. At each exit, every fifty miles or so, Irene and I look for signs of life—a rodeo, a fiesta, a saddle shop, anything. Each town looks the same: a *cantina* housing more horseflies than customers, dirt main streets criss-crossing in perfect grids, and a ballpark. Each would be the grandest stand in all of Nicaragua; in the States, they would be candidates for the wreckers' ball. I'm finding the relative size and condition of stadia as accurate a gauge of development as any World Bank report. None of these are in use—and that's just as well. These dusty bivouacs seem more suited to that Afghan form of polo played with a goat's head. But there's plenty of baseball in Wyoming, isn't there? However urban its origins, baseball speaks of the lure of the frontier's emptiness and shows how desolation can be structured into a form of delight. In baseball, even the most self-sufficient fur trapper, the sharpest-shooting sheriff, must scurry from one base's safe haven to the next. Perhaps that's why baseball has penetrated this country so deeply. The interior of South America is the world's most underpopulated region—and we've just hit its first empty stretch. Venezuela proves that the United States has no monopoly on frontiers.

You can't go too far in these wide open spaces without getting waved
·to the side of the road by soldiers cradling automatic weapons. "If they
don't like your face, pow pow pow!" says Irene, just as I slow down to
honor the first of these checkpoints. "The government they make a big
e-show of looking for gold and cocaine smugglers. Everyone knows, the
government, they are the biggest dealer! Damn Venezuelans!" Irene, too,
is infuriatingly Venezuelan in the glee she takes at spreading alarm.
"Sometimes, they rape girls if they like. Tourists disappear if they don't
give a pay-off." For roadside inspectors, I open my truck with alacrity. By
the third or fourth encounter, these raw recruits look less threatening
than comical. Their camouflage suits barely stay on their scrawny bodies;
their helmets are so oversized that they keep slipping over their eyes. But
I get a little too cocky. When an acne-scarred private demands to know
where I'm from, I answer, "America." Surely, by now I should know
better. "*Qué parte?* North, East, West?" he snaps back with cranky
Venezuelan conviction. "This *is* America," says the boy with the machine-gun.

Except we can't get Hank Williams on the radio. Irene sleeps most of
the rest of the way, and I wish I could. For a hundred miles, I look
forward to a notch on the road with the evocative name of El Tigre. This
supply hub strung out along a single main street has all the charm of an
Oklahoma oil town. The local equivalent of Betty's Luncheonette serves
mango whipsies with swarms of flies for topping. I gun the Chevette
down our last stretch of straightaway, racing the sunset toward the
Orinoco. I want to make Ciudad Bolívar before dark, because every
guidebook warns about the perils of the roads at night. Nothing I've seen
in the daytime maneuvers of Venezculan drivers would make me discount
such advice. In this country, red lights are for wussies; I've yet to see
anyone actually stop for one. "You know," Irene starts up, brought out
of her grogginess by the smelling salt of impending disaster, "the
Venezuelans they drink too much, then they drive along roads like this,
and boom, they go into collision headfirst!" A series of rounded white
plaster nubs, like outdoor bookcases with a single shelf provided for
candles and dashboard-style statuettes of the Virgin Mary, appear so
regularly along the grassy center divider I take them for kilometer
markers. "See the little shrines, look at all the places of accidents! Is too
much!" The scary speeches suggest that Irene is warming up to me.
"Every one a *muerto*," she rhapsodizes. "The families honor the spirits!

They bring fresh flowers, look!" And how many get into wrecks on the way?

An odd assortment of billboards breaks the monotony. They appear to be one-of-a-kind paintings pasted up in three sheets. Captioned only by the names of their creators and some dozen countries of origin, most are geometric abstracts in primary colors. "Oh wow, I heard of this, an international art show. Is too much, no? Some millionaire, he commission these to be put here." This must be the local variant of Amarillo's Cadillac Ranch, where late models are buried, tailfins up, in homage to the endless road. If these works have been placed here to open driver's eyes, or keep them from closing, they've obviously failed. The tombstones offer an instant critique; art alternates with carnage for another hundred miles. Now I know I've arrived in García Márquez country. In this vast stomping ground of visionaries, penitents, and prospectors, one senses that everything can and indeed has happened—at its own sweet, stubborn, nearly imperceptible pace.

As a red sun sinks into a muggy horizon, we cross a suspension bridge, the shiniest and spiffiest artifact for miles. This is the only span across the river's 1,600-mile length. And there below, a brownish flow with hardly a current: the Orinoco! What romance is lodged in these old Indian names, and what deception! Savannah, Dakota, Chattanooga, Tegucigalpa, Tchachapi—these singsong testaments to spirits long departed stand as a legacy of the red man. The shortfall between the poetry of American place-names and their prosaic reality must be the red man's most persistent form of revenge. When Columbus first sailed up the Orinoco's delta of jungle islets populated by tribes with bones through their noses, he believed the river was a pathway up to the heights of a primal earthly paradise. He envisioned his final American destination as one great mound of moisture-giving maternal tit from which all the world's rivers flowed. That section of the river is now best known for a rare and virulent form of malaria. At Ciudad Bolívar, several hundred miles from the Atlantic, the Orinoco looks and smells distressingly like the Hudson just above Spuyten Duyvil.

The river here is but two-thirds of a mile wide, which is why the bridge is named Angostura, from narrow. The colonial settlement on the far side was best known for the angostura bitters first concocted here in the early 1800s. This acrimonious ingredient in a barkeep's repertoire is now manufactured in Trinidad—and the town has been renamed after

Bolívar because everything in Venezuela eventually is. Here, as far as he could get from civilization and the Spanish forces, the Liberator came to rally his troops. The rebels won over this garrison town of six thousand with "manifestoes and tons of fresh meat." In 1819, at the Congress of Angostura, Bolívar galvanized a coalition of armies that eventually crossed the Andes to the Pacific and freed six nations from Spanish control—killing off fully two-thirds of the Venezuelan population. Another Latin icon risen from the blood! How absurd all nationalism looks, especially when the nation in question is someone else's dusty *tierra sacra!*

The unsuitability of old Angostura's architecture to its environment reveals the conceit of colonialism for all to see. This cathedral and plaza seem to have been brought from Spain like a museum's preservation project, stone by numbered stone. The usual rows of rotting stucco boxes coated in pathetically bombastic orange and lavender and lime colors pulsate in the increasing dark. In the town where Bolívar launched his crusade for pan-Hispanic unity, it's hard to grasp why the goal has yet to be achieved. To an outside eye, Latin culture looks remarkably, distressingly homogeneous. This America appears so much more unified than our own in ways that count. If only they weren't divided in the means that pay the bills!

Ciudad Bolívar sits on the bank south of the bridge. The water's at least two hundred feet down. Where I'd imagined a flotilla of Indians in bark canoes hawking pottery and stuffed piranhas, the only riverbank *mercado* is the usually colorful sort featuring twelve kinds of bananas and the local catch of "tiger fish." The Paseo Orinoco is a shady promenade whose main attraction is a kiddie amusement park with bulb-studded merry-go-round. The embankment is faced by a half-dozen uneven blocks with covered sidewalks that come from some backlot replica of a wild west town. We find the Gran Hotel Bolívar, the only one listed in my guidebook. "This is the Gran Hotel?" Irene asks. "Unreal. Before I left, my mother told me this is where she spent her honeymoon!"

No wonder the marriage didn't last. The place has definitely seen better days, or at least less mildewed ones. The receptionist is a pregnant girl in a Snoopy T-shirt, extra-extra large. The lobby has a row of clocks meant to show the time in Paris, Baghdad, and Tokyo—all stopped. This does not inspire confidence in the sightseeing flights into Amazon country advertised underneath. A placard on an easel boasts in English

252

of a ballroom and various convention facilities, but the rest of the first floor looks permanently dark behind opaque doors. I don't care where we stay, so long as I can justify our day's ride with a ballgame. *"No hay béisbol,"* the receptionist insists. *"Esta noche, no."*

We settle for dinner overlooking the river. While hunks of buttery meat called *lomitos* are grilled on tiny hibachis clipped to the side of our table, a series of slides are projected against the back wall of a filthy outdoor patio. A fuzzy soundtrack of parakeets and river crickets and slow boleros accompanies a dizzying tour around the world in no specific direction. The slides appear to have been photographed from old post cards left behind by whoever passed through town. Have we driven all this way just to see Balinese temples, Swiss funiculars, Egyptian digs? Yet nothing could be more distinctly Latin American than this grab-bag of images and daydreams. The place is a planetary flea market.

By the time our flans arrive, the amusement park's been switched off. Our only other choice for entertainment is a hole-in-the-wall cine playing Swedish soft-core porn. About to give up for the night, I spot a poster announcing a dance at the alluring-sounding Club los Mangos. Irene is game and the desk clerk points us in the direction of the airport. It doesn't take us long to find the disproportionately huge rectangular pit. Only in towns of this size does one realize how much room a jet needs to land. We see no signs shaped like mangoes, but notice a crowd of teens in their best Sunday clothes filing toward the single tourist-style hotel bordering the terminal. Before we know it, we're paying for admittance to an event billed as a "Grito del Carnaval," or carnival scream. This must be a warm-up for revels to come. The New World's most distinctive form of partying fits perfectly into the schedule of the New World's favorite form of play—as carnival usually fills the annual lull between February's Caribbean Series and the start of spring training in the States. Held in a brightly lit rooftop ballroom inundated with paper streamers, the carnival seems as innocent as a high school prom. Outside in the warm midnight, groups of young women chatter, awaiting invitations to dance.

While the band sets up, we're accosted by two curly-haired, bleary-eyed fellows who claim to be physical education instructors. Neither seems to react when I tell them I'm researching baseball—except to give a thumbs down assessment of their local players. The drunker of the two refuses to let us go until we've heard his woeful autobiography. "Do you know my grandmother is from the Grand Caymans? What is patois?" he keeps asking. "Where is the 'finger of God'?" Neither Irene nor I can help him. "Do you know how hard it is to get a coil"—an IUD—"for a woman in Manaus?" He keeps repeating these inquiries as if they're his mantra. "A woman in Manaus . . . the finger of God . . . it's not easy to find a coil . . ." The drunk's reference to Manaus reminds me that we're nearing Brazil, and to be near Brazil is to be no more than a samba shuffle from Africa. When the music strikes up, the lilting beat offers no more than a hint of Hispanic remorse. The band is simultaneously called la Misma Gente and the Same People. Same as who is not clear to me: same as last year possibly, but more likely part of the same nation or tribe. Their lyrics also alternate between Spanish and a form of English I can barely follow. "El Callao such a nice place, Everybody live like bruddas . . ." My guidebook tells me that the mud-laned outpost of el Callao, along with el Dorado, was a gold-mining boomtown, stocked with runaway slaves from Trinidad and Guyana. And that the town some hundred miles south has three obsessions: "*Oro, calipso, y fútbol!*" The change in sports is tantalizing.

The band's repertoire includes another gentle calypso-based chant that Irene greets with her own carnival scream. "They're playing your song, mister!" The refrain goes "*Botaste la bola, negro*"—you dropped the ball, brother. Irene tells me this had been the number-one hit for weeks on the Venezuelan charts and that there had even been a popular rock video which showed the band playing, or failing to play, catch. By now, I wouldn't be surprised if Luis Aparicio, the Venezuelan Hall-of-Famer, were elected president. The song drops the names of Armas, Concepción, and Galarraga, and mentions the Tiburones and the other local *campeones*. I take a stab at calypso for all the ball throwers and ball watchers and ball droppers. I keep up the same way I did to the Motown hits at my prom. I dance the dance of America, powered by an African beat. I grip tight the seams of my world. I'm not ready to drop the ball yet. And suddenly, a light tower too high for guiding planes appears across the big runway. Then a second glow comes into view, and a third, all in familiar oval alignment. So there was a game tonight—the receptionist was mistaken. The rule of thumb when traveling in the Third World is to obtain local counsel, then do the opposite. I know I'm closing in on my treasure of the Orinoco. X marks the spot, or at least, home plate.

ARE THERE INDIANS
OUTSIDE CLEVELAND?

There is one Rex to every backwater hotel. His position on the staff rarely has a title. Call him the native guide, house gigolo, professional friend-to-foreigners, and purveyor of the local *éspecialités*, be they gemstones, hides, or ladies. He can always be found in the bar, lurking amidst the potted plants. Irene and I find him over breakfast on the outdoor mezzanine of the Gran Hotel Bolívar. Sunk into rattan chairs that make us feel we've just decamped from weeks in the bush, we're the only patrons enjoying the view of the Orinoco, or more properly, the choking black foliage of the trees along the *paseo*. When the waiter brings our cafés, Irene beckons him closer and begins whispering. Is she trying to find out about the local girlie shows? Maybe she's been inspired by the backwater ambience to set a little intrigue in motion, but she's only trying to please. "Today," Irene announces, "Irene find you the true Venezuelan sport!"

Before I can say Jackie Robinson, or Andrés Galarraga, a middle-aged gentleman bows suavely, flashes a perfect set of teeth, then grabs a chair at the first hint of our admiring response. "I am Rex," he says as though the name were Erich von Stroheim. Rex is dark-skinned, darker than most anyone in sight, but his complexion glows almost golden in contrast with wavy silver hair that's combed straight back à la César Romero. "Welcome to our quiet haven," he declares in unaccented English, his manner half-bedside, half-conspiratorial. "Don't hesitate to let me know how I can be of service!" Little does he know that the word *hesitate* isn't in Irene's vocabulary. Rex looks momentarily taken aback when she slips her shades down her nose and asks for a cockfight. "Well, yes, why not?" I get the feeling that this isn't an item Rex is ordinarily asked to provide. "That should not be a problem on a Sunday. Shall we set out in an hour, then?" Before we know it, we're committed. And would we also like to see the ruins of the old Spanish castle, complete with explorers' bones, only three hours downriver? Or the Guri Dam, one of the world's largest, just completed after a decade's labor? Or Ciudad Guayana, the boom-town described by my guidebook as "thoroughly lacking in atmosphere and infested with water rats"?

When Irene asks if he works at the hotel, Rex answers only, "I keep a room here: one-twenty-seven," as though the number deflates all mystery. After he excuses himself, Irene demands my best guess about what a charmer like Rex might be doing in a hellhole like this. "He's no Venezuelan!" she insists. "He's a fugitive! *Sí!*" This town would make a perfect hideaway, the end of the civilized line where FBI and Interpol dragnets can't reach. "Of course, he's a terrorist!"

"And what would a terrorist have to keep him busy in this place?" I volunteer Rex may be a defrocked priest, a bankrupt plantation squire, the discredited captain of a tramp steamer. Irene vetoes each of my Conradian scenarios. But she, too, has seen *South Pacific*, suggesting that our Rex "murdered a man in a fit of *pasión!*"

Waiting by the embankment, Rex doesn't look nearly so sinister. Maybe it's his dusty Ford station wagon, maybe the company of his ten-year-old daughter. Her looks instantly unlock the secret of her father's genealogy. The dense thickets of black hair, chubby cheeks, and darting almond eyes come straight off some cherubic carving on a Hindu temple. Rex is an Indian, but not the kind Columbus named. Before we've reached the Angostura Bridge, we learn that he was raised in the Philippines and, somewhere along the line, spent twelve years in the Bronx. Everybody in the Caribbean basin seems to have done time along Mosholu Parkway. This peripatetic soul claims to speak twelve languages and plans, among other things, to go to work for the United Nations someday. Rex pulls me aside to say that he's saving his bolívars so he can emigrate to São Paulo. An hour farther on, he's brimming with enthusiasm as he describes the camper he's just purchased for a year's touring through Central America, that picnickers' paradise. At first scandalized by the fact that I've been to Nicaragua, Rex drops odd hints that he'll have no problem driving through its disputed borders. His gypsy daughter smiles at the mention of every projected itinerary. She must know something we don't about her daddy's big speeches.

What Rex really wants to do is drive us to a certain fabled cave where a rare species of tropical bird returns annually. It's amazing how people will manufacture four-star, of-unusual-interest sites out of the most ordinary terrain: a cave here, an abandoned castle there, bat fossils three hundred miles up a trail. Before we begin our search, he can't resist a detour to show us a small lagoon that's formed from river seepage.

"There's something bewitching about the quiet here," Rex tells us, amidst mounds of trash that I take to be the city dump. "Something about the landscape that holds on to you. . . ." Much as he tries to indicate that he's too worldly for this place, Rex is held to Ciudad Bolívar by the sweet succulence of slow rot. These provincial capitals are full of little men with big schemes who end up as big men in little places, and, despite their vast array of qualifications, cannot help slipping back into indolence and quiet and littleness.

Irene looks disappointed. Not only is our guide forthcoming about his past, but he may not be sordid enough to find us our illegal backyard action. Rex admits that he's never actually seen the cocks himself. He heads into the unpaved warren of a *barrio* that he figures is raunchy enough to satisfy our request. Rex ends up driving in circles, slowing for anything that looks like a ring, pausing before every group of malingering youths who look like potential bettors. Finally, he lowers his guide's pride by asking directions to a ring from two ladies sauntering in slippers outside a *grocería*. Never on Sunday, say the señoritas. So we set off in the opposite direction, toward the southern outskirts of town where Rex cruises aimlessly through several more neighbourhoods. I feel sorry for our Fernando Lamas. I wish Irene hadn't picked up on my interest in witnessing Venezuela's second sport. Finally, a couple of teenagers point toward a house whose back wing is a single sheet of tin folded around to form a corrugated igloo. Not exactly Caesar's Palace, but this must be the place. The front rooms are unoccupied shells of mud, but the door that leads into the covered yard is guarded by a boy who has long since become a man. He charges his distinguished visitors three times the going price of admission, in spite of Rex's protests. The L-shaped patio smells like a Four-H Club exhibit at a county fair. There's a red-dirt fighting pit at the back and a kind of staging area alongside the house where future combatants are stacked in wire cages. Before this back wall of prime killer poultry, rugged types in straw hats and floppy mustaches play dominoes at a creaky table. None pays us the least mind. We take our places on the top rung of the concrete amphitheater surrounding the pit. The double-doored metal box which releases the combatants is in place, but there's no sign that it will be put to use anytime soon. Rex's daughter plays with a top. Still trying to show he can deliver, her father shuttles between our seats and the card game. The word he brings back is always *ahorita*. By now, it's the most dreaded word of my journey.

Half an hour later, two handlers in checked cowboy shirts pull out a pair of birds and place sacks over their heads, then hang them at each end of a hand-held scale. The interested parties gather, an unofficial Ciudad Bolívar Cockfighting Commission. This is the prefight weigh-in, meant to determine odds and handicaps. The handlers begin some long-winded, if nonchalant, negotiating. But their attempt to make a fair match is half-hearted. They break off without even bluffing disappointment and go back to their dominoes. All we can do is wait until another pair gets the urge to see blood. In the meantime, a demented, barrel-chested fellow plunks himself down in the middle of the ring and begins filing down the sharp ends of the the birds' silver spurs, giggling all the while. Peasant culture is the hardest culture of all to enter—perhaps because it always seems like there must be more to it than meets the analytic urban eye. The closest I get to this fight game as animal husbandry is the sight of one vanquished champion's stiffened carcass, tossed casually atop a black heap of smoldering trash. Finally, I give the high sign. More than half the day is gone and I may be missing a ballgame. Maybe the last game.

Rex has never been to the Ciudad Bolívar park, but we coax him into making it his final stop on the tour. The cockfight is only a few minutes from the lights we spied last night, and underneath, there's a squat concrete ring like those in the cowtowns, painted in panels of orange and red. The nearly empty lot sets off my panic. I'm sure we've lost our chance to witness the southernmost contest in the Americas. Irene rushes up to a sleepy usher at the gate. *"Hay un juego esta tarde?"* The man says *sí*, but first we have to go halfway around the stadium to the cut-out *taquilla* where paper tickets cost about a quarter. Inside a moatlike area that surrounds the grandstand, an old man in cowboy hat and plastic apron grills kebabs. At my first glimpse of outfield grass, I feel like the mad botanist stumbling on yet another mutation of the cross-pollinated transplant I'm tracking.

I even get a front-row seat. There can't be more than twenty tough hombres sprawled about the dingy orange plastic grandstand. Each has a cross flopping on his chest and everyone's sloshed. They toss half-pints of rum from row to row. Today's contestants represent the amateur champions of the states of Bolívar and Sucre—two teams, two bloody generals—though the backs of their raggedy uniforms advertise local breweries. The hand-worked scoreboard is shot: instead of zeroes, there are holes, permanent goose eggs. The windows of what once was a press box are smashed, too. The aluminum bats, unbreakable and therefore cheaper than wood in the long run, clang rather than crack. The seal of wire fencing that protects the players seems pointless here. Returning from strikeouts with heads hung, these amateurs seem to know that the abuse is part of becoming a player. Encouraged by the hard stuff, these fans practice their time-honored art and supreme duty by razzing almost everything happening on the field. The pervading mood is one of fragrant, well-ripened disgust. "No money! No money!" shouts one drunk eager to work on his English. "Crisis in economy, crisis in baseball!"

Don't I want to tell everyone that this is the place it all ends? Irene keeps asking, "Don't you want to talk to the teams?" All they need to lighten their swings is some stranger barging in to announce, "Congratulations, you're playing at the edge of a precipice!" After a single day, Irene has not only embraced my absurd quest but thrown her considerable zeal behind it. Before I can stop her, my latest Sancho Panza—in her case, Sancha—coaxes a paunchy coach into unlocking the gate onto the field. She doesn't know to wait until the break between innings. We make our way into a dugout that's literally dug out, sitting below field level like elongated burial plots. Once we've descended three dirt steps, Irene announces the presence of *un gran escritor Norteamericano* to the benchwarmers. I hear her say something about how I've spent my life's passion in search of that elusive *fin del béisbol*. The unshaven dudes in their gray jerseys look at her like she's mad. They're less concerned about the end-point of baseball than how they'll acquit themselves in their next at-bats.

The Sucre team is the usual aggregate of Caribbean faces, a mix of brown and white, hard and gentle, horribly wearied yet eager for more. Embarrassed, I play the journalist, as much for their sake as mine. I try an informal poll to ascertain what idols inspire the Sucre team at this farthest-flung point of baseball scuttlebutt. At first, the players seem offended. Do I think they're dummies, just rubes? Yet the names they rattle off are nearly all Venezuelan, including Fred Manrique, an all-field, no-hit utility man who is the first player from Ciudad Bolívar to make the majors. Unlike their compatriots in the Dominican, or even Nicaragua, these weekend warriors can't quote me last year's big-league batting champions or *más valiosos*. Again, Venezuela proves a universe unto itself.

Until a man rises from the end of the bench, instantly recognizable from here to Sioux Falls as *el manager:* grizzled, acne-scarred, with coiled hair prematurely gray from too many ninth-inning losses, eyes in a perpetual squint toward bullpen salvation, a body like a beachball. Stepping forward to protect his troops, he volunteers that he wants to be like Billy Martin. *Por qué?* Because half-cocked Billy the Kid is his kind of guy, an honorary Latin, *"un hombre muy fuerte, un tipo agresivo."* Once more, baseball provides a common reference point: About what other subject could I understand exactly what this fellow means? Irene and I are thanking everyone, retreating from the fray back up the dugout steps, when we're buttonholed by the guy who retrieves bats. I can't call him a bat boy because he's got a five o'clock shadow that makes him look like a cross between Don Johnson and Zapata. He seems to be the only one who's grasped the point of Irene's announcement. "This isn't the last of it." He is anxious to tip us off. "There's more baseball around, in the smaller towns, out as far as Piar. If we want to go to the end, you must go to Piar."

Irene and I have to be back in Caracas by the following night. But having come this far, there is no turning back. When we return to the stands, Rex tells us Ciudad Piar is about forty miles south, a scenic route with "jungle all around." We vacate the ballpark to a smattering of mock applause and head back to the hotel for our rented car. Taking his leave, Rex disappoints us once more with his goodness. For his services, he expects only "whatever we wish to give." As a result, I probably give too much. I know that he's really grown fond of us when he expresses his affection in the time-honored Venezuelan manner. "Be on the lookout for the brigands, my friends!" he warns, just one for the road. "Also the inebriated, returning from picnics on the Río Caroni! You don't want to be traveling after dark. The road is narrow. The road is infamous!"

Are There Indians Outside Cleveland?

Thanks a bunch, Rexxie. Thanks for the apprehensions. Vishnu's smiling handmaiden waves us on our way.

Somebody up there doesn't want me to find the last diamond. Rushing out of town, we forget to check our gas gauge. A soldier at the first checkpoint assures us a station is less than thirty kilometers ahead. As the road grows more narrow and winding, all we find are more and more potholes. There's still no jungle, either. I haven't seen any of the honest-to-goodness gooey, claustrophobic muck since just outside Caracas. Only more of this flat, moonlike plateau, dotted with precariously balanced, seemingly hand-smoothed obsidian boulders that Salvador Dalí couldn't top. Not the Sea of Tranquility but possibly the Sea of Fatalities. The road's slower going than expected, the sun's already starting to set, our promised gas station has faded into the realm of El Dorado. "Let's turn around," I suggest. "We may not even have enough gas to get back."

Just when Irene concedes defeat, we see a small *cantina* perched at the far end of a wide gravel oval. I wait in the car for what seems like hours, watching the light diminish and imagining Rex's "brigands" creeping out of the brush. Irene's voice occasionally wafts through the roadhouse's screen porch. She's trilling away like a little bird, leisurely, infuriatingly. I get out to bring her back into the time-space continuum. I'm greeted by a shaking of the head. "Too much! *No hay* gas on this route," Irene tells me, cool and composed behind her wraparound shades. We've turned toward the door and are heading out to the car when the proprietor casually mentions that he keeps his own tank of ethyl out in the backyard. Irene perks up. More roundabout negotiations follow. For some reason, she's haggling over the price—which turns out to be quite reasonable, considering that we're over a barrel. "Give him anything!" I hiss into her ear. Finally, the barman heads out to the backyard. Beside the rusted tank, a woman with dark braids is bathing herself in an old porcelain tub. I have my suspicions about the quality of this gasoline, but it sure smells like the real stuff. Brimming to the top of a plastic jug, it looks like watered-down grape jelly, this noxious pinkness so essential to our lives! The proprietor begins siphoning the gas into our tank by sucking on a long plastic tube. The last light dwindles.

"If Nature is against us, fight Nature!" Wasn't that what Simón said? But I'm not out to liberate this blasted place or join its pantheon of martyrs. Am I about to get my comeuppance for trying to impose my own mythic boundary on this very real and hazardous terrain? All the

261

horror stories recited these last days are buzzing at once in my ear. I grip the wheel and gun our Chevette. In the meantime, Irene is whistling away like we're out for a Sunday drive. "Not so fast, mister!" she shouts, after I brake precipitously before yet another crater in the blacktop. She's entitled to this one back-seat protest by now. After all I've heard about her countrymen's leaden touch on the accelerator, Irene is right to tell me, "It's you who is making the danger!"

A half hour down, the road branches into two unmarked forks. We can't be sure if the one we've chosen may lead us on a detour to the banks of the huge Guri Dam, undoubtedly another of those Third World ecological blights. For twenty more miles, we ride without a clue. About forty-five minutes beyond what Rex projected, a clump of buildings rises against a stark, reddish bluff at one end of the moonscape. For a wink, the highway becomes a main street by virtue of a single boarded-up trading post. Plunked in the midst of the scrub brush for no obvious reason, there's an elongated, white stucco church, lonesome and austere and straight out of some high desert New Mexico pueblo. The rest of the town consists of a compound of metal Quonset huts that must have been constructed as temporary housing for workers on the dam. It's either that or a relocation camp for shortstops who've failed the mob back in Caracas.

How dare they call this a *ciudad*? Our bump-in-the-road can't be all that got named after Manuel Piar, another of Bolívar's first adjutants. A dashing figure who claimed ancestry of French noble blood, Piar was the bastard son of a Curaçao mulatto and a sea captain. Executed by Bolívar after leading an abortive mutiny, he was among the earliest victims of Latin America's first homegrown junta. The sole inhabitant we can find—an attendant at, yes, a gas station—assures Irene this is the end of the line. I can't help feeling that, in our haste, we may have turned around before determining the exact boundary I've sought. Perhaps I should have done an aerial survey, rented a bush pilot instead of a Chevette. And maybe there can be no absolutes in this most peculiar field of study. This spot is as good as any to quit.

My wanderings finish smack up against the frontier, amidst the unbulldozed emptiness of a continent that goads all stranded here to keep asking why they've come and what they must construct. When I envisioned the search for baseball's final outpost, I had hoped to stumble on a series of fields growing ever more ragged until they turned into faint impressions of diamonds, fossilized imprints of foul lines, ceremonial vestiges of pitching mounds mistaken for Indian burial mounds, infields strewn with carbon-dated shards of bases turned to petrified rocks, pieces of abandoned grandstand ramparts baking unattached in odd formations, enigmatic as Stonehenge. But baseball goes with Coca-Cola and blue jeans, not with canoes and coca leaves—despite the claims of overzealous sports anthropologists or nationalists like Rubén Gómez. U.S. influence ends as abruptly as the asphalt, and from here the roads are unpaved all the way to the Amazon. Beyond this encampment, it may indeed be *puro indio*, presuming there's any such thing anymore. What about those nomadic Braves who've wandered from Boston to Milwaukee to Atlanta? Except in postcards, I never see anyone more indigenous than Chief Knock-A-Homa, the deposed Braves mascot who comes out of his teepee for a home run. He's my medicine man.

In the meantime, this outer boundary of our shared field provides enough ethnography to chew on. How else can any of us know who we are until we've reached the place where we must turn back? Behind the camp barracks of Ciudad Piar, surrounded by a brand-new cyclone fence, is a diamond. This instant field is so shiny and modern compared with everything else in sight that it might have been airlifted in a single piece. A prefab roof shades six rows of aluminum stands along both foul lines, separated from the diamond by more sturdy fencing. A hand-operated scoreboard, all zeroes, marks dead center field. Back home, this would make a passable setting for Little League championships. I can't imagine who uses it out here. This is one lonesome diamond. It's a diamond for a gulag, a diamond for a chain gang, a diamond for Devil's Island. I'm reminded of the prison championships at Tipitapa and the stadium at Havana Psychiatric Hospital, where I was never able to see the inmates play. Now I'm the only *siquiatra* in sight. Nestled against barren hills, this diamond's all mine—the one with my name on it. I'm no longer in the wilds or even on foreign territory. I sprint from the car and do a lap around the bases. I don't care if Irene thinks I've gone mad. I've just hit a home run, rid myself of the last miles' anxieties. I find safety tagging first, second, third, home.

Irene points to show me I've got an audience. Four or five pint-size sluggers have emerged from the back side of the last Quonset down the left-field line. I can't tell if this barefoot Spanky and Our Gang has grown curious or if they're heading out for their customary playtime. If so,

Ciudad Piar's childcare center has provided them with neither supervision nor toys. I've still got one combination kid's red glove and whiffle ball set, lugged from home. I sprint back to the trunk, rummage in my pack. "Tell them to share this mitt. Tell them it's a gift from America in appreciation of all the Venezuelan players." With these children, Irene speaks a Spanish that's not in any textbook, a Spanish that's too fast, too affectionate. An older boy accepts for the rest, who go on glaring the Venezuelan glare, softened only slightly when I mutter, "Tony Armas, Dave Concepción. . . ." Maybe they'll argue over my gift afterwards, but for now, they're just stunned. They sulk off without a *gracias*.

Spreading the gospel of baseball, what values do I inculcate? What stray meanings do I want them to catch with my mitt? Perhaps this is how culture always spreads, unaware of its motives, unknowingly replicating known pleasures. Yet I don't feel I'm imposing anything. These people we persist in calling foreign didn't take to our sporting habit because of the encouraging climate or because they were too poor for higher pursuits. The sport speaks to their conditions as it speaks to ours—at this stage of history, even more. *El béisbol* survives as tradition, not submission.

El béisbol is the face of a comfortable old friend distorted in the funhouse mirror.

El béisbol is Abner Doubleday turning over in his grave.

El béisbol is a Northern weed transplanted to tropical climes, that blooms each winter in a dazzling show of passion and chicanery.

El béisbol is the mambo with ground rules, the cha-cha-cha turned into a double-play pivot.

El béisbol is a pickup game on a cowpatch outside Chihuahua, stickball in the shanties of San Juan, the ghosts of the Havana Sugar Kings versus Castro's barnstorming "Beards," a stadium holding an umpire for ransom in Maracaibo.

El béisbol is played on one huge American diamond, laid out willy-nilly, with home plate near Cooperstown, pitcher's mound in Kansas, and the left-field foul pole somewhere along the Orinoco.

El béisbol is a dream that turned into a nightmare after Teddy Roosevelt ate too many jalapeños.

El béisbol is sending in the Marines, then sending down the scouts.

El béisbol is the Monroe Doctrine turned into a lineup card, a remembrance of invasions past.

Are There Indians Outside Cleveland?

El béisbol is the arcane religion of many million bean-chomping, rum-swilling *fanáticos.*

El béisbol is a catcall in the bleachers of history.

El béisbol is dancing on the dugout.

El béisbol is where error reigns supreme, and perfection is half-heartedly pursued.

El béisbol is a battle for hearts and minds between the foul lines.

El béisbol is taking your best cut, swinging from the heels, because America is all curveballs.

El béisbol is a scrapbook of empire, myth as cheap souvenir.

El béisbol is current events in a dusty uniform.

El béisbol is Spanish for all that is good in America. Baseball *es inglés para todo lo bueno en las Américas.*

Now I saunter up to home plate and strike the same instinctive pose displayed without prompting for my clicking camera by every kid in the *barrio* and the *campo*, on the sun-strewn beaches and trash-strewn lots. Scratching a comfortable hole with my heels, taking my stance, I grip tight my invisible piece of the American forest. Irene humors me one last time by snapping a picture of a bearded, sunburned thirty-six-year-old kid in sneakers taking an imaginary cut at imaginary rawhide. "Too much!" Can she tell I'm doing my Vic Davalillo leg-lift, in homage to his *país natal*? Or is this Mel Ott? How about the swivel-kneed, soft-wristed Carew flick? The Clemente *picador* lunge? The proudly upright Puritan Yaz, bearing his bat a full foot over his head? Sweet swingin' Billy Williams Harold Baines Fred Lynn Lou Piniella? Take a big whiff à la Reggie, uppercutting the heavens, swooning with the pleasure of my own unleashed strength, crossing ankles with the effort and screwing myself into the ground? Can any tribe over the next hill imagine so many sublime ways to clutch a club? If I connect, launch a home run out here, who knows in what peapatch it might land?

All I know is that beyond the last diamond, there is nothing for me. Past this point, I'm even more lost than I think. Out of view of this game's limitless spaces, I have nothing to define me. If no *fanáticos* swap tall tales or trade rumors, I don't speak the language. Out where they've never heard of Darryl Strawberry and Rollie Fingers, Sibby Sisti and Catfish Metkovich, Joaquín and Roberto, Coco Laboy and Candy Maldonado and all the divine crazies, I dare not go.

CATCHER
RECEPTOR
The Reconquest

"It is imperative that our neighbor know us, and know us soon, for the day of the visit is at hand."

—José Martí

They are coming. The bastard children are taking their revenge. The unwanted offspring of all the big leaguers show up on their daddy's doorsteps, insisting upon a fair share of their patrimony. The continental benchwarmers come in to pinch hit for their failing, doddering idols. The bat boys wield the lumber they once toted submissively. The nightmare of every Texas rancher and DAR daughter and officer of *la migración* has come to fruition, as all nightmares must. The midget mascots and the pig-tailed barbecue vendors come streaming across the border until all borders become as blurred as rattlesnake trails in the Sonoran dust. This modern exodus comes carrying graven idols in battered *milagros*, lugging harps and marimbas and blankets and Cangejeros caps. They arrive covered in cocaine dust from out of the holds of unregistered planes. They squeeze through every pipeline and sewer line and regulation. They outnumber us and they already know how to make the pivot at second base.

With the reconquest underway, all the Latin leaguers simultaneously put down their mitts and pick up their machetes. They are aided by a few traitorous gringo left fielders who've been seduced by *señoritas* and favorable exchange rates. These Northerners now coach conspiracy, passing on tips on the fundamentals of destabilizing regimes. As soon as the games are cancelled, dictators waver, regimes topple. With nothing left to root for, the *fanáticos* live up to their name. The banana republics become baseball republics once and for all. And that's when the hot pot

269

that's been cooking for a century boils over. On a given signal, all the big-leaguers with Hispanic surnames announce their retirements before weeping fans. They clean out their lockers and then rendezvous in the *sierra*. To the mountains they go for shelter, like Fidel and Che and Sandino, only this time it's the Rockies west of Denver, the Catskills and the Wasatch, the Appalachians close by the lair of the Peets-boorgh Pirates. Now they aim to be more than late-inning *guerrilleros*.

Roberto Clemente returns to be *comandante-en-jefe*, sparkplug, and chiropractor, complaining on all the long marches about his aching back. Manny Mota is the martial arts instructor, inculcating self-discipline and the fine points of Motaism. Minnie Minoso entertains the troops around the campfire with his imitation of Bill Veeck. Luis Tiant takes over as supply sergeant, rationing out foot-long Upmann cigars for the post-battle celebrations in the locker room whirlpools. Luis Aparicio makes backhanded stabs at stray grenades. Campy Campaneris covers all nine positions in the trenches. Juan Marichal's high kick proves useful for evading the barbed wire on army bases. Pascual Pérez gets lost on his way to the mountains. Chico Carrasquel leads a division of Chicos. Rubén Gómez organizes the kamikaze squad, goes headhunting for umpires and general managers who pass bad checks. Vic Power bearhugs the enemy to death, shouting, "Oh, baby!"

Pedro Guerrero hacks down redwoods like sugar cane. Manny Sanguillén unleashes the world's first lethal grin. Pancho Coimbre tends bar. Tony Fernández is the chaplain. Recruiting sarge Epy Guerrero wields a pen instead of a rifle, keeps his eye out for marksmen and raw-boned cowpokes. The only bonus he offers is a pair of camouflage pants autographed by the '27 Yankees. The Baby Bull, Orlando Cepeda, leads the charge. Joaquín Andújar finally chooses the right moment to go ape, the right enemy. Omar Moreno is a winged messenger, tiptoeing through the forest. The base-stealers steal ammo now, but trot back to first on a foul ball. The Alou brothers organize a squadron of next of kin, the ones nobody ever signed, the ones sent home without even getting a cup of coffee. Fernando Valenzuela does his impersonation of Pancho Villa, swaggering with spent shells girdling his beer gut, blowing on the tip of his smoking *pistola* before his trademarked display of the whites of his eyes. Buck Canel does the play-by-play, shouting, "*Adelante, muchachos! Vámonos, coño! Olivdense, se fue!*" El Norte is going, going, gone!

They swoop down from the hills, spewing tobacco and one-liners, wearing 1890s Redlegs uniforms. The chaos and death squads have come home to roost. North becomes South—the Tijuana border crossing is demolished with a decisive pounding of little league bats. Los Angeles and Miami and L.A. are the first to fall, captured from within. Nueva York finally acknowledges that its boroughs encompass the entire Caribbean. The smell of rotting guava is pumped from Chicago's factory smokestacks. Laughter is heard in the coal mines of West Virginia. Tortillas replace English muffins. The White House becomes the Tan House.

The ballpark turnstiles spin, all attendance records are broken. The tickets are free, of course. The meek inherit box seats. First come, first enthralled. Everyone, not just the midgets, shakes it atop the dugouts. The p.a. announcers do simultaneous translation and turn up the volume so a chorus line of Tropicana dancers can cha-cha-cha along the warning track. Everyone in the bleachers gets a foul ball to cherish, a welfare check in each box of Crackerjacks. Between innings, the children wander out onto the green carpet that goes on forever. The season goes year-round and nonstop. The first worldly World Series pits Monongahela against Huehuetenango in a best of twenty-seven at Anti-Yankee Stadium. The pregame ceremonies commence with Fidel Castro's rendition of Lou Gehrig's farewell address—"I am the luckiest man in the world!"—and end with ten thousand Aztec warriors doing rain dances in synchronization with the Ohio State marching band. Father Ernesto Cardenal leads the benediction. Danny Ortega warms up Ollie North in the bullpen. The mothers of the disappeared throw out a thousand first balls. The colors red, white, and blue are presented on behalf of all the nations they represent. The CIA's Havana bureau chiefs, led by Trafficante, challenge the Venceremos Brigade in an Old-Timers Game; Mickey Mantle loses an arm-wrestling match to the ghost of Martin Dihigo. Pat Boone and Tito Puente, Willie Nelson and the Grupo Moncada, Aretha Franklin and the Orquesta Broadway sing a medley, from "Guantanamera" to "Sometimes I Feel like a Motherless Child." The bleachers rise, caps to their hearts, to sing out, "José can you see . . ."

An inter-American junta reigns beneficently, enforcing no laws but the official rule book. Governors and senators yield to the umpires, who rule even on love affairs and consider every appeal. Governing becomes a matter of prudent general managing. A few handshakes in Florida hotel lobbies, and deals are concluded to swap North Dakota for Costa Rica, New Jersey and the Everglades for El Salvador and a hellhole to be named later, Chile for the Philippines and a puppet regime to be named later, the homeless of New York for the disappeared of Buenos Aires, the electric guitarists for the Peruvian harpists, the Magnificent Seven for the Sandinista Nine, the barefoot *campesinos* for the wing-tipped execs, the carnival dancers for the agronomists, the death squads for the television evangelists, ten thousand nineteen-inch color monitors for one semi-repudiated Aztec deity, fields to plow for songs to sing, the ones whose feet pound the earth for the ones whose eyes rule the sky, the ones who want jobs for the ones who want mythology. A democratically elected commissioner okays a deal giving Puerto Rico back to the Puerto Ricans on waivers. The continent of corn and yucca, cowboys and slaves is finally at peace.

The American game belongs to our neighbors as much as it belongs to us. It has always belonged to all of us. The waiting game must be won by those who wait best, and this game has been going on for five hundred years. Until its two ballplaying halves really come to recognize and embrace one another, America waits to be truly inhabited, just as baseball's lonely sentinel fielders wait for an arcing pop fly. Waiting: for a society of pitchers and catchers, indivisible, with liberty and justice for the ball. Waiting to hear ourselves in the roar, "Wait till next year!" Waiting for America to become America.